Marcus Aurelius and his Legacy

Marcus Aurelius and his Legacy

Seeking Rome's Kingdom of Gold

Judith Stove

First published in Great Britain in 2025 by
Pen & Sword History
An imprint of Pen & Sword Books Limited
Yorkshire – Philadelphia

ISBN 978 1 03610 892 2

A CIP catalogue record for this book is
available from the British Library.

Typeset by Mac Style
Printed in the UK by CPI Group (UK) Ltd, Croydon, CR0 4YY.

The Publisher's authorised representative in the EU for product safety is Authorised Rep Compliance Ltd., Ground Floor, 71 Lower Baggot Street, Dublin D02 P593, Ireland.
www.arccompliance.com

For a complete list of Pen & Sword titles please contact

PEN & SWORD BOOKS LIMITED
47 Church Street, Barnsley, South Yorkshire, S70 2AS, England
E-mail: enquiries@pen-and-sword.co.uk
Website: www.pen-and-sword.co.uk
or
PEN AND SWORD BOOKS
1950 Lawrence Road, Havertown, PA 19083, USA
E-mail: uspen-and-sword@casematepublishers.com
Website: www.penandswordbooks.com

Contents

List of Plates

Introduction

If you happen to mention the Roman emperor Marcus Aurelius, many people will respond: 'Was he the one in *Gladiator*?'

The answer is, of course, yes. The award-winning 2000 film's plot begins with the final days of Marcus Aurelius, the succession to the imperial power, the ascent of Marcus' dissolute son Commodus, and the enslavement of Maximus and his career in the title role of 'gladiator,' a fighter for pay in the arena. The film remains great entertainment, offering the vehicle for Russell Crowe's career-defining performance.

One of the reasons for this book, however, is that the film gives an inadequate account of Marcus Aurelius – and has thus misled millions of viewers. Where his daughter Lucilla (Connie Nielsen) sarcastically observes that 'he has been dying for ten years,' in fact Marcus – while battling ill health – was actively involved in strategy and administration until his death. Where Joaquin Phoenix's Commodus bewails the fact that the basic reason for his failures is that Marcus did not love him, there is ample evidence to the contrary. And similarly, where Richard Harris' Marcus bids Lucilla pretend that she was a good daughter, and he himself a good father, and where Lucilla confirms this to be a 'fiction,' this directly contradicts history. Marcus is on record as a loving and conscientious father to all his many sons and daughters, the majority of whose early deaths caused him severe grief.

More significantly, Harris in the role of Marcus appears confused, at a loss, and questioning everything to do with his own life's work, even questioning Rome itself. Nobody involved in the screenplay or the plot seems to have any knowledge that Marcus reflected deeply yet decisively on such matters. The real-life Marcus did not plan to restore the Roman Republic: it was enough that he tried, at all times, to perform his gruelling duties thoroughly and with justice, and in accordance with Stoic philosophy. The real Marcus, in other words, was a great deal more interesting and impressive than Harris' decrepit depiction in Ridley Scott's blockbuster.

In this book, we will explore some of the many legacies and traces left by the historical Marcus Aurelius. We will discover Marcus fan-fiction from as early as the generation after his death (the Antonine Questions) through, indeed, to *Gladiator* itself. His impact on material culture, evident in such forms as his famous equestrian statue, will be traced.

Aspects of Marcus' life which have been downplayed or altogether ignored will also be probed. These include his interest in a 'golden book,' contrary to previous biographical statements that Marcus had limited interests in the arts; and the surprising lack of attention paid to the problems around the high mortality of Marcus and his wife Faustina's many children ('Losing a Child').

Marcus would also feature as a moral exemplar in such unlikely contexts as the Church of England ('A Superior Genius'), notwithstanding that he was thoroughly pagan, and even reputed to have been a persecutor of Christians (but was he?). The impacts of Marcus' unique and brilliant writings on later literature, from the outset of the English novel ('Marcus Incognito') through to the Russian Formalist school ('Marcus for the Modern Age'), will be sketched.

We will examine the point of view, commonly associated with the great historian Edward Gibbon, that Marcus failed in appointing Commodus as his heir ('Decline and Fall'). And Marcus' relationship with the imperial cult – whereby Roman emperors were considered to be gods after their death – will be addressed. Marcus' reputation ebbed and flowed through the centuries, and we will consider the factors involved, noting that he now enjoys the highest standing, perhaps, since his death in 180 CE.

Finally, 'Walking With Marcus' sections interspersed throughout this book will offer suggestions for readers who may wish to explore for themselves the life and landscapes of Marcus Aurelius, from urban Rome to the wide skies of the Danube frontier.

Thanks and acknowledgements are due to many people, but chiefly to my husband Stuart Wilson, who took a number of the photographs for this book and encouraged my Marcus obsession; my brother Robert James Stove, who located several nineteenth-century references to Marcus; and Harald Kavli, the editor of *Stoicism Today*. I owe particular thanks to Khyel Walker, who translated from the Hebrew and Aramaic material on the Antonine Questions. I am grateful to Australian friends in the Stoic community – Courtney Shipley, Simon J.E. Drew, Will Johncock, Roger Perry, Lyn Vu. Authorities on Marcus Aurelius and members of the Modern Stoicism team, Donald Robertson and John Sellars, were kind enough to offer comments on draft sections. Thanks also to Philip Sidnell, my editor at Pen & Sword Books, for his confidence and patience. Particular thanks to the brilliant editorial team at *Antigone Journal*, for publishing with their customary panache an edited version of 'This is How We Become Godlike: Marcus and His Monuments' (April 2024). All errors are of course my own.

Chapter One

Out of Oblivion

Loss of ancient literature – haphazard survivals – gradual recovery – pagan and Christian views accommodated – twentieth-century disasters – failures of moral authority – twenty-first century reactions – a revival of interest in Stoicism (and other virtue traditions)

How many after being celebrated by fame have been given up to oblivion; and how many who have celebrated the fame of others have long departed.

Marcus Aurelius, *Meditations* 7.6[1]

Imagine that a cataclysmic disruption were to occur, such as a devastating and prolonged world war.

Among other forms of devastation, libraries would be destroyed; intermittent power outages would render the internet patchy at best, possibly for years. Our access to information would be unreliable, and the available data random. Great literary works might have vanished, while car manuals or the odd chemistry textbook might have endured to emerge from the dust. Such an image is inspired by the memorable sketch presented by philosopher Alasdair MacIntyre, in 1981, to indicate the wreck, as he wished to show, of moral theory in the twentieth century.

Yet for students of the classics, it is no mere thought-experiment: rather, it is the actual state of our inheritance from the pre-Christian ancient world.[2] Such texts as we have are very largely the result of one or more chance events, fortuitous preservations, and miraculous escapes.

The fate which overtook ancient Greco-Roman culture occurred in several phases. The first was a series of catastrophic events, notably the fire of March 192, in which several important libraries and archives in the city of Rome were destroyed. In 410, Rome was sacked by Alaric and the Visigoths, and important archives such the Basilica Aemilia, in the Forum, were burned.

In parallel, a separate lengthy phase involved the censorship which took place once Christianity became the major force in Roman culture, during the third to the sixth centuries CE. Much of Rome's wealth and power were being transferred to other centres. The Christian emperor Justinian was to close Plato's Academy at Athens in 529, while Pope Gregory the Great (d. 604) would be blamed, or credited, depending on one's point of view, with the deliberate destruction of much of pagan culture in Rome.[3]

Later phases were gradual. Pagan texts, where they were not actively suppressed, received lower priority for copying and distribution in the monastic *scriptoria* throughout Europe. Survivals were haphazard: much of Cicero's considerable *corpus* was lost, although on the face of it much of his work could fit a Christian worldview; yet the very pagan poems of Ovid continued to be copied, their meanings twisted into acceptable allegorical forms.[4] Plato, inspiration for so much of the later philosophical traditions, some of whose worldview was consonant with Christianity, was far less known and studied than we might have expected. From time to time, ancient manuscripts would be unearthed from monastery libraries or private collections, each contributing to the growth in knowledge about the forgotten world.

This halting and idiosyncratic recovery received impetus from two particular projects. The commentaries on, and translations of, Plato's works into Latin by Marsilio Ficino, in the second half of the fifteenth century, would be central events in the revival of ancient wisdom that we call the Renaissance.[5] Another decisive event at around the same time was the translation into Latin (1472) of the biographical accounts of ancient Greek philosophers, prepared by Diogenes Laertius in the third century CE, still our principal source for dozens of ancient thinkers.

Rediscovered works by Cicero and Seneca, a Roman Stoic, also provided inspiration for statesmen and women, as well as for artists and writers. For the next half-millennium, until the nineteenth century, people studied Latin and Greek in order to read these surviving works, on the understanding that they were among the most beautiful and profound ever written – and that they had the capacity to improve the reader's life and his or her character, by inspiring them to pursue virtue. Accommodations and cross-pollination were made between classical studies and Christianity in its range of forms.

But in the twentieth century, the most recent phase of loss took place. Two world wars and the rise of new tyrannies contributed to a reaction against moral frameworks and scientific certainty. This saw a situation, by the 1970s, of impatience with the old. Psychology – with its pretensions to scientific authority – had usurped much of what had been philosophy, and philosophy in its turn seemed confined to linguistic quibbling and logical argumentation in university departments. Latin and Greek ceased to be taught except in expensive private schools; university enrolments dwindled. Pews were empty, and even most churches abandoned their inheritance of moral authority.

Yet as ever, this situation too prompted a reaction. By the very end of the century, a shift was evident. For thirty years, Western society had got along without formal values, but also seemed to be suffering from mass narcissism, rising crime, and poor mental health. Signs emerged of a renewed interest in ancient virtue ethics, not merely as an academic topic (university philosophy also saw a revival of interest in the ancient schools), but as a means to a better life for ordinary people. Instances from popular culture are representative. They introduced to new audiences two of the three Stoic authors from antiquity whose works survive in any volume: Epictetus (d. 135 CE), and Marcus Aurelius, the second (121–180 CE); the third author is Seneca (d. 65 CE), who had never fallen quite so far into obscurity as the other two.

In 1995, US writer Sharon Lebell published *The Art of Living*, a compendium based upon translations from Epictetus. A slave, born in Hierapolis, now Pamukkale in Turkey (his name simply means 'acquired'), eventually he found his way to the household of the emperor Nero's secretary. At some stage, we are told, a brutal master had broken Epictetus' leg, and he walked with a limp. Yet he was able to study philosophy under another Roman Stoic, Musonius Rufus, in turning becoming a teacher also. Here we find another of these accidents of survival. Epictetus wrote nothing himself, but one of his students, a career administrator called Arrian, took and published extensive notes from his teacher's lectures. These survive as the summary *Enchiridion*, or Handbook, and the longer *Discourses*. These became prized books of counsel, studied by others with a view to helping with practical approaches to life's difficulties. Within a few decades of Epictetus' lifetime, Arrian's book was used in this way.

The Roman writer Aulus Gellius (125–180 CE) reports that on a sea voyage, a storm blew up. Gellius noticed a Stoic philosopher whom he'd known previously, at first apparently alarmed as were all on board. The man then recovered a calm demeanour.

One passenger, 'a rich Greek from Asia,' asked 'in a bantering tone' (*quasi inludens*), what was the man's secret? The Stoic philosopher put off the rude questioner. But when Gellius asked him later the same thing:

> 'Read it' [the calm passenger urged], 'for if you read it you will be more ready to believe it and you will remember it better.' Thereupon before my eyes he drew from his little bag the fifth book of the *Discourses* of the philosopher Epictetus, which, as arranged by Arrian, undoubtedly agree with the writings of Zeno and Chrysippus.[6]

In our surviving versions of Epictetus' *Discourses,* there are only four books, so evidently this fifth book, among others (one account suggests that there were eight), at some stage was lost. Arrian's Epictetus, then, represents one of the lucky survivals from the ancient world. The name 'Stoic' comes from the school's location, in the Stoa Poikile, the 'painted porch,' which was situated in the *agora*, the marketplace, at Athens. Zeno and Chrysippus had been among the earliest founders of the school, in about 300 BCE: once again, their work survives only in very fragmentary form.

Now just as Epictetus' sayings evidently found an enthusiastic readership in the generations after his death, Sharon Lebell's 1995 book became a best-seller, and has since been reissued in numerous editions. Clearly, Epictetus' message once again has struck a chord in the culture. So what is it about the Stoic approach to life which has the capacity to assist people?

We can identify several key Stoic teachings:

a) **The 'dichotomy of control'**: the notion that, as Epictetus said, 'Some things are within our power, while others are not. Within our power are opinion, motivation, desire, aversion, and, in a word, whatever is of our own doing; not within our power are our body, our property, reputation, office, and, in a word, whatever is not of our own doing' (*Handbook* 1[7]). It is appropriate that we concern ourselves only with the former class of matters, because we have no power over the second group.
   - This focus on the controllable has since featured in several schools of psychological therapy, such as Cognitive Behaviour Therapy.[8]

b) **Our emotions come about as a result of our beliefs.** Sometimes those beliefs are mistaken, and so we wrongly experience an emotion. For example, if a man believes that his wife is having an affair, he may experience jealousy and anger. But what if he's completely wrong in this belief? His emotions may cause him to act badly, even to commit a crime, all on the basis of a mistaken belief. It is important, then, for us to take some time to subject our initial impressions about a matter, to ensure as far as we can that our beliefs are well-founded.
   - In Aulus Gellius' anecdote, the Stoic passenger initially felt the same alarm as everyone else on board, but refused to 'assent to' the initial impression of impending death or disaster, thus remaining calm.
   - The Stoics were not the only ancient philosophical group to have this 'cognitive' view about emotions, but they explored the issues most thoroughly.

c) Inspired by the Athenian philosopher Socrates (d. 399 BCE), about whom Plato and others had written, the Stoics maintained that the best life was one spent in the cultivation of four key virtues:

- Courage
- Justice
- Self-control
- Wisdom
- This life, they maintained, was best for both communities (as the Roman writer Cicero, not a Stoic himself, had written in his book *On Duties*), and for individuals. Such a life was most likely to attain a state of *eudaimonia*, well-being. It was also, the Stoics maintained, the life that was most natural for human beings: to live virtuously, they considered, was to live according to nature. We shall explore, through Marcus Aurelius' life and work, some of the implications of this doctrine.

Another pop-culture event which brought some awareness of ancient Stoicism was Tom Wolfe's 1998 novel, *A Man In Full*, featuring a plotline in which a character learns about Epictetus while unjustly incarcerated.[9] The third and perhaps decisive event, however, was the 2000 film *Gladiator*, directed by Ridley Scott.

In the film, the old emperor Marcus Aurelius, played by veteran Richard Harris, is dying, and about to bequeath the empire to his only surviving son Commodus. The film's hero, the fictional Maximus (Crowe), is loyal to Marcus; he is reduced to slavery under Commodus, who – unlike his father – turns out to be a lazy yet terrifying psychopath. The contrast between the virtuous, active, Stoic emperor and general, and his successor son, powers the plot. The film was a popular hit, also winning numerous industry awards, and suddenly Marcus Aurelius and Commodus had once again become household names, for the first time, perhaps, in over a century. In a later chapter we will examine in more detail the film versions of Marcus' final days.

The final accident of survival brought us Marcus Aurelius' single surviving book, usually called in English *Meditations*, but in Greek *Ta Eis Heauton*, 'things [written] to oneself.' (Marcus wrote in Greek rather than Latin as Greek was still, by Marcus' time in the second century of the Christian era, considered the language of philosophy; as an educated Roman, he was fully bilingual.) These are sayings, maxims, reminders, and observations, aimed at consolidating Marcus' Stoic practice.

From internal evidence – Marcus at times jotted down his location – we conclude that he wrote much of the book while on military campaign against the Germanic nations the Marcomanni and the Quadi, in locations now in Austria, Hungary, Serbia and Slovakia. Marcus died of illness on campaign, and it is unclear how his notebook was preserved. As we will learn throughout this book, there are hints and recollections in intervening texts, but the first clear reference to Marcus' book is by a bishop, Arethas (d. 935 CE) of Caesarea (in Cappadocia, Turkey), whose copy (now lost) is believed to be the 'ancestor' of subsequent manuscripts. Yet even among these, the losses persisted. The text of the *Meditations* consulted by scholars today is based on two manuscripts, one of which subsequently disappeared, leaving a single copy surviving at the Vatican.[10]

We may be grateful for this fortuitous survival, because whenever people read Marcus' *Meditations* (usually in translation, as Marcus' Greek is idiosyncratic and technical), they are struck by the beauty, the goodness, and the generosity of its sentiments. They feel as if Marcus is speaking to them, as well as 'to himself.'

To take but one famous example, Marcus regularly reminded himself that the people we meet in the daily round are going to act in less than perfect ways; but as they are closely related to us – the Stoics considered everyone as part of the great network of nature – it would be inappropriate to be angry or reject them:

> Every morning, say to yourself: I will come across the busybody, ungrateful, arrogant, deceitful, defamatory, the unsocial. All these things happen to them because of their ignorance of good and bad. But I, having seen the nature of good, that it is beautiful, and of the bad, that it is ugly, and the nature of him who does wrong, that it is related to me, not through blood or genes, but that it shares in the same divinity – I cannot be harmed by any of them: nobody can involve me in ugliness: nor can I get angry with my relative, nor hate him. For we were born to work together, like feet, like hands, like eyelids, like the upper and lower rows of teeth. To act against one another is against nature: and it is acting against one another to be irritated and to turn away (2.1).[11]

The work seems to illustrate and justify Marcus' reputation of being both a great and a good leader – perhaps the greatest Rome had seen. And for all the forgetting, there seem to have been rememberings of sorts: distorted, confused, but vaguely aware of the greatness Marcus had embodied. Just as historians have located cultural remnants from the campaigns of Alexander the Great, from Greece to Central Asia and beyond, this book will attempt, on a much smaller scale, to trace some of these memories and impressions left by Marcus' remarkable life and work. Concerning the death of Marcus, and the succession of his son Commodus, the historian Cassius Dio remarked:

> Our history now descends from a kingdom of gold to one of iron and rust, as affairs did for the Romans of that day (72.36).

We will attempt to recover what we can of Marcus' 'kingdom of gold,' through myth, legend, coinage, inscription; letters; sculpture, words, and deeds. It will take us from the equestrian statue in Rome to the Ryedale Hoard in Yorkshire, and introduce fan-fiction from antiquity to the digital age: the Talmudic Antonine Questions, Julian the Apostate's *Caesars,* Antonio de Guevara's Renaissance *Golden Book*, and Ridley Scott's *Gladiator*. We will walk on the Caelian Hill, along the Appian Way, and in the Borghese Gardens; further afield, we will explore Roman sites of all kinds, from the Danube to the Antonine Wall.

Marcus only grows in reputation. New editions and translations of *Meditations*, such as those of Gregory Hays (2003), Robin Hard (2011), and Robin Waterfield (2021) have inspired new readers. Over the last decade, the Modern Stoicism non-profit organization has conducted events such as the now-annual Stoic Week, in which participants attempt to live according to Stoic principles, applying suggestions and instructions from the ancient Stoics. Stoicon-X events, held around the world, bring participants together online and in-person. Marcus' legacies are still being created in real time.

Walking With Marcus I: The Caelian Hill

Rome, as everyone knows, has seven hills: the Capitoline, the Aventine, the Quirinal, the Viminal, the Esquiline, the Palatine, and the Caelian. Most visitors today visit the Capitoline for the great museums there, and the Palatine for its access to the Forum and its remnants of the great imperial dwellings. The Quirinal's identity as a hill has long been obscured by aristocratic palaces, and hectic streets. For its part, the Viminal is known mainly as the location of Termini central rail station.

The Esquiline has its most prominent element the southern Oppian spur, site of Nero's Domus Aurea – now deep underground, but accessed through a tunnel and reception area – and Trajan's baths, of which some grand elements remain. The Aventine still rises imposingly above the Circus Maximus, the Pyramid of Cestius and the Protestant cemetery rewarding visitors who make the climb.

By far the least traversed is the Caelian Hill (now known as Celio). It was here that in 121 CE, Domitia Lucilla, wife of Marcus Annius Verus, gave birth to their first child and only son, Marcus Aurelius. The Annii owned property on the Caelian, a convenient location between the Circus Maximus and the Colosseum.

Visitors climb the Caelian via the Clivus Scauri, the ancient road which once connected the Circus and the Colosseum. A museum has recently been opened on the left as you ascend: inside is displayed, for the first time, the Forma Urbis. This was a marble map of Rome, prepared in the reign of Septimius Severus (emperor from 193 to 211 CE), and later broken into hundreds of fragments, many of which have now been assembled and exhibited beneath glass: visitors walk and peer down as if walking through ancient Rome.

The new museum is set within an outdoor exhibition, consisting largely of inscriptions, including grave markers. Several commemorate members of the Annii family or their dependants. The visitor enjoys a peaceful stroll among these carefully arranged memorials.

A short way up the Clivus, under medieval brick archways, you come to the 'Roman Houses.' These are ancient buildings which, through the accretions of time, are now well below ground level. They may have been occupied during Marcus' lifetime. Later occupants included Christians holding underground worship, at the site of a martyrdom. Faded frescoes, both pagan and Christian, illuminate this extraordinary site.

At the hilltop, a gate appears, and through this we find a park (rather rough and scuffed, because this is Italy, not England), woven through with pines and shrubs. It is a de-facto dog park, and the dogs run, sniff, and mark the spot, while their owners talk on their phones. It is a peaceful location to think about young Marcus running and playing with his little sister, Annia, and the household children, on this spot or close to it.

Descending from the hill on the northern side, and heading towards the Colosseum or the Domus Aurea, we pass the Via Annia and the Via Marco Aurelio, commemorating that the ground far below these streets was his and his distinguished family's home turf. Marcus, notwithstanding the Spanish origins of some of his ancestors, was Roman born and raised.

Chapter Two

Succession

A perennial problem – emperors lacking sons – adoption no guarantee – Hadrian's choices – Antoninus and Verus – in sharing power, Marcus ahead of his time

A perennial problem was the imperial succession. Ever since Julius Caesar, winning the civil war which ended the Roman Republic, bequeathed imperial power to his great-nephew Octavian, later called Augustus, the issue of who would succeed was paramount.

Like Julius Caesar, Augustus, who ruled as emperor from 27 BCE until his death in 14 CE, had no sons. He chose as his heir Tiberius, his wife Livia's son by a former marriage. Tiberius, in his turn, lacking sons, adopted his nephew Germanicus as heir, but both Germanicus and his son Drusus died young. Germanicus' son Caligula succeeded, but was assassinated after less than four years in 41, after displaying cruelty and extravagance beyond Roman norms of power.

This highly unstable pattern was repeated, notably when Claudius (Germanicus's brother) was succeeded by his teenage adopted son Nero. Claudius's biological son Britannicus, aged not quite fourteen, was widely believed to have been poisoned at Nero's order. The demise of Nero, again at the hands of a conspiracy in reaction to his crimes, including the murder of his mother, took place in 68.

Chaos ensued, and 69 is known as the Year of the Four Emperors: Galba, Otho, Vitellius and Vespasian, each backed by a different army faction. The last of these brought renewed stability, and on his death, of natural causes, in 79 he was succeeded by his son Titus, the first emperor to be succeeded by his biological son. Titus died of illness only two years later, and was succeeded by his brother Domitian. Once again, harsh rule and curtailment of freedoms resulted in a reaction, and Domitian would be assassinated in 96.

A century of such events had amply demonstrated several points. One, that imperial succession needed to be planned; two, that these plans did not amount to a guaranteed outcome; and three, that neither adoption, nor succession by biological sons, ensured either stability or sound and just rule, *contra* Marcus biographer Frank McLynn's bland assertion that 'adoption ensured a smooth succession.'[1] Nonetheless, recognizing the first of these points, later emperors did their best with the human resources available to them, and with the lessons of recent history in view.

Yet strange decisions continued to be made. On Domitian's assassination, the Roman Senate declared an older, childless and relatively obscure man, Nerva, as emperor. Lacking the support of the army, he ruled only for two years (until 98), forced to share his power in later months with Trajan, who was young, popular, and a successful general. Trajan, ruling with competence both military and administrative, ensuring his stellar and enduring reputation, had no sons, but a promising heir was at hand in Hadrian, who duly succeeded to imperial power in 117. It would be Hadrian to whom Marcus Aurelius would ultimately owe his own succession to power.

If Hadrian – who was an efficient administrator, as well as a creative talent (as demonstrated in his architectural projects) – had had a biological son, the succession would have been very different. Hadrian, however, was undoubtedly same-sex attracted: his best-known relationship was with a teenager called Antinous, whom he showered with honours; Antinous accompanied him on his official travels around the empire. Hadrian even accorded Antinous divine worship, after the young man's mysterious death in 130 before his twentieth birthday. Noting that the categories of sexual identity for ancient Romans were somewhat different from ours, there is reason to classify Hadrian as gay. At the same time, his marriage to Vibia Sabina I was not a happy one; she died in 136, having borne no children. Hadrian's own health was declining, and he saw the pressing need to select a successor.

His first choice was surprising: a fairly undistinguished nobleman called Ceionius Commodus, adopted with the title of Lucius Aelius Caesar. This candidate, however, died within two years, in 138. At this point, Hadrian made what turned out to be an inspired selection: Titus Aurelius Annius Antoninus, known to history as Antoninus Pius, 'the pious Antonine.' A condition of the adoption was that, in his turn, Antoninus should adopt Marcus Annius Verus, the future Marcus Aurelius, just turning seventeen, and the eight-year-old Lucius Ceionius, son of his first choice.

Marcus' biological father had died when he was very young. Hadrian had perceived that this serious and clever youth had the potential for leadership. 'He was,' we read in the *Historia Augusta*, 'a serious child from his infancy' (*fuit a prima infantia gravis*, HA MA 2.1).[2] With the seriousness went a dedication to the truth beyond his years. Hadrian nicknamed him *Verissimus*, punning on his family name of *Verus*, 'true,' 'sincere,' 'honest' – the superlative form of the adjective being used, so that Marcus was 'Mr Honesty' (MA 1.10).

To these promising character traits, the imperial family added an education second to none (which will be covered in greater detail in another chapter). As much an education as his formal studies, was the practical guidance afforded by shadowing Antoninus Pius in his roles. Marcus himself gratefully listed, in Book I of the *Meditations*, what he had learned from the man he called his father:

> From my father, I learned calmness and firm adherence to decisions undertaken; no big-noting about so-called status; love of hard work and persistence; readiness to listen to anyone bringing forward proposals for public benefit; undeviating firmness in giving each person their due…(1.16).[3]

Marcus also celebrates Pius' habit of thoroughly investigating matters, not being satisfied with a first impression. Importantly, Pius exercised constant forethought in administering his vast responsibilities, including being a good financial manager: he showed sensible economy in spending on public infrastructure. There is an implied contrast with Hadrian, when Marcus praises Pius' indifference about 'building houses'; Hadrian had expended huge time and funds on his estate at Tivoli, outside Rome, to which he retired in his final years. This section of the *Meditations* remains a key biographical source for Pius.[4]

Marcus, alongside Lucius Ceionius – now officially called Verus – would act as Pius' assistant until the latter's death in 161. The wisdom of Hadrian's planning would only emerge over time. Pius and his wife Faustina (often called the Elder, to distinguish her from her daughter Faustina the Younger, later Marcus' wife) had two sons and two daughters, but both sons died before their father. This only threw into relief the importance of having Marcus and Lucius Verus in training for power.

On Pius' death, Marcus refused to take the reins unless the Senate also elevated Lucius Verus. We read:

> When Pius died, Marcus bestowed all honours upon Verus, even granting him a share in the imperial power; he made him his colleague (*sibique consortem fecit*), moreover, although the senate had presented the power to him alone (*HA* Verus 3.8).

There were significant precedents for having two partners in power. Republican Rome had featured a pair of consuls having power over the state administration every year, and as we have seen Pius had ruled with the practical assistance of Marcus for nearly two decades. But Marcus' explicit insistence on having Verus as co-emperor was an innovation for the imperial system. It denoted three important things: one, the difficulty and complexity of his conception of the role he faced; two, his preference to share power rather than exercise it alone; and three, his loyalty to the arrangements which Hadrian and Pius had put in place.

No doubt Marcus expected, or at least hoped for, the same kind of practical help with the vast workload of legislation, adjudication, correspondence, and meetings that he had afforded to Pius. It does not seem, however, that Verus was really interested in, or capable of, making such a commitment. Stories soon began to emerge:

> When [Verus] set out for Syria [to deal with emerging problems with governance there] ... his reputation was damaged not only by a dissolute, unrestrained way of life, but also by adulteries and by affairs with young men. Besides, he is said to have been so self-indulgent as to have a tavern installed in his home after he returned from Syria, and to head there after Marcus' banquets and have every type of disgraceful person serve him. It is said, moreover, that he used to gamble on dice all night ... (*HA* Verus 4.4–6)

A half-hearted campaigner, Verus died suddenly in 169 on the way back to Rome from the northern frontier, leaving Marcus as sole ruler. Once again, then, the system of adopting a co-emperor would only be effective when the person was of a virtuous, hardworking, and self-controlled character. The *Historia Augusta*, strikingly, says that Verus:

> Is not to be classed with either the good or the bad emperors. For it is agreed that he neither bristled with vices nor abounded in virtues (*non inhorruisse vitiis, non abundasse virtutibus*, *HA* Verus 1.4).

Verus, then, was no Caligula or Nero: he was just an average, run-of-the-mill, substandard performer promoted above his ability.

Yet the need for workable partnerships in imperial power, which Marcus had thus tried to institute, remained, and would eventually be revived as a practical solution to the ever more challenging role of controlling the Roman world. After another century of chaos, Diocletian would revive the practice, appointing Maximian as his co-emperor in 286, himself ruling in the eastern part of the empire, and Maximian in the west. Diocletian then duplicated the pairing, making Caesars of Galerius and Constantius to assist himself and Maximian. It seems, yet again, that Marcus had been ahead of his time.

Walking With Marcus II: Villa Adriana

From the Ponte Mammolo rail station in Rome's north-east, the visitor can catch a bus towards Tivoli. For forty minutes or so, the bus passes marble workshops and other light and local industries, as must have been practised along this road for centuries. Workers and shoppers get on and off; this is no tourist route. The stop for Hadrian's Villa, Villa Adriana, is scarcely an official one, but the bus driver will let you off at the right place if you ask. Allow plenty of time to explore.

There is a walk of a kilometre or so towards the site. At once its beauty envelopes the visitor. Pines, oaks and olive trees abound; in spring, blood-red poppies spring up. Birds and insects thread through the vegetation. This is surely a haunt of the nymphs and the many spirits of Roman place.

Here, young Marcus spent time during his childhood and teen years, as the ageing Hadrian increasingly retired from Rome proper. Hadrian himself had designed many of the lavish buildings, of which foundations and some other architectural elements survive to impress the visitor. Hadrian was without doubt an architectural and administrative genius, and the villa sees field trips by students of art history at high school and university (and even by pre-schoolers, delightfully holding hands, two-by-two – Italian schools start them young in appreciating their cultural heritage – and requiring frequent snack-stops as they trudge around the extensive site).

Perhaps the most famous feature is the lovely Canopus, a sizeable pool surrounded by statues, named for a region of Egypt, and boasting a shrine of Serapis at its end. Many of the statues were found lying in the water, and have been restored to upright poses. (For its part, the pool is now home to numbers of fish, frogs and other fauna, confirming the enduring life persisting here.)

Less well known is the astonishing Pecile, an open area flanked by a massive wall. This name is a strange one: it is an Italianised version of the Greek Poikile, 'painted,' recalling the original home of the Stoic philosophical school in Athens, the Stoa Poikile, 'painted porch.' Hadrian loved Greek culture; and it is likely that young Marcus, wandering here, imagined the original in Athens, which he was not to visit until many decades later. Perhaps it was after pacing the Pecile that a twelve-year-old Marcus declared his allegiance to philosophy and simple living, until dissuaded by his mother: it was hardly appropriate for an imperial heir to affect a rough cloak and sleep on the ground (HA MA 2.6).

No doubt there were other influences, too. The extraordinary beauty, both natural and man-made, of Hadrian's complex, is likely to have had its impact on Marcus in his impressionable teens. Historians have emphasised that the only mentions of Hadrian in the Meditations are in the context of how readily today's great men become the forgotten figures of yesteryear, concluding that Marcus' opinion of his adoptive grandfather was a dismissive one. They also, reasonably, note that Marcus' emphasis on open rule represent an implied contrast with that of the ageing and increasingly paranoid Hadrian.[5] *These views are consistent, however, with an acknowledgement of Hadrian's idiosyncratic brilliance, of which the finest surviving expression – along with the restoration of the Pantheon which he directed – is this wonderful estate where the imperial family had the privilege of spending time.*

Chapter Three

A Knight Called Marcus

A medieval guidebook to Rome – a mysterious statue – a legend of 'Marcus' – Marcus' northern wars – A Sarmatian war-horse – Marcus' life and work revived – the Sarmatians in Britain

There is extant a small book, called *Mirabilia Urbis Romae*, 'the wonders of the city of Rome,' which was a standard guide to Rome for visitors from the twelfth to the fifteenth centuries of the Christian era. For many travellers of both the active and the armchair kind, there is nothing more delightful than a guidebook. It offers information in digestible bites, and best of all, it invites you to imagine yourself travelling to the destination. Medieval readers throughout Europe – for of course, the little book was written in Latin – must have read, mused, gazed out their window, and planned their own pilgrimage to the Holy City. The *Mirabilia* survived into the age of printing, to appear in several editions. An English version from 1889, by Francis Morgan Nichols, is widely available online.

At the time the *Mirabilia* was written, much of Roman history had been completely forgotten, and where faint recollections were preserved, they were often inaccurate where not entirely fanciful. This, it need hardly be said, only enhances the book's charm. It is as much a tale as a guide, offering entertainment as much as instruction.

The author details Gates, Arches, Churches, Theatres and Bridges, as they were known and understood a thousand confused years after their heyday. Among these marvels one was allocated its own chapter: 'Wherefore the Horse was Made, that is called Constantine's.' Our author begins:

> There is at the Lateran a certain brazen horse, that is called Constantine's Horse; but it is not so, for whosoever will know the truth thereof, let him read it here.[1]

The Lateran complex, on the Caelian Hill, had become an important site of papal residence, but in earlier times as we have seen it had been the site of family property of Marcus Aurelius' family, and probably Marcus had been born there.[2] Our author in fact fails to clarify why the horse was not Constantine's, but rather goes on to relate a truly medieval legend:

> In the time of the Consuls and Senators, a certain full mighty king from the parts of the East came to Italy, and besieged Rome on the side of the Lateran, and with much slaughter and war afflicted the Roman people. Then a certain squire of great beauty and virtue, bold and subtle, arose and said to the Consuls and Senators: If there were one that should deliver you from this tribulation, what would he deserve from the Senate?[3]

The squire – riding a horse 'without a saddle' – sets a trap for the besieging king, taking him captive, while the city's troops defeat the king's men.

> And the Romans had from that field an untold weight of gold and silver … and all that they had promised to the aforesaid esquire they paid and performed, to wit, thirty thousand sesterces, and an horse of gilded brass without a saddle for a memorial of him, with the man himself riding thereon, having his right hand stretched forth …[4]

Here we see a typical confusion of actual traces of classical Rome – consuls, senators, sesterces – overlaid with a medieval apparatus of the individual questing squire and his reward.

A later writer, indeed, offers additional detail. In the tradition of guidebooks, the *Mirabilia* became a key source for many later works. One of these was by an English writer, Ranulf Higden (1280–1364), whose historical compendium *Polychronicon* was widely read and influential for centuries. Higden describes the brazen horse, offering competing theories about it:

> Also there was another statue before the palace of the pope, a horse made of brass, and the rider as speaking to the people with his right hand, and controlling the horse with the left … whom pilgrims call Theodoric, the common people Constantine, but court officials call Marcus or Quintus Curtius. This statue used to stand under four bronze pillars before the altar of Jupiter on the Capitol, but the Blessed Gregory [the Great, in the sixth century CE] removed the rider and horse, placing the columns in the Lateran church. The Romans later placed the rider and horse in front of the papal palace.[5]

Higden thus neatly indicates the state of confusion about the statue's identity. Theodoric (454–526 CE) and Constantine (c. 272–337 CE) were of course much later than Marcus Aurelius. Curtius was a figure from remote Republican Roman legend, a horseman who – at some distant time – had thrown himself into a marshy pit or pool in the Forum, the so-called Curtius Lake (dried up as early as classical times) in order to save the city.

Higden explains that those who call the rider 'Marcus' gave the following account: Rome was being attacked by a dwarf magician called Nanus (the Latin word *nanus* simply means 'dwarf,' 'miniature').

> This Nanus left his camp early before sunrise, to employ his dark arts. Having realized this, the Romans made a promise to Marcus, a strong and fit soldier (*strenuo militi Marco*), that he would have control of the city and a perpetual memorial, if he could liberate the city. Marcus tunnelled through the city wall at the point where Nanus had performed his magic ... Marcus captured Nanus, whose powers were lost, and brought him by hand to the city, and so that Nanus would not use his spells to free himself, Marcus ground him beneath the horse's feet, thus earning this monument.[6]

We can see that in the medieval imagination, a genuine trace – the name of the emperor – has been attached to a 'strong soldier,' as with the 'squire' of the *Mirabilia*. A hint, a suggestion, then, survived of the legendary virtue of the Stoic leader.

If only the statue had really commemorated something as quirky as the outwitting of a diminutive magician. (The detail of Nanus being trampled beneath the horse's hoofs has been taken to indicate that at an early stage, a figure of a defeated foe may have formed part of the statue group.[7]) In reality, the statue was probably set up around 176 CE, to announce Marcus' hard-won victory after eight years of gruelling war over Germanic tribes, from northern Italy to the Danube, at the cost of thousands of lives and immense resources.

Marcus had become emperor in 161, with Lucius Verus as co-ruler. Before long, Verus was despatched to the eastern part of the empire, to deal with disturbances fomented by Rome's perennial rival, the Parthians. With the support of experienced commanders, such as Martius Verus (no relation) and Avidius Cassius, slowly recapturing territory, Verus was eventually able to claim victory during 165, and a triumph was celebrated at Rome in the following year.[8] Prudently, during this period, Marcus prepared for the creation of two new legions within Italy.

In this period, the peoples generally called Germanic, but also allied with groups originally from the Black Sea region, had made repeated incursions into Roman territory around the Rhine and Danube rivers. In 167, attacks into the Roman province of Pannonia were accompanied by strikes into Dacia.[9] At the same time, the pandemic called the Antonine Plague was killing troops and civilians alike throughout the empire, delaying a formal response. In 168, Marcus and Verus advanced to Aquileia and made a successful foray across the Alps to ensure compliance by the Marcomanni and Victuali groups. Verus died in early 169 on the way back to Rome.[10]

This left Marcus as sole commander-in-chief. With his son-in-law (married to Marcus and Faustina's eldest surviving daughter Lucilla) and trusted colleague Claudius Pompeianus, he set out again from Rome late in the year. The chronology of events is unclear, but several Germanic groupings were launching attacks: the Iazyges in Dacia; the Marcomanni around Carnuntum (now in Austria), and even in Italy proper, destroying Oderzo northeast of Venice, and besieging Aquileia.[11] A new Alpine command was formed, and the Danube fleet was reinforced. The Marcomanni were at length trapped at the Danube. Diplomatic work also took place, with agreements being signed with tribal leaders. The success is denoted by Marcus taking on the title of *Germanicus*, and the inscription *Germania subacta*, 'with Germany defeated,' appearing on coins of 172.[12]

Over the following two years, however, incursions and counter-strikes took place around the Rhine and Danube, in addition to the ongoing diplomacy, whereby Marcus, now based at Carnuntum east of Vindobona (modern Vienna), at times aggressively supported one or other rival group.[13] By 176, the Quadi were defeated, forced to provide hostages and auxiliary troops for the Roman army. The following year, the Iazyges were overcome in the Hungarian plain, the terms of their defeat including having to supply 8,000 cavalrymen, of whom 5,500 were sent to Britain.[14] After this decisive victory, Marcus took the title *Sarmaticus*, denoting the defeat of the Sarmatian people.[15]

We are told that Marcus wished to turn the Marcomannic and Sarmatian lands into Roman provinces, and would have done so, but for the fact that at around this time his friend and general Avidius Cassius raised a revolt in the east.[16] In the event, Cassius' own troops put him to death before the revolt could spread beyond Syria and Egypt. Marcus grieved at Cassius' death, saying that he had hoped to complete his reign without shedding the blood of a single senator – an optimistic aim.[17]

The betrayal by Cassius followed upon personal tragedy. Marcus' departure for the Marcomannic War – probably in its final phase – took place just after the death of his seven-year-old son, named Marcus Verus, from an operation on a tumour under his ear. Marcus mourned for five days, still working on public affairs. There was no public mourning as Marcus did not wish to interrupt the games of Jupiter Optimus Maximus, then in progress; he ordered that statues should be made for his son, a golden image of him carried at the Circus Maximus, and that his name should be included in sacred songs.[18]

Coming hard after the plague and devastating floods, the German wars had exhausted Rome's treasury. Marcus' method of attempting to recoup finances was to sell off the valuables belonging to the imperial house itself.

> When he had drained the whole treasury for this war, moreover, and could not bring himself to impose any extraordinary tax on the provincials, he held a public sale in the Forum of the Deified Trajan of the imperial furnishings, and sold goblets of gold and crystal and murra [a precious stone], even vessels made for kings, his wife's silken gold-embroidered robes, and, indeed, even certain jewels which he had found in considerable numbers in a particularly hidden cabinet of Hadrian's. This sale lasted for two months, and so much gold was acquired, that after he had conducted the remainder of the Marcomannic war in full accordance with his plans, he gave the buyers the ability, if any of them wanted it, to return their purchases and recover their money.[19]

We are also told that in 176, Marcus, on returning from a tour of the east after Cassius' death, and holding a triumphal procession to mark the end of the German/Sarmatian war, made public donations of unprecedented generosity:

> Then upon his return to Rome he made an address to the people: and while he was saying, among other things, that he had been absent many years, they cried out 'Eight!' and indicated this also with their hands, in order that they might receive that number of gold pieces for a banquet. He smiled and also said 'Eight!' and later he distributed to them eight hundred sesterces apiece, a larger amount than they had ever received before.[20]

Here, Marcus' smile, from the podium, and the raised fingers of the listeners, are captured as if in a snapshot the beloved leader celebrating, with his people, his long-awaited return home. (It is even possible that our source, Cassius Dio, born in 165, either was present at this memorable scene, or heard about it from an eyewitness.[21]) And so it is probably from this phase of joyful deliverance of the empire, after years of trouble, that the statue of Marcus dates.

Indeed, it has been convincingly argued that Marcus' mount is a Sarmatian war-horse. The highly mobile peoples of the Black Sea regions were above all brilliant horsemen, and the horse was not merely a form of transport but a close household companion and economic asset.[22] Children learned to ride as soon as walk – we are told that one of the leaders with whom Marcus negotiated,

Battarius, was a boy of twelve – and on defeat, tribute in the form of horses and cattle formed part of treaties.[23] As we have seen, the Iazyges were obliged by the terms of their defeat to supply 8,000 cavalrymen to the Roman army, putting their expertise and assets at the service of Rome.

As noted earlier, the *Mirabilia* stresses that the brazen horse has no saddle (accounting for this by suggesting that the heroic squire, likewise, had lacked one), but in fact Marcus' horse bears a saddle-cloth with a striking zig-zag fringe. It is this feature which is likely to identify its origin among the steppe peoples; by contrast, Roman saddle blankets were depicted on Trajan's and Marcus' columns as a plain rectangle.[24] On this view, Marcus rides a Sarmatian horse with its local felt saddle-cloth, a representation – like the title *Sarmaticus* – of his personal and imperial authority.

The significance of the Sarmatian-horse image is confirmed by its inclusion in a carved panel which, until the sixteenth century, formed part of the pedestal of the column of Marcus Aurelius. A sketch of this panel, made before its destruction, shows a Sarmatian-saddled horse at left, Marcus in the centre extending his hands in a gesture of clemency, and a group of defeated barbarians to the right. When the column was new, in the 190s, this panel is likely to have been the very first image seen by the viewer, conveying a sense of forgiveness and unification after the battle scenes shown further up on the column frieze (see a later chapter for detailed discussion of the column).[25]

We have noted the confusion which attended the statue by the time of Ranulf Higden, in the fourteenth century. It would be over a hundred years before the facts about its identity became clearer. Two major factors were involved, with impacts across educated Europe: the rediscovery of one of the major sources for Marcus' biography in the *Historia Augusta*; and the publication of new versions of Marcus' own *Meditations*. The *Historia Augusta* is an enigmatic text for a number of reasons, but it remains uniquely valuable as a source of biography of the Roman emperors from Hadrian through to the late-third century. From 1475 onwards, new editions appeared, with the famous scholar Erasmus publishing a definitive text in 1518.[26]

In coming years, the Spanish author Fray Antonio de Guevara (c. 1480–1545), court historian to Holy Roman Emperor Charles V, wrote two highly successful books, the *Libro Áureo de Marco Aurelio* (The Golden Book of Marcus Aurelius, appearing first in Seville in 1528), and the *Relox de Princípes* (The Dial of Princes). The first was a biography based firmly on the *Historia Augusta* account, emphasizing Marcus' justice, leniency, and philosophical life. The second, aimed at the young prince Charles V, includes much of the same material, but with the focus on Marcus as an example whom any prince might well emulate. Both works were popular and appeared in numerous editions.[27] De Guevara was a skilful writer, and his Marcus fan-fiction, with its overtly didactic purpose of educating leaders, was effective. From the *Historia Augusta* he derived a certain amount, and he elaborated on key themes, such as the critical influence exerted by a prince on the conduct of his people.

Translations soon appeared in many European languages. An English version was prepared by John Bourchier, second Baron Berners (1467–1533), a soldier and statesman, as well as translator of note. Berners served Henry VIII on several diplomatic missions, but contracted serious debts and was forced to borrow money from the king. It was against this background that Berners was asked to translate De Guevara's 'Golden Book of Marcus Aurelius' from a French version, and Berners' work appeared posthumously in 1535.[28] This was the tumultuous period of Henry's marriage to Anne Boleyn, and the dissolution of religious houses, with the appropriation of their property: it appears unlikely that Henry profited greatly by Marcus' examples of clemency and frugality.

The popularity of De Guevara's work, among other factors, reflected the fact that throughout Europe, there was a deep longing for what had been forgotten. A mood of regret for the loss of pagan culture, both material and written, was expressed movingly by the artist Albrecht Dürer. In his *Treatise on Painting* (1512), he deplored the widespread destruction of ancient art and literature: 'I have often been grieved that I have been deprived of the teaching of the ancient art masters.' For this personal loss, Dürer blamed 'the enemies of Art' (*die Feinde der Künst*).[29] A few years later, for his part, Raphael reproachfully reminded Pope Leo X of the role of the papacy, over centuries, in the obliteration of pagan masterpieces.[30]

In 1474, Pope Sixtus IV had placed Marcus' equestrian statue upon a new pedestal.[31] But the next century brought war between Charles V, and Pope Clement VII and his allies: 1527 saw the sack and plunder of Rome itself, torn apart in the conflict. Charles entered the city in triumph in April 1536, accompanied by Fray Antonio de Guevara (by this time nicknamed 'Marco Aurelio' because of his advocacy).

Before long plans were afoot to move the equestrian statue, by now recognized as none other than the great Stoic emperor, to the Capitoline Hill. For Pope Paul III, this formed part of a project of restoration of past greatness, which included moral renewal. Nothing less than a reform of Christendom was planned, and a key element would be the assimilation and exaltation of the most virtuous of the pagan emperors. As part of Michelangelo's plan for a complete redesign of the Capitoline complex, the statue, restored from its lowly setting at the Lateran, would stand tall at the Capitoline as an *exemplum virtutis*, an exemplar of virtue.[32]

There followed a vogue for leaders to have themselves depicted adopting not only the equestrian stance, but Marcus' outstretched right hand. This was interpreted to depict the attitude of a *pacificator*, bringer of peace, a reading supported by the *Historia Augusta* account that Marcus had wished the Marcomannic and Sarmatian lands to join the Roman empire as full civilian provinces, rather than as occupied and garrisoned war zones. The gesture would appear, apparently for the first time, in the effigy of Paul III on his own tomb, and also on numerous portraits of other grandees, including Philip II of Spain.[33]

By now Marcus' own great book, the *Meditations*, was reaching a wide audience. There is evidence that it had not been completely forgotten in the Middle Ages. Joseph Bryennius (1350–1431), a monk and diplomat who lived in Crete and Constantinople, prepared works of theology which quote, without attribution, extensively from Marcus' book (not the last time Marcus would be put to use in Christian contexts).[34] Wilhelm Xylander's translation into Latin appeared in 1559; translations into modern languages would follow. Now there was no longer any doubt about the identity of the rider, his exploits as a leader, or his character and writings.

Marcus' statue continued to inspire, to provoke emulation, and to evoke the greatness of Rome. Equestrian statues would soon be created, of leaders such as Charles IX of France.[35] In the eighteenth century, the French philosopher Denis Diderot would have a celebrated quarrel with the sculptor Étienne Falconet about the statue's merits.[36] Under commission from Catherine the Great of Russia, Falconet would depict her predecessor Peter the Great in equestrian mode (the statue unveiled in 1782). This successor to Marcus would be the subject of a poem by Alexander Pushkin (1833) and become an iconic symbol of St Petersburg.

One final legacy deserves our consideration here. We recall that 5,500 Iazyges/Sarmatian cavalry were dispatched to northern Britain by the victorious Marcus. In a permanent camp at Bremetennacum, near Ribchester, they would raise horses and train cavalrymen.[37] Without doubt they will have married local British/Celtic women, and settled. They will also have brought their mythical tales and legends of their heroes, the Narts.

Traditional tales of the Narts, as recorded among the Ossetian people of Central Asia by folklorists in the nineteenth and twentieth centuries (notably the French polymath Georges Dumézil, 1898–1986), included one where the hero Batradz, on dying, urges his reluctant friends to hurl his sword into the sea. Also related are tales of a magical cup, Nartyamonga, 'the cup of the Narts.'[38] While there is also likely to have been influence the other way – perhaps from Celtic tradition on the Central European body of lore[39] – it may thus be that there was Sarmatian influence upon that central and most evocative of medieval cultural streams: the Arthurian canon. Just as the *Mirabilia* and Ranulf Higden had refracted Marcus through the chivalric lens of their age, it may just be that this very lens had, in part, been created, and later organically developed, as a result of Marcus' own far-reaching strategy.[40]

Perhaps now, dimly, we can see a continuum and pattern among the waves and ripples of the intervening ages, just as our author of the *Mirabilia* seems to have done in writing the wistful conclusion to his lovely little book:

> These and many more temples and palaces of emperors, consuls, senators and prefects were in the time of the heathen within this Roman city, even as we have read in old chronicles, and have seen with our eyes, and have heard tell of ancient men. And moreover, how great was their beauty in gold, and silver, and brass, and ivory, and precious stones, we have endeavoured in writing, as well as we could, to bring back to the remembrance of mankind.[41]

And although Marcus, according to the Stoic worldview by which he lived, considered that all such currents and cycles would rapidly pass and be forgotten, he and his brazen horse – its original safely and suitably housed in a special part of the Capitoline Museums, a copy above in the Campidoglio to greet the tourists – are likely to be known, to stand, and to be visited, as long as is the Eternal City herself.

Chapter Four

Marcus in the Hands of the Sophists (Or Were They in His?)

Recovery of texts beneath palimpsests – Mai discovers Marcus-Fronto correspondence (1815) – Fronto a sophist – Sophists and philosophers – Herodes Atticus, archetypical sophist – Herodes' chaotic career – His contempt for Stoicism – Is Stoicism an 'apathy cult'? – Marcus as reconciler – Literary roles in the correspondence – Imperial home life (Foucault's misreading) – Marcus rejects the sophists for philosophy

To an extent which may surprise us – used as we are to inexpensive paper - in late antiquity and the Middle Ages, writing surfaces were at a premium. Papyrus from Egypt, parchment, and vellum were all rare and expensive; and the distribution of Christian texts was the priority of the writing centres, *scriptoria*, in monasteries. Older, usually pagan texts were more or less erased, leaving a surface for the reception of a later, usually Christian copy (a 'palimpsest'[1]).

By the eighteenth century, scholars wished to retrieve, as far as possible, the earlier texts. This was also the period in which the towns of Pompeii and Herculaneum, preserved at a moment in time by the eruption of Vesuvius in 79 CE, were beginning to be excavated, and a trove of scrolls from Herculaneum – carbonized in the pyroclastic flow – were subject to a range of interventions in the attempt to render them legible.

It was against this background of exciting recovery that a scholar of classical texts, Angelo Mai (1782–1854) discovered, in the Ambrosian Library in Milan in 1815, some of the correspondence between Marcus Cornelius Fronto and his students, Marcus Aurelius and Lucius Verus. Mai quickly published an edition. Some years later, he located a second batch in the Vatican Library, which he published in 1823. The two caches of letters appeared to have belonged to a single collection, which had become separated during the seventeenth century. Over the letters had been written a history of the Acts of the (Christian) Council of Chalcedon in 451.[2] Mai, as was customary at the time, used a range of chemical agents such as Gallic acid to assist in revealing the underlying text, a practice which caused damage and rendered the manuscripts – ironically – at points now permanently illegible.[3]

From mentions in a range of authors, it seems that Fronto's letters were published, widely known, celebrated, and even imitated, from the third to the fifth centuries, but the last writer to refer to them was John of Salisbury in the twelfth century.[4] Then followed 700 years of oblivion, until Mai identified the Milan collection. For us, the correspondence must be far more valuable for the light it sheds on the youth and adulthood of Marcus Aurelius than for the merits or otherwise of Fronto's literary style. In addition, there is no other ancient author for whom we have a comparable corpus of juvenilia, as well as the mature work represented by the *Meditations*. In the correspondence with Fronto, we see the young Caesar experimenting with Latin styles both casual and formal, with the poetic and with the everyday, in a way we would love to be able to observe for many ancient writers.

Marcus Cornelius Fronto took up the role of a teacher to Marcus on his adoption, aged seventeen, by Hadrian in 138. The earliest letter which can be dated is from 139, when Marcus became Caesar.[5] At this time, Fronto, who had been born in Numidia in Africa, was in his thirties, a renowned orator who had held important administrative roles. In Book I of *Meditations*, Marcus would credit Fronto not for teaching him to be a great Latin stylist, but, rather curiously:

> From Fronto, I learned to observe what kind of badmouthing, and deviousness, and hypocrisy go along with absolute power, and that those of us who are called 'upper-class' tend to be lacking in family love (1.11).

It almost looks as if Marcus was scratching around for something for which to thank Fronto; he could hardly omit the famous orator from his list of debts, yet the implication is that he learned more from the life of Fronto the man than skills from Fronto the teacher. After all, philosophy was, for the Stoics, a way of life, of which a willing student will find even unwitting teachers. He may mean that Fronto provided a living example of family love, which might have been somewhat scarce on the Palatine Hill with the busy Antoninus Pius, or earlier at Tivoli with the fading and unwell Hadrian. In any event, Marcus himself seems to have been, or become, a very affectionate son, father, and friend.

Indeed, the impression which emerges from the correspondence is that even by his early twenties, Marcus knew all that Fronto could teach him about writing, and more. It seems that Fronto sensed this, and was forever attempting to retain his special place with his student, who by now was learning to rule the world. He certainly knew that the young man was unusually gifted: 'Farewell, my lord, with your rare abilities' (*cum eximio ingenio, Ad M. Caes.*iii.8.3[6]) is a typical expression.

By this time, also – indeed, from his early adolescence – Marcus had fallen in love with philosophy; and in his thanks to his teacher Rusticus, Marcus' mature contempt for 'sophistical' eloquence – Fronto's speciality – was plain:

> From Rusticus, I got the impression that my character needed correction and therapy, and learned not to be lured into competitive sophistry, nor writing on theoretical issues, or delivering persuasive lectures, or pretentiously displaying myself as a man of simple living and good deeds (*Meditations* 1.7).

He adds, at the end of Book 1, his gratitude that 'when I had an inclination to philosophy, I did not fall into the hands of a sophist' (1.17). This is pointed: in fact, he was 'in the hands' of two of the most celebrated sophists of the age, but here he repudiates their influence. Marcus' own mature style, in the *Meditations*, is as memorable and pithy as his one-time teacher might have appreciated, but it is almost anti-rhetorical: Marcus conveys meaning through brief and pointed instructions to himself.

But who were the sophists, and how were they different from philosophers? Or were they? Was it just a matter of context?

As always, the background of Socrates is key. In fifth-century BCE Greece, life-coaches such as Gorgias of Leontini (in Sicily) and Protagoras of Abdera (in northern Greece) would travel around, teaching paying students the skills of public speaking and some training in reasoning and debate. They claimed to have knowledge which, in return for money, they would impart. By contrast, Socrates insisted that he himself knew nothing, and would charge nothing to talk about philosophy (*Apology* 31b-c). Almost by convention, then, a sophist laid claim to expertise; a philosopher in the Socratic tradition did not.

In Rome, public speaking was a key skill to be mastered. By the second century, a new batch of experts held public office, gave lectures, and were rivals for acclaim throughout the Greco-Roman world. We are well informed about these men of the so-called 'Second Sophistic', because the lives of over fifty of them were written by Philostratus of Athens in the early-third century. For Philostratus, in contrast to the Socratic tradition, the term 'sophist' is one of praise.[7] For our purposes, of most interest are those two 'sophists' who were engaged to teach Marcus: Fronto and Herodes Atticus.

I: Herodes Atticus

Herodes Atticus (101–177) was in some ways the archetypal sophist of this era: rich, aggressive, successful, egotistical, quarrelsome, but public-spirited on occasion. Antoninus Pius thought so highly of Herodes that he invited him to Rome in 140 to assist in teaching Marcus (then nineteen) and Lucius Verus (just ten). There was a family connection: Herodes had been brought up in the house of Marcus' maternal grandfather Calvisius (*Ad M. Caes.*iii.2), which might assist in explaining the appointment. In the event, however, it is quite possible that Marcus' identification with philosophy, and particularly with Stoicism, was in part a reaction against the hyper-emotionalism, complete with anger and even violence, which Herodes represented.

It was not long before strife ensued, and Marcus was barely in his twenties before Herodes faced charges by the people of Athens, to be heard at Rome, with none other than Fronto as a participant in the trial. Noting the awkwardness of the situation, Marcus professed his affection for both his teachers (*Ad M. Caes.* iii.2). Fronto acknowledged the problem, but insisted that 'shocking charges are made and must be shockingly discussed (*atrocia enim sunt crimina et atrocia dicenda*, iii.3).

Notoriously, Herodes, on returning to Greece in the period after 160, once more antagonized the people of Athens over several scandals, including the accusation that one of his household had attacked Herodes' pregnant wife Regilla (a relative of Marcus' family), causing her death (Philostratus 2.9/555–6). Regilla's brother brought an action for murder against Herodes, who ridiculed the charge, adducing his own extreme grief at Regilla's death: this seems to echo a pattern noted by researchers that intimate-partner violence may be accompanied by intermittent remorse.[8] Herodes was, Philostratus adds, 'by nature prone to deal harshly with his freedmen and slaves' (2.5/549).

Herodes, like many another wealthy citizen, sought immortality through funding important public works. He organized projects such as a stadium for Apollo, an aqueduct at Olympia in honour of Zeus, and a water-supply for Canusium in Italy. His ambition even extended to the long-projected plan of cutting a channel through the Isthmus of Corinth:

> Poseidon, I aspire to do it, but no one will let me! … For a long time I have been striving to bequeath to men that come after me some proof of an ambition that reveals me for the man I am, and I consider that I have not yet attained to this reputation (2.6/552).

A century earlier, Nero had begun this massive project, directing a workforce of perhaps 10,000 slaves, political prisoners, troops, and forced labourers. One of the political exiles forced to work had been the Roman Stoic philosopher Musonius Rufus, the teacher of Epictetus (in turn a key influence on Marcus). Another philosopher, Demetrius the Cynic, reported:

> Demetrius said he had seen Musonius at the Isthmus working in chains and compelled to dig. [Demetrius] himself, naturally, had expressed outrage, but Musonius clutched his pickaxe and struck the ground vigorously, and then stood up and said, 'Does it pain you, Demetrius, to see me digging the Isthmus for the good of Greece? What would you have felt if you had seen me playing the lyre like Nero?' (Philostratus, *Life of Apollonius* 5.19).

In other words, the Isthmus project was associated in the public mind both with Nero's oppression and his vanity projects, and with the unjust treatment of philosophers. For Herodes Atticus to aspire where Nero had failed, was indeed to indicate 'the man he was.'

Such was Herodes' reputation for violence, that it was even rumoured that he had struck his patron, Antoninus Pius, on a visit to Mount Ida (2.8/554). Reading between Philostratus' lines, we can see that Herodes' relationship with Marcus also had its difficulties and differences, notwithstanding Marcus' repeated attempts to salvage it through his personal tact. One of Herodes' intimate friends was a wit known simply as Lucius, who ridiculed Marcus' interest in philosophy (the references to Marcus' age perhaps date this exchange to the 170s, prior to Marcus' final departure for the northern frontier):

> The Emperor Marcus was greatly interested in Sextus the Boeotian philosopher, attending his classes and going to his very door. Lucius had just arrived in Rome, and asked the Emperor, whom he met going out, where he was going and for what purpose. Marcus answered: 'It is a good thing even for one who is growing old to learn. I am going to Sextus the philosopher to learn what I do not yet know.' At this Lucius raised his hands to heaven, and exclaimed 'O Zeus! The Emperor of the Romans is already growing old, but he hangs a tablet round his neck and goes to school, while my King Alexander [the Great] died at thirty-two!' (2.11/557)

The constant drama and tragedy in Herodes' life went on. Regilla's death was followed by those of Herodes' daughters Panathenais and Elpinice. (Philostratus, perceptively, suggests that Herodes' excessive grieving for his daughters was a reflection of his disappointment in his son Atticus, who may have had learning difficulties: 2.13/558.)

Indeed, Herodes explicitly rejected Stoic views about endeavouring to remove harmful emotions. The Roman writer Aulus Gellius, who was on friendly terms with both Herodes and Fronto, reports that he once heard Herodes criticise Stoic *apatheia*, absence of passion. (As Cicero and Seneca had done before him, attempting to convey Greek philosophical concepts in the Latin language, here Gellius translates into Latin what he recalled of Herodes' Greek address: *Attic Nights* 19.12). Gellius writes that Herodes was responding – we might say retaliating – as he had been subjected to an attack (*lacessitus*) by a Stoic philosopher. The claim was that Herodes had behaved with little wisdom and barely even like an adult (*minus sapienter et parum viriliter*) during a period of mourning after the death of a beloved young man. It is typical of Herodes to have framed the issue around a personal grievance – his life was a series of dramas, feuds and enmities – and to have cast himself as the wronged party.

We can see from Gellius' account what a compelling public speaker Herodes must have been, and his argument is an interesting psychological one. The discourse was aimed at illustrating Herodes' contention that no normal person can be wholly free from the emotions which the Stoics called *pathē*, but that even – *per impossibile* – he or she could be, their life would be hopelessly impoverished. For such a person, Herodes claimed:

> His mind would grow weak and sluggish (*langueret animus et torperet*), being deprived of the support of certain emotions, as of a highly necessary stimulus (*necessaria plurimum temperie privatus*, 19.12.6).

Those feelings and faults of the mind, Herodes said, although they become problematic when excessive, are connected and involved (*innexos inplicatosque*) with activities of the intellect, and that, therefore, if 'we in our ignorance eradicate (*convellamus*) them altogether,' we risk losing the good and useful powers of our minds.

To illustrate this potential problem, Herodes told a vivid story about a 'man from Thrace,' an area of northern Greece notorious, at least in the southern states, for backwardness:

> When a man of Thrace ... from a remote and barbarous land, and unskilled in agriculture, had moved into a more civilised country, in order to lead a less wild life, he bought a farm planted with olives and vines. Knowing nothing at all about the care of vines or trees, he chanced to see a neighbour cutting down the thorns which had sprung up high and wide, pruning his ash-trees almost to their tops, pulling up the suckers of his vines which had

> spread over the earth from the main roots, and cutting off the tall straight shoots on his fruit and olive trees.

The knowledgeable neighbour, of course, is conducting standard pruning and maintenance, trimming and reducing. The Thracian, however, deciding to imitate the practice, unwittingly removes all his productive branches and shoots:

> Then he took his sickle and axe; and thereupon in his pitiful ignorance the fellow cuts down all his vines and olives, lopping off the richest branches of the trees and the most fruitful shoots of the vines, and, with the idea of clearing up his place, he pulls up all the shrubs and shoots fit for bearing fruits and crops, along with the brambles and thorns, having learnt assurance at a ruinous price and acquired boldness in error through faulty imitation.

'Thus,' Herodes finished, 'those apathy-cult members (*apathiae sectatores*), who want to seem calm and brave and consistent, desiring nothing, sad about nothing, angry about nothing, rejoicing in nothing, have surgically removed (*amputatis*) all the most vigorous functions of the mind (*animi officiis*), and grow old in the coma of a sluggish and low-energy existence.' Gellius must have enjoyed rendering this thundering conclusion in colourful Latin (19.12.10).

Herodes' contention was deliberately offensive in likening the Stoics to the most ignorant and unskilled of labourers; not only that, but as seeking to render themselves less capable, and as seeking a low-effort, low-intellect life. Perhaps, if we are students of Stoicism, we are obliged to respond to his claim.

Was Herodes right in suggesting that key emotions are connected in some deep and vital way with intellectual power? The Stoics may seem particularly open to such an assertion in view of their insistence that emotions are intimately linked, or even identical, with cognitive judgements. '[The Stoics] consider the emotions to be judgments (*kriseis*), as is stated by Chrysippus in his treatise *On the Passions*: love of money being an assumption that money is a good' (DL VII.111).[9] To offer another example, a man gets angry when he judges that he or someone close to him has been harmed: 'anger is a craving or desire to punish one who is thought to have done you an undeserved injury' (DL VII.113). In this way, the Stoics might seem to have conceded, up-front, Herodes' central claim.

But let us examine this impression more closely. For one thing, we may dispute Herodes' assertion that the 'apathy cult members' 'rejoice in nothing.' The Stoics recognised joy. 'They say that there are three emotional states which are good, namely, joy, caution, and purpose' (*boulēsis*, DL VII.116).[10] They also promoted family love, friendship, and community, all sources of *eupatheiai*, good emotions.

It is only the 'bad emotions,' then, which are in question. Let us take them separately. Could fear really be linked in a crucial way with effective problem-solving? It seems implausible; if anything, fear – which often comes about through a faulty estimation – is likely to result in further distortion of judgement. Fear, we are told, is an expectation of evil (DL VII.112). A person afraid to walk down the street because he or she fears that a barking dog might escape and attack them, may well go on to regard dogs in general as a threat. Such a fear might cause more difficulties for the person in everyday life – rather than, on Herodes' view, stimulating productive activity.

The same principle appears even more relevant to anger and jealousy. Stoic treatments, such as Seneca's *De Ira*, emphasised that a person possessed by anger is likely to make any situation far worse. In fact, as Seneca writes, anger can – far from stimulating effective mental capacity – appear to be the opposite, 'temporary madness' (*brevem insaniam*, I.2). Seneca here also carefully distinguishes between emotions which have an element of peace and calm (*quieti placidique*, 1.1), and anger. In other words, the original wrong judgement (about the ostensible basis for anger) is likely to be exacerbated by subsequent judgements distorted by the powerful emotion.

Jealousy is even more likely to aggravate whatever problem was perceived in the first place. A person who thinks, mistakenly, that their spouse is having an affair, will not only suffer themselves: they are quite likely to make the spouse, and/or third parties, suffer too. The original mistaken belief is not likely to lead to more productive beliefs and actions; in fact it is very likely to lead to worse results all around.

In this way, we can grant Herodes' premise about the intimate connection between emotion and intellect, while preserving the Stoic insistence that the destructive emotions are both involved with and productive of unreasonable (*alogoi*) impressions; good emotions are connected to and productive of reasonable (*eulogoi*) ones (to borrow terms from the extended discussion at Diogenes Laertius VII.111–116). In this case, we have reason to attempt to extirpate the bad emotions, while seeking every opportunity to experience the good.

It seems likely that Herodes Atticus advanced his derogatory opinion about the Stoic doctrine as a self-serving justification of his own volatile conduct. On this view, Herodes framed his critique to defend himself, suggesting that if he had, in accordance with Stoic ideals, moderated his extravagant behaviour, he would have lost his 'edge,' unthinkable for a public intellectual.

Philostratus reports that the philosopher Sextus, one of Marcus' teachers, commented on Herodes' outbursts of grieving, this time on the death of his daughter Elpinice (disaster seemed to attend a great many people in Herodes' orbit):

> No small gift will you give your daughter if you control your grief for her (*Lives of the Sophists* 2.12/558).

Sextus may have been a Stoic but perhaps was a Platonist; in any event, we feel that we know him best from Marcus' praise:

> From Sextus, kindness: the role-model of a family run in a fatherly way; the concept of truly living according to nature; genuine dignity…never showing anger or being in the grip of any other passion, but both being unmoved and at the same time very affectionate… (*Meditations* 1.9)

It is almost as if Marcus drafted this remembering Herodes' specific critique of Stoicism. Stoic impassivity did not preclude great affection for others.

For his part, Herodes could not even control his anger in the presence of Marcus. One of his ongoing feuds was with the powerful brothers of the Quintilius family, who held official positions in Greece. There were disputes about public events and expenditure. The Athenian people protested, and several of their leaders made their way to Marcus, by now in camp with his family far away in Pannonia:

> Not only was [Marcus] himself convinced that he ought to treat [the Athenian representatives] with … benevolence, but he listened as well to his wife and his little daughter who could not yet speak clearly; for she especially used to fall at her father's knees with many sweet sayings and implore him to save the Athenians for her (2.15/560).

The presence of Faustina in the tale dates it to between 170 and 175 (she died in 176 at the latest), and since the youngest princess Vibia Sabina II had been born in 170, the episode is unlikely to date to later than 173 or 174 (one imagines Marcus' daughters being early and proficient talkers). Marcus unquestionably had his hands full with the campaign, but took the time to seriously consider the Athenian grievances.

> Let us consider Marcus' conduct in this trial among the most outstanding examples of his philosophical practice. For he never frowned or changed his expression, as might have happened even to a magistrate, but he turned to the Athenians and said 'Make your defence, Athenians, even if Herodes does not give you leave.' And as he listened to the speeches … he was greatly pained, though without showing it … and when they exclaimed: 'Alas, what bitter honey!' [about Herodes' attempts to pervert the course

> of justice] and again, 'Happy they who perished in the plague!' his feelings were so profoundly affected by what he heard that he was moved openly to tears (2.14/561).

Marcus, then, was far from unemotional, particularly in consideration of people suffering under injustice. It was with the perceptiveness we would expect that, following this dispute with the Athenians, Marcus responded to Herodes' reproaches that 'he no longer wrote to him.'

> For yourself I wish you good health, and that you should think of me as well disposed to you. And do not regard yourself as unjustly treated ... (2.15/562)

That, of course, was *exactly* how Herodes regarded himself. Marcus finished with a request that Herodes assist in initiating him in the Mysteries at Athens, an elegant tribute to his old teacher's standing in the city – and overlooking his quarrels with his fellow citizens. As Philostratus admiringly adds: 'This was Marcus' defence, so generous and so firm' (2.15/563).

In the event, perhaps what Marcus learned principally from his celebrity teachers was to live in a completely different way from theirs. In Book 1 of *Meditations*, in which Marcus carefully lists those to whom he owed debts of gratitude, Herodes is notable by his absence, and we have seen the slight and curious acknowledgment of Fronto. Perhaps, however, in writing Book 1, Marcus was recalling one of Fronto's elegant rhetorical images from the early days of their studies, back in 139:

> The more generously disposed a man shows himself, the more persons will he praise, nor those whom others before him decked with praises; but he will choose out gods and men that have been most passed by in the praises of others, and there give proof of his generous disposition; just as a farmer shows his industry, if he sows a field never before ploughed, and a priest his devotion, if he sacrifices at a desolate and inaccessible shrine (Fronto, *Eulogy of Smoke and Dust* 6).

The most surprising thing is that Antoninus Pius, whose judgement Marcus rated so highly, had selected Herodes Atticus – that violent, bullying, melodramatic man – to teach young Marcus and Verus.[11] Verus, indeed, may have found a role-model in Herodes: but Marcus seems to have learned rapidly to reject everything Herodes represented. As Philostratus highlights, it is in his mature dealings with his old teacher that Marcus embodied the philosophic precepts of that school which Herodes had misguidedly, if brilliantly, attacked.

II: Marcus Cornelius Fronto

Whatever Fronto and his heirs may have imagined – one theory about the preservation of the correspondence invokes the desire of Fronto's successors to burnish the reputation of the sophist and his family, for posterity – the star of the corpus is not Fronto, but his student.[12]

Even as a youth, Marcus showed extraordinary abilities. Fronto writes, when Marcus was around twenty years old:

> But if ever anyone by his character had so much influence as to unite his friends and followers in mutual love for one another, you assuredly will accomplish this with far greater ease, for you were formed by nature (*natus es*) before you were fitted by training for the exercise of all virtues. For before you were old enough to be trained, you were already perfect and complete in all noble accomplishments, before adolescence a good man (*ante pubertatem vir bonus*), before manhood an experienced speaker (*Ad M. Caes.*iv.1, 140–143 CE).

Aulus Gellius writes in passing that Fronto suffered from the gout, and we find Marcus writing from the resort town of Baiae that he would like to come and massage Fronto's foot himself:

> [Let me] run at once to my Fronto, to my most beautiful of souls, above all to be with him at a time when he is so unwell, to clasp his hands, and most of all, as far as possible without discomfort, to massage the poor foot itself, soak it in the bath, and support him as he steps in (*Ad M. Caes.*i.2).[13]

Marcus' official duties must frequently have prevented him from social meetings, and letters offered the chance to converse. Some modern readers have interpreted the expressions of love in these letters as evidence of a passionate affair between the young Caesar and his teacher. Amy Richlin's introduction to her 2007 edition of the letters, *Marcus Aurelius In Love,* has asked: 'Were Marcus and Fronto in love? Were they lovers?' Such a reading may obscure the very literary nature of the letters. Plato is always in the background (as Richlin, to her credit, notes), and any sensitive reading of Plato on love, in dialogues such as *Phaedrus and Symposium*, admits no simple matter of 'sexuality.'[14] There is also the fact that

Marcus is evidently playing a series of roles, 'trying out' the languages of passion in a humorous way, as he experimented with other genres.[15]

Fronto's gout is hardly the occasion for an epic confession of love, yet Marcus plays it up in order to cheer and amuse. Fronto responds in kind, naturally with a fresh collection of similes and metaphors: he makes it into a poetic lesson:

> For that seems to me no love at all which springs from reason and depends on actual and definite causes: by love I understand such as is fortuitous and free and subject to no cause, conceived by impulse rather than reason, that needs no services, as a fire logs, for its kindling, but glows with self-engendered heat. To me the steaming grottoes of Baiae are better than your bath-furnaces, in which the fire is kindled with cost and smoke, and soon goes out … (*Ad M. Caes.*i.3).[16]

Marcus had mastered all the genres which Fronto considered so vastly important: metaphor, mock-epic, complete with quotes from Homer and Hesiod, and appropriate snippets from the great tragedies and the ancient Latin authors favoured by the sophists of the time. Already, however, we see that he regards this kind of thing as a rather pointless pastime. With the frankness which had earned his nickname 'Mr Honesty (*Verissimus*),' he concludes a long letter full of such features:

> That's enough of this game, which I've played more for love of you than from my own confidence in it …. for I've spun all this out for you this evening (*Ad M. Caes.*i.4, 143 CE).[17]

Fronto, however, took it rather more seriously, responding that Marcus had used 'many happy arguments', 'so subtly and cleverly' (i.5).[18]

Public speaking, however, was a different matter, based as it was in practical realities, and Marcus confides that he feels nervous about an upcoming address to the Senate.

> But about my *athumia* [Greek in original, 'misgivings'], my spirit is still nervous and a little bit sad (*tristiculus*), lest I should say something in the Senate today unworthy of you as my teacher (iii.17).[19]

It is striking that Marcus uses a diminutive (*tristiculus*): this will be a feature of his mature style in the Greek of the *Meditations*, used to downplay the significance of the thing to which it is applied: in this case, his low mood.[20] It is a self-deprecating move, lest he should – like Fronto, perhaps – take himself too pompously. We recall that decades later, Marcus would remind himself not to be *Caesarised (mē apokaisarōtheis)*, not to be seduced into playing the great leader: here, already, in his early twenties, he is taking steps to avoid it.[21]

Readers who see a love affair for the ages would also do well to note Marcus' mock-bestowal of an honour on Fronto:

> [Original in Greek] M[arcus] Cornelius Fronto, consul, is the winner! He is crowned in the contest of the Great Friendship Games! (ii.2).[22]

With rare humility (expressed as an anxious, self-deprecating 'yes, I'm that shameless', *quae mea impudentia est*), Fronto ventured to write a letter in Greek to Marcus' mother Domitia Lucilla, asking Marcus to check it first for any 'barbarism' (*barbarismus*), as Marcus' Greek was fresher than Fronto's own (i.8).[23] The letter turns out to be a highly-literary production, showcasing Fronto's similes and self-satisfied, laboured, reflections.

To be sure, Fronto must have suspected, at times, that Marcus was making gentle or not-so-gentle fun of him. Here, Marcus praises Fronto's eulogy of Antoninus Pius in the Senate:

> Oh, happy you to be gifted with such eloquence! Oh happy I to be in the hands of such a master! Oh what impressive handiwork! [Greek in original, *epicheirēmata*]! Oh what orderly arrangement [*taxis*]! Oh what elegance! What charm! What beauty! What language! What brilliance! What expressiveness! What graces! What discipline [*askēsis*]! What everything [*omnia*]! (ii.3).[24]

Marcus also manages to satirise Fronto's love of obscure archaic Latin, writing:

> [My longing for you] is daily renewed and flourishes, and as Laberius says of love, in his own way and according to his unique 'muse' [original phrase in Greek], 'Your love as fast as any onion grows, as firm as any palm-tree' (ii.6).[25]

Onions and palm-trees? Fronto must have tut-tutted to see such vulgar and old-fashioned items feature in his Caesar's prose, but will also have acknowledged his student's grasp of the relevant literature.

It is certainly the case that Marcus liked, on occasion, to shock. He writes to Fronto the story (*fabula*) of how he and some friends played a prank on local farmers:

> I, as usual, mounted my horse and set out on the road, and had gone a little way, then right on the road there was a flock of sheep clumped together, as happens in confined spaces, with four dogs and two shepherds, and that was all. Then one shepherd, when he saw our mini squad (*plusculos equites*), 'Watch out for those riders,' he said, 'they're the ones who've made all the big raids!' When I heard that, I spurred my horse and rode into the flock – they dispersed in panic – running everywhere, bleating and fleeing every which way (*aliae alibi palantes balantesque oberrant*). The shepherd hurled his crook – it hit the rider who was following me. We made our getaway … (ii.12).[26]

It is as if Marcus is trying to show that he is not always the serious young leader, and that he is prepared to engage in the kind of entitled, graceless stunt so often associated with young aristocrats. The anti-Caesarising Caesar seems also rather pleased to have been mistaken for a local crime boss. He anticipates that Fronto will scarcely believe the account, adding 'True story (*res vera est*)!' The fact that the passage has caused discomfort even to today's scholars (as doubtless it will have to Fronto), only confirms that the young master knew what he was about.[27]

Marcus was, indeed, attempting to change public perception of his character, which he suspected – rightly, as it would turn out – his teacher shared. Fronto would confess – with an honesty which does credit both to him, and to the student he knew had a soul greater than to take offence – that he had previously found fault:

> I have occasionally criticised you behind your back in somewhat strong terms, among a few of my closest friends. Time was I did this, when you went about in public gatherings with too serious a face, or when you used to read books either in the theatre or at a dinner … then I would call you a harsh and unreasonable, even at times, stung by anger, a disagreeable sort of person. But if anyone else found fault with you in my hearing with similar criticism, I could not listen to him with any patience. So it was easier for me to say this of you myself than to allow others to speak ill of you: just as I could more easily strike my daughter Gratia than see her struck by another (iv.12).[28]

Illustrating Fronto's compliment that he brought people together, on Marcus' request, Fronto wrote to Herodes on the death of his infant son.[29] This must have been a challenge, since as we have seen Fronto was not confident in his Greek, but he rose to the occasion, including a recommendation of acting calmly and moderately. We may imagine Herodes, as he read this, exploding with annoyance, even if Fronto's Greek (perhaps vetted by Marcus and/or Domitia) passed his exacting standards.

As with the sheep anecdote, Marcus at times underlines the normality – the anti-Caesarism – of his family life. In a celebrated passage (made famous, *inter alia*, by Michel Foucault in his work on the 'technologies of the self') Marcus describes an evening at the imperial home:

> Then I had a long chat with my little mother as she sat on the bed. My talk was this: *What do you think my Fronto is doing now?* Then she: *And what do you think my Gratia* [Fronto's wife, Domitia's friend] *is doing?* Then I: *And what do you think our little sparrow, teeny Gratia* [daughter of Fronto and Gratia], *is doing?* Whilst we were telling stories in this way and disputing which of us two loved the one or other of you two more, the gong sounded, which meant that my father [Antoninus] had gone to his bath. So we had supper after we had bathed in the oil-press room; I do not mean 'bathed in the oil-press room,' but when we had bathed, had supper there, and we enjoyed hearing the locals bantering with each other … (iv.6).[30]

Foucault reads the passage as reflecting the period's obsession with the body: 'All the details of taking care of oneself are here, all the unimportant things he has done.'[31] Yet Foucault's is a superficial take: none of the features of the letter is unimportant.

Marcus is underlining several things in this passage: his closeness with his mother; the family friendships which they discuss; Antoninus' routine; and, finally, supper with the local people, in whose piquant Latin, and cheerful mood, Marcus and Domitia take pleasure. In all these aspects, Marcus is likely to have been attempting to puncture the more pompous concerns of Fronto. There is no literature here, no formal oratory, and no polished language; just family conversation (complete with Marcus' trademark diminutives) and everyday themes.

Relaxing in the evening was the more essential, as performing his duties as Caesar and Antoninus' assistant was no sinecure. In his next letter, Marcus mentions that he is worn out from dictating nearly thirty letters (iv.7).[32] The next letter mentions health concerns: chest pain and an ulcer, declaring he is under doctor's orders (iv.8).[33] Fronto, however, always outdoes Marcus in complaining about his health (v.6).[34]

Once again, Marcus paints a vivid, and almost slapstick, picture of the ordinary dramas of family time:

> My sister was seized suddenly with such pain in her 'female parts' that it was terrible to witness. My mother in her agitation accidentally hit her side against the corner of the wall, causing us as well as herself great pain. As for myself, when I went to lie down I found a scorpion in the bed, however I was able to kill it before lying on it. If you [Fronto] are doing better, that is a comfort … (v.8)[35]

For all Fronto's pomposity and his attempts to impress, we come away with affection for him, simply because his own love for Marcus was deep, and because he freely acknowledged that his student was exceptional. He tells us, too, with artless pride, how popular young Marcus was, his portrait placed everywhere:

> You know how in all the money-exchanges, shops, bookstalls, eaves, porches, windows, anywhere and everywhere, there are pictures of you on show, badly enough painted most of them, for sure, and modelled or carved in a commonplace or off-colour style of art, yet at the same time your picture, however poor the likeness, never when I go out meets my eyes without making me part my lips for a smile and dream of you (iv.12).[36]

In a letter of the later 140s, Fronto reveals how loved Marcus already was by his people:

> The last time you were setting out, when your father [Antoninus] had already got into the carriage, but you were delayed by the crowd of those who were saying goodbye and kissing you … (iii.13).[37]

Evidently, Marcus' bodyguard must have been relatively relaxed about his public appearances, with his popularity a guarantee of his safety.

Yet shortly Fronto's importance in Marcus' life would be overtaken by the influence of philosophy. Having encountered the work of Aristo of Chios, an early Stoic, Marcus writes to Fronto in consternation:

> Ariston's books just now treat me well and at the same time make me feel sick (*bene accipiunt, atque eidem habent male*). When they teach me a better way, then, I need not say, they treat me well; but when they show me how far my character falls short of this better way, time and again does your student blush and grow angry with himself, as, twenty-five years old as I am, no draught has my soul yet drunk of noble doctrines and purer principles. Therefore I do penance, am angry with myself, am sad, compare myself to others [Greek in original, *zēlotupeō*], starve myself …(iv.13).[38]

Just as Fronto had criticised the Caesar he loved so much, there is surely here, in return, an implied critique of Fronto and his other teachers: that they have not provided what Marcus' soul craved: a way of life, not a way of writing or public speaking; humility and goodness of heart, not an impressive turn of phrase. Herodes was more obviously an anti-role model, but even Fronto, for all his gentleness, experience, and literary skill, was no more influential.

But the correspondence of Marcus and Fronto is incomparably valuable. It enriches our understanding of Marcus as a young man: his talent for all the literary techniques which Fronto had been engaged to teach him, but more importantly, we now understand how early and how sound were Marcus' judgments about what was most important in his life: his friendships, his family, philosophy, and his duties as a man and a leader.

Walking With Marcus III – Via Appia and Borghese Gardens

A popular activity for visitors in Rome is to either walk or cycle along the ancient Appian Way. Visitors may take the metro to San Giovanni and then the 218 bus to the Appia Antica park, alighting at the bike hire shop just along from the park headquarters.

Close by here, the Almone, an offshoot of the Tiber, crosses beneath the road. This is the stream in which the priests, each year in March, would wash the image of Cybele the Great Mother (Magna Mater), whose cult (as we see in another chapter) was patronised by Marcus and his family.

An e-bike obviously helps negotiate the hills, notably the steep climb as you first enter the park. The road surface varies from relatively smooth, to rough ancient flagstones, to bare earth and tree roots, so care is required, particularly around walkers and dogs. The road can be followed for several miles.

Much of the area around the road was owned by friends of Marcus Aurelius. These included Herodes Atticus and his wife Regilla. Herodes erected a monument to Regilla which survives in the Caffarella Park, within the larger park of the Appian Way. Another property belonging to Herodes was opposite the great tomb of Caecilia Metella, one of the highlights along the first section of the road.

Caecilia Metella was part of the great Roman clan of the Caecilii, wife of Marcus Crassus (son of the famous triumvir of the same name, partner with Julius Caesar and Gnaeus Pompey in the first century BCE*). On the same side as Metella's memorial, but further along, is a property which belonged to the Quintilii brothers, consuls in 151, friends of Marcus, and bitter rivals of Herodes. No doubt being neighbours along the Via Appia afforded fresh occasions for dispute.*

The Villa of the Quintilii was noted as the largest in all the suburbs of Rome. Its associated buildings included a vast nymphaeum, a shrine to the water-dwelling nymphs, usually constructed around a natural spring or watercourse. There was also, of course, a baths complex, as well as several memorial structures. An aqueduct, of which some arches can be seen, brought more water to the estate. Under Commodus, the Quintilii brothers were dispossessed of their beautiful property, and executed, perhaps as early as 182.

Once again we are reminded of Herodes Atticus, as a cross road bears his name (Via Erode Attico). Along the road are funerary monuments, some of which underwent restoration in the nineteenth century. One is traditionally called Seneca's Tomb. Among the pines and cypresses, with fields beyond, this is a peaceful stretch where it is easy to imagine the monuments in their entirety, each attended by family members who, in Roman custom, included the dead in the celebrations of the living.

Back in Rome proper, there is a 'Temple of Antoninus [Pius] and Faustina [I]' in the Borghese Gardens in Rome. But this turns out to be no ancient ruin: it was erected in the 1790s, during a craze for 'Roman ruins' (the ruin in the gardens of Schönbrunn Palace, Vienna, dates from the same era).

Alongside this 'temple' stand two stelae, bearing lengthy Greek inscriptions. These turn out to be copies of the memorial inscriptions for Regilla, which Herodes Atticus had commissioned from a distinguished poet, Marcellus of Side. The originals of these were removed from Regilla's monument during the Napoleonic Wars, and remain (somewhat damaged) in the Louvre, but copies were made at various periods. So the 'temple' is a fake, but the inscriptions, albeit copies, reproduce genuine documents from about 160.

Herodes, as we would expect, must have directed Marcellus to lavish poetic praise upon Regilla, her ancestry, himself, his ancestry, and their children. There are numerous links and references to Greek mythology, particularly to figures representing fertility such as Demeter (of whose cult Regilla had served as priestess).

Perhaps most interestingly, for our purposes, one of the inscriptions mentions Marcus' mother:

> *'The grain-giving mother of powerful Caesar [Domitia Lucilla], who rules over the heroines of the past, will not despise [Regilla] as she goes to the chorus of earlier semi-divine women, she whose lot is to rule over Elysian choruses of women, and with her Alcmena, and the blessed daughter of Cadmus [Semele].'*[39]

This surely implies that by the time of Regilla's death, Domitia Lucilla was herself already in the next world (her death is usually placed in a range from 155 to 161). No doubt Herodes' strategy (on this as on other occasions) was to involve Marcus and his family, enrolling them as powerful allies in the context of widespread outrage over Regilla's death.

Even in the Elysian Fields, the many contacts of Herodes Atticus were not immune from his attempts at manipulation.

Chapter Five

A Golden Book

Marcus was interested in nature – Halieutica: A Book About Fishing – The always interesting deep – Shared Creation – Cetacean intelligence – Stoic necessity –Human parallels – Epic battles – Surprising octopus behaviour – Dolphin friendship – Marcus' golden reward

> Many other things – though far from beautiful if seen separately – still, as formed by nature, help to enrich and please the mind; so that if someone should have a feeling for nature, a deeper insight, they will give pleasure… and other things will present themselves, not to everyone, but only to him who is truly familiar with nature and her works.
>
> Marcus Aurelius, *Meditations* 3.2–3[1]

In Chapter One, we observed that the preservation of works from antiquity was haphazard, with many great books known to have been lost for ever, while others of less obvious merit have survived. Many of these are the province of specialists only, and are never likely to be read even by people interested in the ancient world.

Yet one of these books which does survive is one for which Marcus Aurelius gave its author a magnificent gift. It is a book about the denizens of the ocean, literally a book about fishing: *Halieutica*, 'fishing matters.' In fact, one tradition claimed that Marcus himself had written a surviving book *On Fishing*, probably a confusion arising around this very work, but plausible on the basis, as I will argue, that its contents were agreeable to Marcus' philosophical views.[2] We can usefully, at the outset, dismiss McLynn's slipshod generalization that 'Marcus was incurious in artistic matters [and] had a narrow range of interests … He was not interested in mathematics, astronomy, poetry, art or sculpture …'[3]

The book's writer was a man called Oppian. He was probably from Cilicia, now in the far south-east of Turkey, but at that time under the control of far-distant Rome. We are told in brief surviving accounts that Oppian was a 'grammarian and epic poet.'[4] A 'grammarian' is a wordsmith, a writer, and traditionally philosophers, particularly Stoic ones, had little patience for a devotion of that precious resource, time, to words rather than to good actions. Seneca, active a century before Marcus, wrote dismissively about people who focus on definitions rather than pursuing virtuous action. Indeed, Marcus himself famously wrote: 'Stop talking about what a good man is; just be one' (*Meditations* 10.16).

But the *Halieutica* must have appealed deeply to Marcus. The study of animals and plants was an accepted part of philosophy: Aristotle had been a pioneer here as in so much else. In Aristotle's work, the study of animal life was central to the study of nature as a whole. Aristotle and his successors looked at those characteristics which were shared by different animals and species, and those which were different. Such examination helped with classifying animals into groups, but ultimately it led to consideration of traits and functions – respiration, locomotion, egg-laying or live birth – in a manner which influenced the entire later history of biology.[5]

Aristotle's work seems to have given rise to a whole genre of popular scientific writing. Several works on fishing were known by the second century CE. These fell into two kinds: with a focus on cooking and eating the fish; or on capturing the fish in their natural habitat.[6] There was a *Halieutica* supposedly by the great Roman poet Ovid (early-first century CE; known only in fragments today), and Pliny's *Natural History* (before 79 CE). Not long before Oppian, a writer named Leonidas wrote a *Halieutica* which was highly influential. It has recently been argued that Leonidas had drawn on first-hand investigations of marine animals in the Red Sea region.[7] All these works, then, preceded Oppian's.

Parallel to this tradition in natural philosophy, there was also an unfavourable metaphorical tradition with which Marcus will have been familiar. Plato, in the dialogue *Sophist*, has his character the Visitor draw a comparison between the 'sophist' and a fisherman: the latter is 'known to all and unworthy of any great interest' (218e). The fisherman practises his art which is one of force and deceit, using a range of implements (nets, tridents). This is hardly a flattering account of the fisherman's trade, but it is a realistic one. We may note another Socratic link with a variety of fish: Socrates himself, in debate, was accused by young Meno of being like an electric ray, *narkē*, because the effect of his questioning was to render his interlocutor numb just as a strike by the ray affected a fisherman (80a-b). Philosophers, including of the Stoic school, were interested in what we now understand as electricity (Seneca refers more than once to lightning, Letter 57.8–9); Oppian several times refers to such an interesting fish.

With all this background in mind, as it would have been in Marcus', let us turn to the text of Oppian's poem. First, we should consider that sea life remains perennially interesting. Aquariums have a timeless appeal: people love to watch fish, sharks, rays (at a safe distance) swimming in a quasi-natural setting. Scuba-diving and snorkelling allow people these days to experience marine animals at first hand. And for others, books, documentaries and films offer knowledge and pleasure to the armchair viewer. The strangeness of many fish species, even those in fresh water, is exploited in such popular television series as *River Monsters*. Roman society was far less visual and far more auditory than ours, so Oppian's achievement can perhaps be considered as if David Attenborough were to deliver a sea-life documentary in hexameter verse: an impressive feat.

Secondly, Oppian's poem offered parallels between marine life and human life on land. These served to underline the links between human and other species. Humans are not simply observers of the array of sea animals: we are participants in a shared environment; human life is a subset, and a reflection, of animal life. Stoicism, for its part, insisted upon our assimilating to ourselves, as if members of our own family, people further afield, a process called *oikeiōsis,* from *oikos*, 'home.' The same can be said about other species, as fellow-members of nature's great network. Recognising this, Oppian's work falls into the genre of didactic verse: it offers lessons to the reader or listener, opportunities for reflection, and not only about the sea.

For example, the habits of the lobster remind us of human affection for our native places:

> The lobster again holds in his heart a love exceeding and unspeakable for his own lair and he never leaves it willingly, but if one drag him away by force ... in no time he returns to his own cleft eagerly ... [and] seeks the home that he left and his native haunts and his feeding-ground ... Thus even to the swimming tribes their own house and their native sea and the home place where they were born instil in their hearts a sweet delight, and it is not to mortal men only that their fatherland is dearest of all; and there is nothing more painful or more terrible than when a man perforce lives the grievous life of an exile from his native land, a stranger among aliens bearing the yoke of dishonour (i.263–279).[8]

Oppian emphasizes the links between different inhabitants of the world, and their shared creation by Father Zeus:

> O Father Zeus, in thee and by thee all things have their roots, whether thou dwellest in the highest height of heaven or whether thou dwellest everywhere, for that is impossible for a mortal man to declare. With what loving-kindness (*philotēti*) although thou hast marked out and divided the bright sky and the air and the fluid water and earth, mother of all, each apart from the other, yet hast thou bound them all to one another in a bond of unity that may not be broken, under a shared and unshakable yoke! For neither is the sky without air nor the air without water nor is the water

> sundered from the earth, but they inhere each in the other, and all travel one path and revolve in one cycle of change (i.409–420).

We do not know whether Oppian openly belonged to one or another of the philosophical schools, but this address to Zeus is entirely consonant with the Stoic worldview, which emphasized the creative beneficence of Zeus and the radical interconnectedness of all species. It also maintained that the regular cycles of the cosmos constituted evidence for this benevolent creation.

Oppian takes seriously these inter-species links and correspondences. We find him calling fish colonies by the same name as the Greek city-states: *polēes* (i.438). In a flowery passage describing the effects of spring on all living things, Oppian makes the point that the processes of gestation and birth are difficult and painful, and not only for human women:

> So not even on the fishes have the Fates bestowed easy birth, and not alone to women upon earth are there pains, but everywhere the birth-pangs are grievous (i.485–7).

Again, here is a Stoic observation around necessity, an outcome which could not be otherwise: and even in our technologically advanced era, pregnancy and birth remain zones of serious difficulty, pain, and danger for women (as, to echo Oppian, for non-human females).

One particularly evocative section describes the behaviour of dolphins.

> Now all the viviparous denizens of the sea love and cherish their young but diviner than the dolphin is nothing yet created; for indeed they were aforetime men and lived in cities along with mortals, but by the devising of Dionysus they exchanged the land for the sea and put on the form of fishes; but even now the righteous spirit of men in them preserves human thought and human deeds (*phronin ēde kai erga*) (i.646–654).

Strikingly, modern science has confirmed both that cetaceans – whales, dolphins and porpoises – are descended from land mammals, and that they share a very high level of intelligence. While modern writers avoid anthropocentric language, they confirm essentially Oppian's point: one recent article notes that cetaceans solve problems, show empathy, teach their young, and exhibit grief, joy and playfulness.[9] Oppian continues:

> What a marvel shall you contemplate in your heart and what sweet delight, when on a voyage, watching when the wind is fair and the sea is calm, you

> shall see the beautiful pods of Dolphins, the desire of the sea; the young go before in a troop like unmarried youths, even as if going through the circles of a dance. Behind and close by come the parents great and splendid, a guardian host, even as in spring the shepherds attend the tender lambs at pasture. As when from the works of the Muses [e.g. from cultural events or gatherings] children come trooping while behind there follow elders, to watch over their hearts and minds; even so also the parent dolphins attend their children, lest any danger occur (i. 670–685).

Dolphins, then, are celebrated for their careful parenting. So are seals, whose mammalian nature is likened to that of humans. Vividly, Oppian portrays the mother seal, after giving birth to her babies on dry land, taking them 'home' to the ocean:

> Even as a woman that has borne a child in an alien land comes gladly to her fatherland and to her own home; and all day long she carries her child in her arms and hugs him while she shows him the house, his mother's home, with unceasing delight; and he, though he does not understand (*ou phroneōn*), gazes at each thing, the hall and the haunts of his parents; so that wild thing of the sea brings her children to the water and shows them all the works of the deep (i.694–700).

This is a sensitive observation of both the human and the non-human mammalian experience, of both the adult and the baby. There follows a general statement about the love of parents for children across the animal kingdom, and indeed in the Stoic worldview, parental love was one of the key building-blocks of cosmic order. This important principle had been expressed two centuries earlier, by Rome's greatest philosopher and interpreter of Greek thought, Cicero, in his book *On Duties*, which was based upon a work (now lost) by the Greek Stoic Panaetius. Cicero wrote that humans, sharing with other animals care for their young, also have the ability to conceive of the past, and plan for the future, and to form communities for the greater benefit of their families (I.11–12). As Oppian expresses it, the love of offspring is 'inexplicable and self-taught' (*amēchanos autodidaktos* I.705): natural, essential, and profound.

Book II of Oppian's masterpiece opens with another statement which has clear Stoic overtones. What, he asks, can mortals accomplish without the gods? Not even walking a step, or opening the eyes.

> The gods themselves rule and direct everything, being far, yet very near. And fate unshakable constrains men to obey, and there is no strength nor

> might whereby one may arrogantly wrench with stubborn jaws and escape that fate, as a colt which resists the bit. But always the gods who are above all turn the reins all ways even as they will, and he who is wise (*saophrōn*) obeys before he is driven by the cruel lash unwillingly (ii.5–14).

From the Stoic perspective, the god or gods created a cosmos which consisted of a vast network of causes and effects. On the other hand, the Stoics were also careful also to insist on the ability of human reason to make choices, and the wise man, in their view, would choose to follow willingly what is evidently meant by the gods to be. The most famous illustration of this principle was attributed to several of the early Stoic thinkers (Zeno and Chrysippus): humans are likened to a dog tied to a cart, who must follow the cart either reluctantly or willingly (Oppian has changed the animal image to a colt and a bit).[10]

Book II describes many of the ways in which sea creatures entrap and devour one another. One of the most remarkable fish is the *narkē*, the electric ray (mentioned by Plato, as mentioned above, in the dialogue *Meno*). As also used of several other fish powers, we are told that the ray's power is *autodidakton*, 'self-taught.' The implication is always of innate capacity, what the Stoics called *hormē* or *impetus*, 'instinct' (it is often suggested that the Stoics had a blank-slate view of animal capacity, but this is entirely a misapprehension). Indeed, the ray's ability to immobilize its prey is said to have been gifted by the gods. Finally, Oppian describes the unfortunate victim's paralysis:

> Even as in the dark phantoms of a dream, when a man is terrified and keen to flee, his heart leaps, but, struggle as he may, a steadfast bond as it were weighs down his eager knees: even such a chain does the *narkē* contrive for [other] fishes (ii.81–85).

The octopus is of particular interest, as indeed we find it in our time: as documentaries such as *My Octopus Teacher* attest, as well as the work of philosophers and animal-behaviourists which has confirmed the animals' practical intelligence. Oppian tells us that the octopus at times eats its own feet, but that the feet can re-grow (ii.243–6). Surprisingly, both these claims are correct; octopuses have been observed to practise autophagy in several situations (such as where one limb is trapped; or during mating), and limbs can re-grow.[11]

As this is an epic poem, traditionally it should include battle scenes: Greek and Roman audiences expected this from their epics, such as Homer's *Iliad* and Virgil's *Aeneid*, and Oppian (tongue a little in cheek, perhaps) does not disappoint. He includes a dramatic account of a 'battle' for supremacy between an octopus and the Mediterranean moray eel. The moray had a special prominence in Roman popular culture; there are records of morays being kept as pets, and even having their heads pierced for the purpose of inserting ear-rings.[12] That the moray-octopus encounter remains a popular theme can be confirmed by an online search: videos abound of contests between octopus and moray.

Oppian's present tense suggests the urgency of the struggle:

> The octopus is not unaware that the moray is at hand. First in terror he turns to flee, but he has no means to escape the moray ... speedily she catches the octopus and fixes her deadly teeth in him. The octopus is forced to fight and twines around her limbs, contriving all manner of twists, now this, now that ... Even as two men skilled in valiant wrestling do at length display their might against each other; already from the limbs of both pours sweat warm and abundant, and the varied wiles of their craft are on show, and their hands are surging round their bodies; so do the octopus' suckers, randomly deployed, labour in futile wrestling (ii.258–283).

Oppian even puts words into the moray's mouth:

> 'Why do you skulk, you clever one? Whom do you hope to trick?' (ii.305)

Inevitably, the moray drags the octopus off his rock, and Oppian likens his sad situation to that of a child being dragged away from a defeated city, even as he clings to his mother: in such creative ways does Oppian include many of the traditional features of epic. It is not long, indeed, before the moray meets her nemesis the lobster, and once again – confirming Oppian's choice of theme – enthusiasts can readily find video records of lobster-moray fights. In his turn, however, the lobster may be eaten by an octopus (ii.389), a restoration, perhaps, of cosmic balance overall.

After detailing battles between his favourites, the dolphins, and others, Oppian includes an account of dolphin beaching, a phenomenon poorly understood even today. He presents it as a kind of willing Stoic suicide: the dolphins, realising that disease and death (*terma biou*) are upon them, head for the shore to die:

> That so, perhaps, some mortal man may take pity on the holy messenger (*hieron trochin*) of the Earthshaker [Poseidon], as he lies, and cover him with a mound of shingle, recalling his gentle friendship ... Excellence and majesty attend them even when they perish, nor do they shame their glory even when they die (ii.634–642).

Book II concludes with a prayer for the health and continued reign of Marcus and Commodus, as preservers of justice in the human world (ii.680–688). Book III outlines the methods of catching the sea's bounty, supposedly first revealed by Hermes. The fisherman, Oppian insists, should be strong and smart:

> Daring also should he be and bold, and self-controlled/wise (*saophrōn*), and he must not love sleep overmuch, but must be keen of sight, wakeful of heart, and open-eyed (iii.44–46).

Heroic virtue, thus, attaches to the humble fisher's role. Oppian goes on to describe the reactions of different fish to capture, and the varying kinds of bait – generally another species of fish – which attract different species (iii.183–193). These sections have been of great interest to historians of ancient technical practice. Of course, there are also lessons about human vice and virtue; a catch of numbers of fish in basket traps affords an observation about the bad choices of fatherless youth (intended, perhaps, to compliment the imperial father Marcus, now watching closely over his son, but acquiring poignancy from the downfall which would be represented by the career of Commodus after his father's death):

> As when to the house of a fatherless youth his age-fellows, lacking sound judgment (*outi saophrosunēsi*), gather all day invited and uninvited, wasting forever the goods of the masterless house, in such pursuits as foolish young men are incited to by youth's thoughtlessness, and in their poor judgement (*kakophrosuneēesi*) come to a bad end: even so for the gathered fishes, doom stands by (iii.358–364).

Book IV covers the ways of love among the sea creatures, and its exploitation by fishermen, using a female fish to attract many males of the same species, the lessons here for humans being all too obvious. Oppian takes the opportunity to identify jealousy as a destructive passion (iv.211–218), a message once again consonant with Stoic judgments about the deadly nature of anger and jealousy.

Our friend the octopus re-enters the narrative, this time because of its love of olives. Oppian describes the octopus detecting the proximity of olive-trees by scent, coming ashore, and climbing the olive tree in order to eat the fruit (naturally, a weakness exploited by fishers who trap the animal: iv.268–307). This would seem to be too extraordinary to be true, yet researchers have established that several species of octopus, in various parts of the world, at times come ashore and climb trees (including the Pacific Northwest Tree Octopus).[13] As so often, it seems that Oppian's information may well be accurate.

An even more surprising episode has also received cautious critical acceptance. Oppian claims that the sea-bream, *sargus*, loves to be around goats, and gathers enthusiastically when goatherds bring their flocks to the shore (iv.308ff). This anecdote had a curious subsequent history, while also attracting learned scepticism; but may reflect ancient herding practices including seasonal washing of goats in the sea. Specialist on ancient fishing lore, Ephraim Lytle, pointing out that Oppian's text conjures 'a cosmopolitan world of interconnected *poleis*', has suggested that his claims about the strange phenomenon should be treated seriously.[14]

In a chapter which includes so many triumphs of human ingenuity over fish, it is pleasing that Oppian – while celebrating successful fishing – also pities the victims. He writes:

> Beholding [a school of captured Pelamyds, bonitos] even a stone-hearted man would pity them for their unhappy capture and death (iv.549–550).

And in discussing the use of poison, Oppian seems strongly to disapprove of the method, partly because of the wider pollution it entails (iv.663). He likens the practice to siege warfare in which one side poisons the wells of the other (685–688).

Book V, climactically, describes the monsters of the deep. The techniques of whalers, and the agonies of the harpooned whale, are presented as a sea-battle. Sharks and turtles are fair game. But dolphins are, as we have seen, sacred, and to kill them is to invite moral and religious contagion:

> The hunting of dolphins is immoral and that man can no more draw nigh the gods as a welcome sacrifice, not touch their altars with clean hands, but pollutes those who share the same roof with him, who so willingly devises destruction for dolphins. For equally with human slaughter the gods abhor the deathly doom of the monarchs of the deep (v.416–421).

Oppian recalls the famous story of the musician Arion, rescued by a dolphin from the clutches of pirates. His listener, Marcus the emperor, will have affectionately recalled that his old teacher, Fronto, had retold the much-loved tale of Arion as a set literary piece, in their correspondence years before, no doubt as a model for his student's style.[15]

Oppian adds an anecdote from recent times – a friendship between a young man and a dolphin, over a period of years. The dolphin would come when called by name (474–476). The youth would ride on the dolphin's back:

> No colt for its rider is so tender of mouth and so obedient to the curved bit; no dog trained to the bidding of the hunter is so obedient to follow where he leads; nay, nor any servants are so obedient, when their master bids, to do his will willingly, as that friendly Dolphin (*delphis philos*) was obedient to the bidding of the youth, without yoke-strap or constraining bridle (497–504).

Oppian recalls the two animals which live most closely with humans, horses and dogs, and even other humans, in the dolphin's behaviour; and its willing submission is a representation of its wisdom, if we recall the preamble to Book II. Wicked fishermen from Thrace, however, even target the dolphin as prey.

The poem concludes with a beautiful wish for Marcus:

> So much I know, O Wielder of the Sceptre, nursling of the gods, of the works of the sea. But for you, may your ships be steered free from harm, sped by gentle winds and fair; and always for you may the sea teem with fish; and may Poseidon, Lord of Safety, guard and keep unshaken the deep foundations which hold the roots of Earth (675–680).

The Stoic interest in the natural world was important in several ways. As Marcus wrote (in the epigraph to this chapter), deeper insight into nature's bounty brings pleasure on its own. But further: the more we know about animals, plants, and natural processes, the more readily they manifest to our senses: and this, in turn, leads us to learn still more. Thus, the cognitive and the phenomenological interact in a positive feedback. Readers of Oppian will come away better informed, and likely to notice many new things of which they had been oblivious. As Seneca had written, we aim to see nature as if for the first time (*tamquam spectator novus*, Letter 64.6).

The tenth-century CE Byzantine encyclopaedia, the *Suda*, tells us:

> When [Oppian's] poems were read in the presence of the emperor, he gave him a golden *stater* for each line of verse, so that he received 20,000 coins in all (omicron 452).[16]

A *stater* was a highly valuable coin. Presumably Marcus was delighted with the work's depiction of the many wonders of the marine world. Doubtless, however, he was also conscious of the cruelty involved in much human treatment of animals – and of other humans. In one enigmatic entry of the *Meditations,* he reflects:

> A spider thinks it's great to have caught a fly; someone when he's caught a little hare, another catching a fish in a net, another a wild boar, another bears, another Sarmatians. If you look closely at their 'principles', aren't these all criminals? (10.10)[17]

Marcus was probably recalling the opening part of Plato's *Sophist*, which explores the varieties of hunting, as, characteristically, he reduced the activity to its essential elements. His and Rome's own quest against the Sarmatians, then, was just another form of lethal pursuit.

Chapter Six

Roman Joy: Marcus and Hilaritas

Joy in Stoicism – Hilaritas – Roman abstraction into 'gods' – The Cybele cult and Hilaria festival – Hilaritas and Marcus' family – Commodus debases the currency

It seems a commonplace of Marcus scholarship to announce that there has been no perceptible influence from philosophy upon various aspects of his reign. Scholar of coinage Susanne Börner has found an issue featuring the goddess of wisdom, Minerva, as the only series possibly influenced by Marcus' philosophical interests.[1] But by contrast, early in the twentieth century, Harold Mattingly announced, in connection with imperial coinage:

> We are on the edge of a large and interesting question – that of the place of the virtues in Roman religion and thought.[2]

It certainly seems to be the case that Marcus' coinage celebrated virtues such as *Pietas*, dutiful conduct, and *Honos*, honour.[3] We have seen that the ancient Stoics applauded and promoted three positive emotions: caution, joy, and a sense of purpose. Against this background, we find a remarkable series of coins from the lifetime of Marcus Aurelius featuring *Hilaritas*, meaning 'cheerfulness', 'merriment'. This seems an unlikely trait for the truly serious and practical Romans to have celebrated on coinage, so let us explore a little further.

The Romans were famous, or notorious depending on one's point of view, for making gods of many things; and the Stoics were particularly singled out for it. In his work *On the Nature of the Gods*, the writer Cicero, in the voice of a dialogue participant, critiqued this impulse:

> And if [Saturn] is a god, we must also admit that his father Caelus is a god. And if so, the parents of Caelus, the Aether and the Day, must be held to be gods, and their brothers and sisters, whom the ancient genealogists name Love, Guile, Fear, Toil, Envy, Fate, Old Age, Death, Darkness, Misery, Lamentation, Favour, Fraud, Obstinacy, the Parcae, the Daughters of Hesperus, the Dreams … (III.xvii)

There were few abstract entities which were not, one way or another, considered as a lesser or greater god or goddess. It was prudent to be on the safe side, and worship more, rather than less, widely and generously.

This is how *Hilaritas* appears; like other deities, she has a set of recognisable attributes: a cornucopia (horn of plenty), sometimes a sceptre, and a long palm frond. At times she is depicted with two small children, apparently representing the Roman people. Some coins specify *Hilaritas Aug.* (the joy of Augustus or Augusta), *Hilaritas P(opuli) R(omani), Hilaritas Temporum* (joy of the times).[4]

This seems highly general, but there was a more specific application. Late in the month of March, Romans celebrated the festival called Hilaria, for the Great Mother Cybele. This was a cult originally imported from the eastern reaches of the Mediterranean world, Anatolia, the region now part of Turkey. Cybele was considered a mother of the gods, a deity of the mountains, and she had a strong connection with animals. A myth told of how her lover, the youth Attis, castrated himself in a fit of madness. Attis died somewhere in the story, but at a later point he was resurrected, along with the changing season, and a re-enactment of these events formed the core of the *Hilaria* festival. The cult priests were eunuchs, in honour of Attis.

The cult had been adopted at Rome in the second century BCE, and by the time of the early empire, the popular festival lasted for much of March. On 15 March, *Canna intrat* (the Reed enters), referring to baby Attis being hidden among river reeds; 22–3 March, *Arbor intrat* (the Tree enters), a pine tree being felled and brought into Cybele's temple, commemorating the death of Attis beneath a pine tree; 24 March, *Dies Sanguinis* (Day of Blood), violent mourning in which participants scourged themselves, scattering blood on Attis' altar; 25 March, the spring equinox, and the symbolic resurrection of Attis, the *Hilaria* proper, with all rejoicing. There followed a day of rest, then the *Lavatio* (Washing) on 27 March, during which the sacred stone of Cybele was transported to the Tiber river and ritually washed; and the final event was on 28 March, the *Initium Caiani*, which may have involved initiations into the cult of Cybele and Attis.[5]

While the cult had come to Rome centuries earlier, it seems to have gained popularity under the emperors. In fact, the wife of Antoninus Pius, Faustina I is shown on coins in character as Cybele in a carriage drawn by lions. Her daughter, Marcus' wife Faustina II, and their daughter Lucilla, are also depicted on coins with the *Magna Mater*, Great Mother, one of the associated names of Cybele. Later, Commodus would celebrate her as 'Preserver of the Emperor.'[6] There seems, then, to have been a close family relationship with the worship of Cybele.

Even prior to his reign, however, as a young Caesar, Marcus seems to have issued coins marked *Hilaritas*, as a companion to issues celebrating *Honos* and

Iuventas (youth). It references a general rejoicing accompanied by elements of the natural world, notably plants, along with the mother figure. On some issues, a maternal figure holds branches; in others, she holds a drinking cup, in others a spear; but most often a palm frond.[7]

Hadrian had issued some *Hilaritas* coins in the 120s, but the theme may have lapsed until about 140, a time when, as we have seen, Marcus was in his late teens and growing more active as an assistant to Antoninus Pius. One gold aureus shows Marcus with bare head, and distinctive curls, on the obverse (AVRELIVS CAESAR AVG PII F, 'Aurelius Caesar Son of Augustus Pius'), on the reverse *Hilaritas*, holding a palm frond and a cornucopia. Similar issues appeared through until the 160s.[8] These issues offer a series of portraits of the young Marcus comparable to the sculptured busts on display at the National Archaeological Museum in Naples. Variant issues from a similar period show Faustina II (FAVSTINAE AVG PII AVG FIL, 'Faustina Augusta daughter of Pius Augustus').[9] No doubt the fact that both Marcus and Faustina are shown in parallel issues was intended to foreground the joy in their marriage and family connections with Antoninus and the elder Faustina.

A later series of *Hilaritas* appears, perhaps surprisingly, after the victory over the German and Sarmatian people in 176–7. The mood is no longer of young married rulers and their happy family life; but rather of a leader recovered to his people after the gruelling northern campaign. We recall that one facet of Stoic joy is *boulēsis*, intention, purpose, focus; and Marcus, with his generals, had exhibited these qualities in order to bring about the hard-won victory. On a denarius minted at Rome, a now bearded Marcus appears on the obverse, M ANTONINVS AVG GERM SAM ('Marcus Antoninus Augustus Germanicus Sarmaticus'), and on the reverse, *Hilaritas* with her palm and cornucopia once more: we recall Marcus' generosity to his people on triumphant return. Commodus, too, at this time only about 15, begins to appear: COMMODO CAES AVG FIL GERM SARM, 'Commodus Caesar, son of Augustus, Germanicus Sarmaticus'), as does Faustina II on a fresh set of issues, shown in a vivid portrait with her hair in waves. Lucilla appears too in a denarius from some time in the 170s.[10] Once again, the family is asserting their *Hilaritas*, their joy and their united front, after the difficulties of the past years.

Following his father's death, Commodus made several issues of the type.[11] The great irony here is that at the very time, the late 180s, when these issues appeared, Commodus was undermining the entire concept. By this time, he had experienced several plots against him, including by his sister Lucilla and men close to her such as her cousin Ummidius Quadratus, who were executed. Increasingly uninterested in governing, Commodus had effectively delegated power to freedmen such as Saoterus who sold privileges and brokered influence.

More conspiracies followed, as did more reprisals and judicial killings: Lucilla herself, exiled to the island of Capri, had been put to death as early as 182, while brothers-in-law, sisters, and cousins both male and female were also killed over the rest of Commodus' reign, before he himself was, at length, assassinated in 192.

Commodus' physical resemblance to his father had offered a superficial likeness only: and his ascension as sole ruler plunged both his family and the empire into an orgy of bloodshed and personal vengeance. The promise of *Hilaritas*, so confidently promoted under Hadrian, Antoninus, Marcus, and Faustina, seems a cruel joke on the coinage of Commodus. Stoic and family joy has given way to the ugliest forms of vice, alongside the utter abuse of power by a ruler who was an enemy to those he ought – naturally, on the Stoic view – to have cherished. The only echo of happier times was that now each day – not only that one in March – was a 'day of blood,' and there would be no joyous resurrection on the morrow.

Chapter Seven

Losing a Child

Marcus gives thanks – Cousin marriage in Rome – Demography and child death – Emperors with few or no children – Marcus and Faustina an exception – Stoic approaches to high child mortality – Herodes and Fronto (not for the first time) offer 'how-not-tos' – The post-surgery death of Marcus Annius Verus – Commodus' limitations – Heritable childhood disorders – Did Marcus or Faustina bequeath a genetic problem to their children?

> [I thank the gods] that my children have not been born stupid, or with a physical disability.
>
> (*Meditations* 1.17.4)

The Greek reads: *To paidia moi aphuē mē genesthai mēde kata to sōmation diastropha*. Literally: '[that] my children were not born unnatural or distorted in their little body.' *Aphuē* means 'without talent, dull, unintelligent,' and *diastrophos* 'twisted, distorted.' Marcus is thankful that his children were not physically or mentally disabled from birth; and once again we note his use of the diminutive, 'little body,' here, surely indicating *philostorgia*, family affection.

In our time, to be thankful for such a thing is considered to be in somewhat poor taste, insisting as our society does that, broadly speaking, 'disability' does not exist, or – if acknowledged – should not be regarded as unfortunate, or its absence something for which to be grateful. We should note that in Roman society, babies born with evident deformities were, at least in some cases, put to death; so perhaps Marcus is grateful that he was not confronted with that horrifying task.[1]

There are two general points, both striking, about Marcus' children. The first is that he and Faustina had so many: she was pregnant at least twelve or thirteen times, more than once with twins. This was extraordinary, compared with every previous imperial family, whose offspring had been sparing, and had often not survived to adulthood; Vespasian, with two surviving sons Titus and Domitian, represented the previous most prolific emperor. In McLynn's summary, characteristically both careless as to the facts and bizarre in its formulation:

> Marcus and Faustina, with fifteen [sic] children and six surviving into adulthood, were the ancient equivalent of those heroes of the revolution and those heroine mothers who used to be celebrated under the old Soviet system.[2]

Birley, a far better authority, lists fourteen live births (including several pairs of twins), with six reaching adulthood.

The other point is that so many of Marcus and Faustina's children died: eight out of fourteen.[3] What was going on? Marcus evidently believed that his children had escaped physical and mental disability; but could they have been affected by other congenital problems? Historical diagnosis is of course impossible, but the situation seems to call, at the very least, for some investigation.

The extent to which cousin marriage was common in pre-Christian Roman society has been the subject of scholarly disagreement.[4] The historian Tacitus reports a debate in the Roman Senate about the legality or otherwise of the emperor Claudius' plan, in the late 40s, to marry, as his fourth wife, his niece Agrippina the Younger. During the debate, it was claimed that cousin marriage, once upon a time considered incestuous, was now common. But this claim, on its own, in a polemical and literary context, tells us little. In their now-classic 1984 survey, Shaw and Saller studied the family trees of several aristocratic Roman clans, finding that cousin marriages were rare among aristocrats.[5] More recently, specialist demographer of ancient Rome Bruce Frier concludes from a range of (admittedly sparse) evidence that Shaw and Saller were somewhat off the mark in their conclusion: cousin marriage seems, in fact, to have been common, or at least unremarkable, in both the later Republic and early Imperial periods.[6]

It is curious that one of the family trees which Shaw and Saller claim to have examined in order to reach their conclusion that close-kin marriage was not a common feature of Roman aristocratic life was that of the Anni Veri.[7] This, of course, is the family of Marcus' father, of Marcus himself, and of central interest to this chapter. The relevant section of the family tree is given by Birley.[8]

Marcus' biological father, Marcus Annius Verus II (d. 120s), was the son of Marcus Annius Verus I (consul for the third time in 126). M. Annius Verus I's daughter was Annia Galeria Faustina I, whom we have met as the wife of Antoninus Pius. Antoninus' and Faustina I's only surviving child and daughter, Faustina II, as we know, became Marcus' wife. Marcus and his wife Faustina II were therefore cross-cousins, i.e. children of different-sex siblings (the other form of cousinship relevant to pedigree matters is parallel-cousins, children of same-sex siblings). Using the *gradus cognationis*, 'relationship scale,' we count back two generations from Marcus to Annius Verus I, then two generations forwards to Faustina II, arriving at 'cousinship in the fourth degree.'[9] The situation is of course complicated by the fact that Marcus, following his adoption by Antoninus, is regularly called his 'son,' as indeed he called Antoninus 'my father.' (While conveying the dynastic closeness of the relationship, this convention also has the unfortunate result of making Marcus' marriage, thus formally viewed, as being to his sister.)

As first cousins, then, Marcus and Faustina married in the early part of 145. Their first three children – a daughter, and twin boys – all died over the next four years.[10] What were the demographic factors involved? It would appear that socioeconomic conditions for the Imperial family were as good as for anyone in the period, so they can be put to one side. We do, however, need briefly to consider one key demographic matter: general child and infant mortality in Roman society, as far as it can be established. Can we have any idea whether the mortality of Marcus and Faustina's children was in alignment with, or excess of, contemporary norms?

The study of ancient Roman demography became fashionable in the 1970s and 80s. Unfortunately, as usual with surviving remains from the classical world, the evidence was patchy. Tombstone inscriptions were of some help, but were unlikely to be representative of the population at large.

In lieu of systematic ancient data, 'life tables' – estimates of life expectancy at different ages – compiled in the nineteenth and earlier twentieth centuries for particular communities have been used to attempt to establish comparable data sets.[11] However, as these life tables are based on quite different communities, and feature a life expectancy at birth of no less than 35 years, it is not clear that they represent an accurate proxy for ancient Rome.[12] Noting a range of caveats, Frier has estimated that 'normal Roman life expectancy at birth is perhaps more satisfactorily set in a broad range from twenty to thirty years.'[13]

Infant and child mortality have proven even more difficult to assess, except to conclude that it was high relative to our society and time. One more recent (nineteenth/twentieth-century) data set from Southern Europe and East Asia indicates that between 36 and 43 per cent of all deaths are/were likely to fall in the 0 to 4 years age group.[14] However, these are estimates largely inferred from age distributions in later parts of life.[15]

The causes of child mortality are also hard to ascertain, although it is clear enough that water- and food-borne diseases were common: typhoid, cholera, diarrhoea and dysentery occurred; malaria was rife in certain locations; bubonic plague, measles and smallpox outbreaks also were known.[16] As we know, the so-called Antonine Plague – often identified as smallpox – was a feature of Marcus' reign. In addition, the nineteenth and twentieth-century databases identified pneumonia and tuberculosis, so *a priori* they will have been a factor in ancient Rome also.

An important 1999 survey by Walter Scheidel of the demographics of the imperial family, from its inception with Augustus to the sixth century CE, takes particular note of Marcus and his family.[17] Scheidel notes that the case of Marcus was unique in that there is no other imperial family for which we have a similar level of information even about the number of children born.[18]

Was Marcus, Scheidel asks, 'just unfortunate' in having so few children surviving out of so many? He concludes that very many of the children of Roman imperial family members died at young ages, and that 'a complete lack of surviving children is far from unusual.'[19] Strikingly, in the two-and-a-half centuries since Augustus, Vespasian and Septimius Severus were the only emperors to leave two living sons.[20] (Notably, one of Septimius' sons, Caracalla, would execute the other, Geta, perhaps highlighting one of the factors involved.)

Scheidel has speculated that in view of the successive deaths of Marcus and Faustina's children, leaving Commodus the sole male heir by the end of the 160s, they may have then attempted to have more, and little Vibia Sabina (born, as we saw in an earlier chapter, in about 170) may have been the result.[21] (Surely he goes too far in describing her arrival as 'unwelcome': the anecdotes about her cute behaviour during Herodes Atticus' visit to Marcus in camp suggest that, like all of Marcus' and Faustina's children, she was very much loved and appreciated.) He draws attention to a poem by Martial, who died early in the second century CE, mentioning a woman all of whose ten children were alive at her death, for which she received public recognition at the games. This, then, must have been an extraordinary outcome, worthy of a public occasion.[22]

In addition to Marcus' own family, we should turn to the evidence from his friend Fronto (highlighted by Scheidel), and the Roman and Stoic literary traditions, which may shed light on the situation. Rome's greatest philosopher, public speaker and statesman, Cicero, had written about the grief he felt on the death of his adult daughter Tullia, not long after the birth of her second child. He turned to writing philosophy in a move of self-consolation.

In the next century, Seneca several times mentions the loss of children as being one of those events which regularly test our character. His own consolation to his mother Helvia is a case in point. Helvia had lost grandchildren, including Seneca's own young child. Then there is the consolation to his friend Marcia: in the course of this work, Seneca compares Marcia's loss of her young-adult son to similar losses experienced by other noblewomen. The point was that this was far from a unique experience, indeed Seneca insists that, rather, it is Marcia's prolonged grieving which is out of step with the expected course of events.[23]

For his part, Epictetus – in one of the passages which today is least understood and accepted – lectured that we should regard our wife or child as likely to be taken away by death at any moment. His words, as reported by Arrian, were:

> From now on, whenever you take delight in anything, call to mind the opposite impression; what harm is there in your saying beneath your breath as you're kissing your child, 'Tomorrow you'll die'? (Discourses 3.24.88)[24]

Today's readers tend to regard this attitude as perverse, with McLynn, as so often, making an anachronistic misinterpretation: 'It is perhaps fortunate for human sanity that a greater genius than Marcus Aurelius [he means Shakespeare] has adequately refuted this stance.'[25] But we can regard it as a practical, even constructive, approach in a society with a high rate of child and young-adult mortality. For the Stoics, and indeed also for their rivals the Epicureans, as death was inevitable, it was wise to anticipate that it might occur at any time, on any day. This preparation of the mind for less pleasant events was a Stoic practice, *praemeditatio malorum*, 'thinking ahead about evils.'

Coupled with another practice, the insistence that for the Stoic, all the world's events are part of an intelligible causal chain, and thus not to be considered as surprising, this was a powerful preparation against the death of a loved one. The final weapon in the Stoic armoury was recognition that as all events are part of nature, all occurrences are fundamentally good. Birth would not be possible without death: both form part of the repeating cosmic cycles which are ordered, rational, and divine. If our child dies, he or she is taken back by Nature, which had only lent them as a beautiful but temporary gift. Again, this perception of a benevolent cosmic order finds few adherents among 'modern scientific' people, but it was central to the worldview and practice of the ancient Stoics.

With these attitudes brought to the fore, we can see that – not for the only time – Marcus' teachers had provided him with a how-not-to. As noted in an earlier chapter, Marcus' Greek public-speaking teacher, Herodes Atticus, was notorious for his extravagant displays of grief when – as often occurred – he lost a friend, relative, or, most famously, his wife, Regilla, in whose violent death he himself was implicated.

The satirist Lucian reports another of Herodes' psychotic stunts which purported to commemorate a young man, Polydeuces. Herodes ordered a chariot and horses to be prepared, along with an elaborate meal, as if Polydeuces were still around to enjoy them. Lucian adds the detail that most people played along with Herodes' charades; understandably, given his volatile temper. The philosopher Demonax (it is not clear whether this person actually existed, or was a Lucianic fantasy of the ideal philosopher) pretended, also, to 'play along': announcing he had a message from Polydeuces, and on Herodes' eager query, said Polydeuces wondered why Herodes didn't come to join him (in death).[26] Brutal though this may seem to us, it encapsulates the realism about death which was, Lucian reminds his readers, a key feature of the true philosophical attitude to living.

Marcus' other public-speaking teacher, Fronto the Latin specialist, provided Exhibit B of a faulty response to deaths of loved ones. Not one to indulge in Herodes-style performances, Fronto however was far from accepting his bereavements with grace. Scheidel quotes from one of Fronto's letters to Marcus, from 165, bemoaning his situation:

> I have lost five children under the most distressing circumstances possible to myself. For I lost all five separately, in every case an only child, suffering this series of bereavements in such a way that I never had a child born to me except when bereaved of another. So I always lost children without any left to console me and with my grief fresh upon me, I conceived others (*cum recenti luctu procreavi*) ... Then afflicted by the most distressing calamities I have lost my wife, I have lost my grandson ... Even if I were made of iron I could write no more for now.[27]

Fronto's later comments underline his falling short of the philosophical ideal:

> Often I even find fault with the immortal Gods, and upbraid the Fates with reproaches.

He goes on to question Providence's arrangements: worthless people see their children grow up, but his son-in-law (and Marcus' friend), the blameless Aufidius Victorinus, has seen his son die.

> Be the immortality of the soul ever so established, that will be a theme for the disputations of philosophers, it will never assuage the yearning of a parent.[28]

Fronto's remarks here were nothing if not tactless. Marcus and Faustina had, by this time, already lost six children: Domitia Faustina (147–151), twin boys T. Aurelius Antoninus and T. Aelius Antoninus (born and died 149), another T. Aelius Antoninus (born and died 152), another son (born and died 157/8), and Commodus' twin brother T. Aurelius Fulvus Antoninus (161–165).[29] Perhaps Fronto thought he was expressing solidarity with Marcus, but his insistence on having lost his children one-by-one – with an implication that Marcus was comparatively fortunate in having some children surviving those who were deceased – seems pointed, if not graceless.

It is no surprise, then, that Marcus credits neither Fronto nor Herodes with one of his most important lessons, but rather the philosopher Apollonius of Chalcedon, whom Antoninus Pius had invited to the court to teach Marcus and Verus.

> From Apollonius, I learned freedom and unambiguous resistance to random events, focusing without the slightest distraction on reason; to be always the same, in the face of acute pain, losing a child, or chronic illness... (*Meditations* 1.8)[30]

Here Marcus places the experience of losing a child between two bodily conditions, underlining both its corporeal nature in Stoic theory, and its equivalence in impact to bodily pain. This surely (*contra* the hostile account of Herodes Atticus) tends to contest any notion of Marcus, or the Stoics in general, as unfeeling, or insufficiently concerned by loss. Rather, as always with them, the key issue is one's rational response, which will be acceptance of death as both inevitable and providentially ordained.

Further, Marcus tells himself, mere length of life is unimportant, as Seneca had told Marcia that her son's life had been as long as it needed to be:

> Look behind you at the yawning gulf of time and see the other immeasurable stretch ahead. From this point of view, what's the difference between a baby who lives for three days and someone who lives three times as long as Nestor [an aged Greek hero from Homer's *Iliad*]? (4.50)[31]

Finally, Marcus repeats the sentiments of Epictetus about reactions to the loss of children:

> It is crazy to look for figs in winter: just as crazy to be looking for your little one, when this is no longer possible (11.33).

> A person kissing their little one, Epictetus used to say, should whisper to himself: Maybe you'll die tomorrow. – 'That's bad luck!' – Nothing is bad luck, he said, which implies a work of nature: otherwise, harvesting grain would be bad luck (11.34).[32]

Of Marcus' and Faustina's bereavements, we only know the medical background to one, Marcus Annius Verus. As noted in an earlier chapter, his death, at the age of seven, took place in 169, while Marcus was preparing to campaign in the north. Young Verus died after an unsuccessful operation on a tumour behind his ear, *exsecto sub aure tubere* (*HA MA* 21.4). At first glance, a surgical approach seems unusual; the physicians of the day generally used remedies and plasters, or in some cases cauterisation, to treat tumours. Marcus' own physician, Galen, attributed the growth of tumours to an excess of 'black bile,' suggesting that cancerous tumours were only treatable at their commencement. He advised extreme care in attempting to excise a tumour, noting the high risk of haemorrhage, and the side-effects of cauterisation.[33]

Did Galen perform this operation? Did the boy bleed to death? Was there any attempt at anaesthesia? Perhaps Galen learnt caution after this disastrous event. It is recorded that one of Commodus' sadistic pranks in later years was to stage 'surgeries,' that is to say, mutilations, of victims. Perhaps the circumstances of his little brother's demise had been preserved in the historical record – unlike the multitude of normal child deaths, even imperial ones – simply because they had been so horrifying and traumatic for all concerned.[34]

Our hearts ache for poor little Marcus Verus, and for his parents and siblings, seeing him suffer. And yet, of course, surgical treatments for tumours are standard today: so perhaps here, in some terrible way, yet again Marcus, as a father, was ahead of his time, just as Galen was a pioneer in many fields of medicine. And in all probability whichever condition caused the tumour would, before long, have led to little Marcus' death; surgery was thought to have been worth trying.

After this, only one more child of Marcus and Faustina was to die before, or around the same time as, Marcus himself. This was little Hadrianus, hopefully named after Marcus' adoptive grandfather. We only know of his existence from two inscriptions, one at Ephesus, the other from the Propontis near the Sea of Marmara. Born no earlier than 161, he seems to have died in about 180.[35]

By the time of Marcus' death in March that year, only Lucilla, Cornificia, Commodus, and Vibia Sabina (and possibly Annia Galeria, b. 151, and Fadilla, b. 159, as their death dates are unknown), were still alive. Lucilla would only survive until 182, killed by her brother in a general purge. Cornificia would live until about 213.

Commodus proved to be one of the very worst of the Roman emperors, a violent psychopath whose interests were in sex, violence, and the gladiatorial arena. There are hints in the sources that, prior to their deaths, both his parents had misgivings about his mental capacity. During the uprising of Avidius Cassius in 175, Cassius Dio writes, Faustina – whom the author depicts as having knowledge of the conspiracy – feared that Marcus' death might leave Commodus, about fourteen at the time, unable to cope (with the added result that she herself would lose power). Cassius Dio writes:

> [Faustina], who was the daughter of Antoninus Pius, seeing that her husband had fallen ill and expecting that he would die at any moment, was afraid that the throne would fall to some outsider, inasmuch as Commodus was both too young and also rather simple-minded, and that she might thus find herself reduced to a private station (72.22.3).

The Greek here translated as 'rather simple-minded' is *haplousterou tous tropous ontos*, literally 'being somewhat simple as to his habits.' The habits remain unspecified, so the phrasing would appear to be a euphemism for unfortunate tendencies already observed in the youth's behaviour. A recent monograph about Commodus translates the term as 'rather naïve.'[36] This obscures Cassius' point that even for his age, Commodus seemed to have limited ability: after all, people of normal or even high intelligence can be naïve.

For its part, the *Historia Augusta* relates that in the years after Commodus was married to Bruttia Crispina, that is to say during the 170s, the youth's decline was evident:

> During this time the behaviour of his son steadily fell away from the standard the emperor had set for himself (*labentibus iam filii moribus ab instituto suo*, *HA MA* 27.10).

The term *moribus* expresses the same idea as *tous tropous* in Cassius' Greek: observable, established habits of life. The *Historia* continues:

> Two days before his death, it is said, [Marcus] summoned his friends and expressed the same opinion about his son that Philip expressed about Alexander when he too thought poorly of his son, and added that he was not particularly sorry to die, but rather to die while leaving such a son as heir. For already Commodus had made it clear that he was dishonourable and cruel (27.11).

The reference to Philip of Macedon's comments is a little unclear; the Loeb editor refers us to Plutarch's life of Alexander section 9. This chapter recounts two possibly relevant matters: Philip's excessive indulgence of the still-teenage Alexander, followed by an open quarrel between the two which threatened to break into actual violence. We conclude that, like young Alexander, Commodus was spoilt, volatile, and had a hair-trigger temper – the very opposite of his father, although Marcus might have had a temper in *his* youth, too, prior to absorbing the guidance of philosophy: he writes that he was 'often angry' (*to chalepēnanta pollakis*) with his teacher Rusticus.[37] Perhaps, however, Marcus, even now, retained some hope that the resemblance between the youths might yet presage greatness rather than, or perhaps alongside, disaster. After all, Alexander's teacher had been Aristotle, and Alexander – even while prosecuting war and conquest – had retained philosophers 'on staff,' at least paying lip-service to their counsel (although the fate of one, the unfortunate Callisthenes, who died on campaign after speaking plainly to the king, was surely ominous).

For his part, Cassius Dio is explicit in his belief that Marcus was aware of Commodus' incapacity. While scholars routinely dismiss Cassius' testimony as 'biased' against Commodus, here we see the historian as understanding that the impending disaster was not the young man's fault:

> [He] was not naturally (*ephu*) evil, but, on the contrary, as guileless (*akakos)* as any man that ever lived. His great simplicity (*pollēs haplōtētos*), however, together with his cowardice, made him the slave of his companions, and it was through them that he, at first out of ignorance, missed the better life and then was led on into lustful and cruel habits, which soon became second nature. And this, I think, Marcus clearly perceived beforehand (*saphōs prognōnai*) (73/2.1).

A member of the senatorial class, Cassius witnessed at first hand the many killings of men and women during Commodus' reign, which surely may account for his hostility (among the victims were the brothers Quintilii, in happier times, under Marcus, the courtroom adversaries of Herodes Atticus). As we see, however, even this was tempered by a recognition that the new emperor lacked the ability to do better – and that his father was all too aware of the problem.

It is likely enough that Marcus, in many respects influenced by Epictetus, would have followed him also in taking a Socratic view of the relationship between cognition and virtue. Socrates famously considered that nobody does wrong willingly: every person who does wrong, imagines (mistakenly) that he or she will gain something beneficial by so doing (*Protagoras* and *Gorgias* are key dialogues here). Relevant to this are other Socratic notions, that all the virtues are interlocked, and impossible, ultimately, to separate; and that virtue is a kind of knowledge.[38] The wise person will also be courageous and just. The converse form of the concept, that the foolish person may well also be unjust, cowardly, and without self-control, is a phenomenon far more commonly observed; we note Cassius' mention of Commodus' cowardice as well as his limited intelligence (as a member of the educated senatorial class, Cassius, no less than Marcus, will have been familiar with these Socratic principles).

Among criminologists – even though they are unlikely to be following Plato, Socrates, or Epictetus – it is widely considered that there may indeed be an empirically observed connection between low intelligence and violent offending. In the words of a 2012 survey, 'Research has consistently found lower cognitive ability to be related to increased risk for violent and other anti-social behaviour.'[39] Studies – not without controversy, during the twentieth century – have specifically concluded that there exists a strong negative correlation between intelligence and chronic offending.[40] We may conclude, then, if Commodus was indeed 'somewhat simple-minded,' this may have been related to his pursuit of violence and cruelty.

It remains to be considered whether the consanguineous marriage of Marcus and Faustina may have contributed to whatever conditions resulted in the deaths of their children. The ancients had no notion comparable to modern understanding of inheritance of genes. Obviously humans have observed from time immemorial that children often resemble, in appearance or mannerisms, a parent or grandparent. But the tendency of certain medical conditions to be inherited was an idea which arrived late. It was not until the early-twentieth century that specific study of inherited conditions began to take place. It took until the mid-century – that is to say, within the lifetimes of many people living today – for scientists to conclude that many juvenile conditions are the result, largely, of genetic factors.

Recent official advice in the United Kingdom – with high populations from South Asia, in which cousin marriage is culturally prevalent – notes that for every 100 babies born to unrelated couples, fewer than three have a birth disorder, whereas for every 100 babies born to closely related couples, five to six have a birth disorder.[41] In other words, cousin marriage increases by 100 per cent the chance of a birth disorder in the child. Heritable disorders include several groups, including chromosomal disorders (such as Down syndrome), and disorders linked with recessive genes (such as cystic fibrosis). Such disorders may result in early death: a recent Canadian study has indicated that 'marrying a cousin leads to more than a three-year reduction in offspring life expectancy [and that] this effect is strikingly stable across time, despite large changes in [adult] life expectancy and economic environment.'[42]

It is perhaps worth noting that one of the effects of cystic fibrosis, along with lung problems and chronic infections, is (in males) infertility. We note that Commodus' health had always been of concern (*HA Comm.* 13 describes him in general, despite his gladiatorial efforts, as 'weak and unhealthy,' *debilis et infirmus*), and that his marriage at seventeen to Bruttia Crispina had resulted in no children by the time of his death at thirty-one.

While, as we saw, Marcus Verus, of all the child deaths in the family, is the only one accorded a formal cause, there is some evidence about the first-born, little Domitia Faustina. Sometime around 147, Marcus writes to Fronto (and this seems to be well before he had learned to manage his fears for a child's health):

> Thank the gods we seem to have some hopes of recovery. The diarrhoea is stopped, the feverish attacks got rid of; but the emaciation is extreme, and there is still some cough (*Ad M. caes.*iv.11).

Haines notes that little Faustina died not long after this, and the egregious Herodes Atticus – never busier than around death – set up a memorial at Olympia.[43]

Some final observations may be in order. Marcus was well known to suffer from poor health, although scholars differ on its nature. Faustina II, we are told by Cassius Dio, suffered from gout (72.29.1), although this may be a catch-all term for problems we might recognise today as neuropathic, which can result from other conditions such as diabetes.[44] Faustina II was the only one of Antoninus' and the elder Faustina's four offspring to survive childhood (*contra* McLynn's careless statement that Antoninus '[did] not beget children'[45]).

She and Marcus, then, may have been carriers of a recessive gene which, among their own children, resulted in a high incidence of one or more fatal conditions. As we noted earlier, general child mortality at the time has been estimated at about 40 per cent; but in losing eight out of fourteen live-born children, Marcus and Faustina II experienced a loss of 57 per cent. Genetic factors, in addition to all the usual illnesses now known as viral (such as the Antonine Plague), bacterial (such as tetanus and tuberculosis, among a multitude of others), in addition to possible environmental factors such as lead poisoning, suffered by the population at large, may indeed have been involved.[46]

Chapter Eight

Marcus and his Monuments

Rituals of imperial death – Marcus and Verus commission the Antoninus Pedestal – familial, national, cosmic imagery – function and form of Marcus' column – a Platonic inspiration? – the death of Marcus: confusion or misinformation? – funerary rites – a lost triumphal arch

Imagine – instead of the luxury shops of Rome's Corso, the gritty streets and grand palaces which surround its piazzas – the Campus Martius, Field of Mars, as it was in the 190s CE: a vast and beautiful open parkland, dotted with temples, massive altars, and, dominating the landscape, two towering columns, those of Antoninus Pius, and of Marcus himself. Rainbow-painted friezes spiralled up each tower, leading the eye all the way to the gleaming statue atop the height. Across the Via Flaminia (as the Corso was then called), triumphal arches of Antoninus and of Marcus also stretched. Of these many commemorative and honorific structures, all have vanished except the mighty column of Marcus Aurelius in the Piazza Colonna, and the pedestal of Pius.

An Emperor Dies

As Penelope Davies has detailed in her classic study, *Death and the Emperor* (2000), from Julius Caesar and Augustus onward, the rituals around imperial death, agreed divinity, and formal cult honours followed a strictly observed script. It was the responsibility of the nominated imperial successor, in cooperation with the senate, to ensure both deification and commemoration of the deceased.

Hadrian, who in adopting Antoninus Pius on condition of his also adopting Marcus Aurelius and Lucius Verus, initiated the dynasty, asserted his position upon the death of Trajan in 117. Trajan had died in Cilicia, in the far east of Turkey. Hadrian received Trajan's remains and sent them on to Rome. These, in all probability, were his ashes following cremation, which were brought back to Rome and interred within Trajan's Column.

When Hadrian, in turn, died at Baiae, the fashionable resort town near Naples, in 138, it fell to Antoninus Pius to bring back his remains. Antoninus had Hadrian buried 'in the gardens of Domitia [wife of emperor Domitian];

moreover, he had him placed among the deified emperors, although everyone opposed it,' the *Historia Augusta* says, a reflection of how unpopular Hadrian had become by the end of his reign.

Marcus Aurelius, still only in his teens, was tasked with making appropriate arrangements for his (adoptive) grandfather, which included organising gladiatorial games. For his part, Antoninus built a temple for Hadrian at Puteoli, 'by way of a tomb' (*pro sepulchro*).[1] Evidently the vast mausoleum which Hadrian had designed for his own interment, was not yet complete. In 140 Antoninus arranged for Hadrian's remains to be exhumed and interred in the mighty mausoleum, which would be the final home for men, women and children of the imperial house, and survives today as the Castel Sant' Angelo.

By the time that Antoninus himself died more than twenty years later, in 161, Marcus and his co-heir Lucius Verus were old hands at the rites:

> They laid the body of their father (*corpus patris*) in the Tomb of Hadrian with elaborate funeral rites (*magnifico exsequiarum officio*), and an official funeral procession marched in parade on a holiday which came after.[2]

Presumably the 'body' on this occasion was actually Antoninus' ashes, post-cremation.[3] We also note that the interment and the celebratory procession seem to have taken place on different days.

The Antoninus Pedestal

In addition to the customary cult arrangements, Marcus and Verus ordered the creation of a permanent memorial: the column of Antoninus Pius. As Davies puts it, this was 'their first recorded artistic venture.'[4] Students of history and of Stoicism have often regretted that all of Marcus' creative writing, other than *Meditations*, has vanished. Yet here, in the pedestal, we have a work which, chronologically, sits between the juvenilia of the correspondence with Fronto, and the mature work of the *Meditations*. Let us appreciate the pedestal of Antoninus' column as a surviving creative work probably designed by Marcus, in collaboration with Verus, and attempt to 'read' it in this light.

The four sides of the pedestal are presented as follows: on the north face (noting that the pedestal is no longer in its original setting), the dedicatory inscription: DIVO ANTONINO AUG. PIO/ANTONINVS AVGVSTVS ET/VERVS AVGVSTVS FILII, 'To the Divine Antoninus Pius, Antoninus Augustus [Marcus] and Verus Augustus [Lucius], his sons [dedicated this].' We are to assume the verb, which is not included (Latin being more succinct than English), and we should note the emphatic placement of *filii*, 'sons,' at the end of the message. Marcus and Lucius are presenting a united front in their piety to their (adoptive and now deified) father.

The eastern and western panels are carved with a pair of matching and similar reliefs. These both appear to show some of the complex cavalry (*decursio equitum*) and infantry manoeuvres which featured in imperial funerals, of which we have a detailed account in several authors including Cassius Dio, who took part in the funeral of Pertinax in 193. The horses and their riders are shown in such high relief that they appear to be surging out of the panel, in places given small protruding brackets to support one or more legs. For their part, the foot-soldiers in the centre are also perched on a narrow bracket, as if defending a narrow defile or pass. They look in all directions as if anticipating an attack. In some ways, this work anticipates depictions on Marcus' column, in its explicitly military mood, and the capture of frenetic action through the use of high relief and a range of perspectives. Unlike the column, however, its focus is funerary, as underlined in the south-facing relief.

Recalling the reminder by the great scholar of Roman reliefs, Mario Torelli, that we are to read a relief, as if a Latin text, from left to right, at bottom left is a male figure personifying the site of apotheosis, the Campus Martius.[5] Resting on a pile of stones, he holds up an obelisk, the central feature of the Horologium of Augustus. A link is thus made with Augustus' funerary complex, his mausoleum, and his cosmic concerns.

Here we see at the top, and slightly off centre, Antoninus and Faustina I, facing slightly across one another in a naturalistic pose. Between two eagles, they are borne aloft on the wings of a large, nude male figure, shown facing and engaging the viewer. At bottom right is a female representing Rome, with a war helmet and resting on a shield, a reminder (if anyone were likely to forget it) that Rome's greatness and her future depended on her legions. Roma's shield depicts the babies Romulus and Remus suckling from the wolf, another reminder that Romulus himself was translated to heaven as a deity, the great prototype of Augustus and the rest.

This, then, is Antoninus' and Faustina's apotheosis, the ascent to heaven as gods. The figure carrying them has been interpreted as Aion, Greek for 'age,' and often understood as representing 'eternity.'[6] A predecessor in the genre was the apotheosis shown on the Arch of Titus, where the emperor soars vertically, awkwardly supported by a single eagle.[7] Another precursor was the panel commissioned by Hadrian for his wife Sabina, showing Sabina carried aloft by a winged figure, apparently female although given the damaged state of the piece, there is some doubt.[8] On the Antonine pedestal, the main agent of the ascent is Aion/time/age/eternity, personified at centre stage, and all-powerful. As Davies explains, the scene underscores the familial: Faustina carries Juno's sceptre; family continuity is being emphasised. Marcus, after all, was married to the pair's surviving daughter. The focus on Aion, however, connects the familial to the eternal.

A key intertext on that theme is Cicero's *Somnium Scipionis*, 'The Dream of Scipio,' in Book VI of *De Re Publica*, a work surviving to us only in fragments but doubtless familiar to Marcus in its entirety. The *Dream* is more particularly a key intertext here because of its strongly Stoic overtones.

In the surviving sections, Cicero has the younger Scipio have a dream in which he meets his (adoptive) grandfather, Scipio Africanus. The older man prophesies future greatness for the younger, but he also outlines important principles of the future life, particularly as a prospect for earthly leaders:

> All those who have preserved, aided, or enlarged their fatherland have a special place prepared for them in the heavens, where they may enjoy an eternal age of happiness (*beati aevo*, 6.13).

> Imitate your grandfather; ... your father; love justice and duty, which are indeed strictly due to parents and kinsmen, but most of all to the fatherland. Such a life is the road to the skies, to that gathering of those who have completed their earthly lives, and been relieved of the body, and who live in yonder place which you now see (it was the circle of light which blazed most brightly) (6.16).

Here, then, we see explicitly the link between the familial (adoptive as well as biological) and the eternal, as well as the patriotic Roman, expressed in the Antonine pedestal. There is also stress upon the key virtues for rulers, 'justice and duty,' which, we know from the eulogy in *Meditations* Book I, Marcus considered that Antoninus had embodied. This is, once again, both a personal and a universal connection.

Including as a 'character' the location, the Campus Martius itself, underlines its importance as the setting for imperial apotheosis. The inclusion of Augustus' Horologium obelisk provides both another reference to the imperial location – the Horologium was sited to the south of Augustus' mausoleum – and to its important function, which was to measure and in some sense capture time itself.

That time – its extent, its meaning, its passing – was a preoccupation with the Stoics and with Marcus in particular, as we find in many reflections from the *Meditations*. To take but two examples:

> The cosmic cycles are always the same: up and down, from age to age (and here the word Marcus uses is indeed *aiōn: ex aiōnos eis aiōna*, 9.28.1).

> Everything which is beneficial to the whole, is beautiful and in season. So the end of life for each person is not bad or anything ugly, as it is not a matter of choice and is common to all: it is good, as it is in-season, beneficial, and productive (12.23).[9]

This section ends with a statement about becoming divine:

> And this is how we become godlike, moving towards god and towards sound judgment (12.23).

Bringing the interconnections full circle, so to speak, the red granite from the broken shaft of Antoninus' column would, in the eighteenth century (not without incompetence, scandal, and controversy) be utilised to repair the obelisk from Augustus' Horologium.[10] This now stands for both in the Piazza del Montecitorio, ancient site of altars to the deified Antonines.

Temple and Column: Function and Form

Because of the *damnatio memoriae* applied in 193 to his own monuments, few of Commodus' own public buildings survive, but he ordered the construction of a temple complex to his parents, the deified Marcus and Faustina.[11] The temple complex has completely vanished, but is believed to have been located to the west of Marcus' column, that is to say, roughly where the Palazzo Wedekind (1838) now stands, on the western side of the Piazza Colonna.

Scholars differ on the dating of the column. It may have been planned as early as the victories of 176, or possibly begun only after Marcus' death.[12] The absence of any depiction of Commodus, who was present on the campaigns of the late-170s but not the earlier tours, may suggest the earlier date. It seems to have been completed in about 193, when Adrastus, the *procurator* or supervisor of the project, requested permission from emperor Septimius Severus to use the leftover building materials for a new house for himself.[13]

The *Mirabilia Urbis Romae*, which we met in an earlier chapter, refers to Marcus' column, along with Trajan's, as a *columna cochlis*, 'snail-shell column,' a description which highlights the fact that there was a spiral staircase inside.[14] Martin Beckmann suggests that the column's functions were twofold:

> One, as an honorary monument of unprecedented size; two, as an architectural wonder, a class of monument that was normally solid but now had been turned into a building that one could enter and ascend.[15]

That the spiral staircase remained a drawcard for visitors is confirmed by the historian Ammianus Marcellinus, writing in the late-fourth century. He describes the first visit of the emperor Constantius to Rome, in 357, as consisting of one impressive sight after another:

> It seemed to him that whatever his eye first lit on took the palm. It might be the shrine of Tarpeian Jupiter ... or the buildings of the baths as big as provinces, or the solid mass of stone from Tibur that forms the amphitheatre [Colosseum], with its top almost beyond the reach of human sight, or the Pantheon spread like a self-contained district under its high and lovely dome, or the lofty columns with spiral stairs to platforms which support the statues of former emperors ...[16]

As Beckmann adds, the visitor who climbed the hundred-foot column to the viewing platform would have been treated to a panoramic view, including over three monumental altars which were discovered to the west of the column, beneath the buildings of the Palazzo del Parlamento (Montecitorio). These altars were identified as early as their first discovery in the eighteenth century as 'Antonine,' probably commemorating Antoninus Pius and Marcus; scholarly opinion has varied, but Beckmann concludes that Antoninus, Marcus and Faustina II may well have been commemorated with these altars. Whether the altars represent the sites of their cremation is another much-debated question.[17]

One of the Stoic practices employed by Marcus himself was 'the view from above,' zooming out in order to place mundane matters in their proper (insignificant) perspective, so the idea of a panoramic viewing platform seems to have been a most appropriate tribute. Its location was appropriate. Most people now approach the column via the Corso, past luxury shops; but in antiquity, this road was the Via Flaminia, the main way north out of Rome. It was along the Via Flaminia that Marcus, at the head of his legions, set out for the northern campaigns. The 'setting-out,' *profectio* in Latin, and the 'arrival,' *adventus*, were recognised set-pieces in commemorative art.

Marcus' column has been the subject of less scholarly scrutiny than Trajan's column, its far better-known predecessor. Scholarship about the earlier column, indeed, is likely to assist us in several respects to understand Marcus'. Firstly, in addition to offering a monument and an architectural feature, Marcus' column could potentially have been intended as a mausoleum. This, it is believed by many scholars, was the intention of Trajan, which was begun well within his lifetime.

It was against convention for burials to take place within the *pomerium*, the ancient boundary of Rome, so it has been suggested that plans for Trajan's interment within the column may have been sensitive and confidential. In particular, the plan would indicate that Trajan's respect for tradition, including the authority of the senate, might have been less than supposed.[18]

Several imperial mausolea, such as Augustus' and Hadrian's, involve the spectator walking around a circuit before reaching the central chambers, so the spiral staircase inside, and the winding frieze outside, may both be related to directing the visitor's attention towards the centre and the ascent. Indeed, as Beckmann concludes, the function of the structure was principally the turning and the ascent, both aspects important for the effect on the visitor.

Beckmann is adamant, however, that Marcus' remains were not interred within his column, and that the column was never intended as a funerary monument: 'the Column of Marcus Aurelius did not contain a tomb,' 'Marcus' Column had no funerary chamber …'[19] Beckmann, curiously, remains silent about an alternative burial location for Marcus, while asserting that Marcus had Faustina cremated on a pyre in the Campus Martius, then her remains interred in Hadrian's Mausoleum.[20] He points out that the imagery on the column's friezes in no way relates to an apotheosis (deification) of Marcus, as might be expected on a funerary memorial.[21]

Yet Péter Kovács declares that the Adrastus inscription, cited by Beckmann, 'clearly shows' that the column's purpose was originally funerary. In this inscription, the column is called *columna centenaria Divorum Marci et Faustinae,* 'the hundred-foot column of the divine Marcus and Faustina,' and *columna divi Marci.* It must be the inscription's emphasis on the divinity of Marcus and Faustina which leads Kovács to this conclusion.[22]

While devoting considerable space to later references to the spiral form of Trajan's and Marcus' columns, Beckmann does not speculate on its inspiration. Here, Davies' analysis is illuminating. She explains that the staircase offered the visitor a phenomenological experience of ascent, 'designed to draw visitors into a dialogue involving them in an active process of commemoration.'[23] While this is undoubtedly the case, we may be able to contribute further thoughts about an ultimate source for the design.

Trajan's column was probably designed by the remarkable Apollodorus of Damascus, about whose background – apart from his expertise as a military engineer – little is known. We do know, however, from the Roman writer Vitruvius, another military engineer from Julius Caesar's reign, that the working architect was expected to be educated in the great Greek theorists, including

Plato and Pythagoras. Their principles of geometry, calculation, and proportion, afforded essential tools for design and execution in an age without formal training in the discipline.[24]

We also know that one of Trajan's intimate entourage was the Greek-background philosopher and sophist, Cocceianus Dio, also known as Dio Chrysostom (golden-mouthed). His famous speeches on kingship, delivered with Trajan in the audience, survive, revealing his considerable reliance on the classic Greek authorities: Homer, Plato, and Aristotle. In Oration 1, Dio Chrysostom at length retails a 'myth,' which – much in the manner of Plato's myths – retails a lesson through a reported narrative: a version of the 'choice of Hercules,' here offering a message about the difficulty of good kingship.[25]

Perhaps one of Plato's own myths may, through the influence of Dio Chrysostom, have inspired Trajan's spiral column. Cicero's *De re publica* had been inspired by Plato's *Republic*. In the tenth book of this we find the famous myth of Er, evidently the key precursor to Cicero's *Dream of Scipio*: in the later work, as in the former, the myth rounds out the entire work. Plato has Socrates tell the tale about a man from Pamphylia (now southern Turkey), who 'once upon a time was killed in battle,' his body brought home, and twelve days later placed on a funeral pyre, at which point he came to life. The tale, then, like Cicero's after it, is about survival and translation following death, and being purportedly from an eyewitness, brings an inbuilt claim to authenticity.

For our purposes, the key section of the myth, in which Er explains the process of judging the dead, the various locations involved, and the punishments for wrongdoers, is this:

> After four days [newcomers to the next world] arrived at a place from where they could see clearly a straight shaft of light stretched out from above through the whole of the sky and the earth like a column (*hoion kiona*), closely resembling the rainbow, but brighter and purer ... Stretching down from either end was the spindle of Necessity by which all the circles turn ... The nature of the whorl (*sphondulos*) is as follows: its shape is like the ones we use, but you have to imagine what it's like from his description of it, just as if in a large hollow whorl, scooped out right through, another of the same sort inside it ... The total number of whorls is eight, each lying inside the other. Their edges seen from above are circles, forming from the back a continuous single whorl around the shaft, the latter being driven right through the centre of the eighth (616b–e).[26]

There are considerable obscurities here, both verbal and conceptual, and scholars have offered varying interpretations. Nonetheless, several elements clearly emerge:

a shaft of light like a column; a 'spindle of Necessity,' controlling the constant cosmic cycles; and, somehow relating to the shaft of light or surrounding it, a 'whorl,' that is an helical structure which contains a sequence of smaller helical structures fitted within it. That this structure is related to the three Fates emerges in a later passage, in which we are told that Clotho, the Fate of the present, turns the spindle, Atropos of the future touches the inner circles, and Lachesis of the past touches both (617c).

So Plato's shaft of light is a column, uniting the earth and the heavens for the benefit of the newly dead, while a closely involved helical structure expresses the constant cosmic revolutions, the inscrutable influences of Fate, and the passage of time. Could Dio Chrysostom have suggested to Trajan and to his resident architectural genius, Apollodorus, that they might attempt to express a revolutionary – in two key senses – form in funerary architecture, one inspired by no other than this vision in Plato?

A small piece of corroborating information may be that Dio Chrysostom's final appearance in recorded history is indeed concerned with a funerary monument, that of his own family. In about 111, the writer Pliny, governor of Bithynia at the time, wrote to Trajan about a dispute in Dio's home town of Prusa. Dio had returned from Rome to his home town, and apparently had caused great controversy by placing a statue of Trajan within a temple, close by the graves of his (Dio's) wife and son. Opponents claimed that Dio had not submitted the correct planning documentation. Pliny had inspected the site, finding Trajan's statue safely in the library of the complex, while Dio's family burials were at a safe distance in the courtyard. Trajan, no doubt recalling Dio's rhetorical prolixity, advised Pliny to dismiss the to-do, simply reiterating that correct documents must be provided.[27]

Whether or not Plato's myth was an influence in Trajan's decision to commission an helical column as his funerary monument, it may well have been a factor in Marcus'. Undoubtedly, Marcus knew the myth of Er. Marcus may well have memorised sections of Plato's work, as he quotes them at several points in the *Meditations*.[28] We also know that Marcus, in the Stoic tradition, was ever conscious of the approach of death. On these bases, one of Plato's most famous and evocative – if enigmatic – tales about the afterlife, in combination with the precedent of Trajan's, is very likely to have entered Marcus' deliberations about an appropriate way for posterity to remember him.

The Death of Marcus

Affording space for a range of approaches to the issue of Marcus' death arrangements, is the considerable uncertainty which persists around the facts.

Doubtful matters include the location and date of Marcus' death, cremation, funeral and deification (possibly involving multiple ceremonies), Commodus' role in proceedings, and Marcus' ultimate interment.

Marcus biographer McLynn offers a colourful account of events directly following the emperor's death:

> In the first place, [Commodus] was criticised for showing scant honour to his father's burial rites by remaining in Germany instead of returning to Rome with the catafalque ... While Marcus had a funeral in Rome, was deified and was given the title *Pius* to go with *Divus*, Commodus bided his time in Germany ... [29]

McLynn end-notes this assertion with references to the *Historia Augusta*, Herodian, and Cassius Dio, none of which actually supports it. Herodian, close in date to the events (as was Cassius), explains that directly after Marcus' death, 'During the next few days [March 180], Commodus' advisers kept him busy with his father's funeral rites,' before much deliberation around a return to Rome.[30] This strongly suggests that Marcus' cremation took place on the northern frontier, not in Rome. Herodian adds nothing about a 'catafalque' travelling to Italy, with or without Commodus.

In the next section, Herodian reports Commodus' departure, implying that it was relatively prompt:

> He sent off letters, and after assigning command of the Danube to men whom he considered capable, he announced his departure for Rome (1.6.8).

Cassius Dio, also, offers no detail about the funeral, but suggests the opposite of McLynn's version: that Commodus, far from 'biding his time,' was in haste to return to the city:

> But [Marcus' advisers'] suggestions and counsels Commodus rejected, and after making a truce with the barbarians, he rushed to Rome, for he hated all exertion and craved the comfortable life of the city (73.1.2).

The *Historia Augusta* is even brisker:

> [Commodus] abandoned the war which his father had almost finished, and submitted to the enemy's terms, and then he returned to Rome (*HA Comm.* 3.5).

Marcus died in March 180, but Commodus did not appear in front of the Senate in Rome until October. This complicates the sources' implication of a hasty return by Commodus: in fact, six months of negotiations with the northern nations took place, prior to his departure. While apparently a contradiction, there need be none: Commodus' impatience may have been evident, but there was no speeding up a very delicate diplomatic situation.

Leaving the role of Commodus to one side, confusion extends even to the location of Marcus' death. Was it at Vindobona (Vienna, as claimed in the *Epitome de Caesaribus*), or Sirmium (Sremska Mitrovica, in the Christian writer Tertullian)?[31] This vagueness may have been strategic in the first instance, as relations with Rome's enemies were at a sensitive juncture: information about the emperor's death may have been selectively massaged and disseminated for different audiences. As Herodian claimed, Marcus himself seemed apprehensive about the enemy nations' response to his imminent demise, as 'the barbarians are likely to be stirred up even for quite haphazard reasons' (1.3.5).

That inaccurate messaging took place around the death, whether deliberate or, as Tertullian would have it, incompetent, is confirmed, as he declares:

> After the loss to the State of Marcus Aurelius at Sirmium, on the sixteenth before the kalends of April, that most sacred high priest [of Cybele] was offering, a week after, impure libations of blood drawn from his own arms, and issuing his commands that the ordinary prayers should be made for the safety of the emperor already dead. O tardy messengers! O sleepy dispatches!
>
> *Apology* 25.5.

The formal process of an emperor's funeral at Rome was highly elaborate, as detailed by Cassius Dio in his eyewitness account of the funeral, held in Rome, for Pertinax in 193. On this occasion, some months had chaotically elapsed between Pertinax's murder by a group of troops in March, after a reign of only weeks, and the similarly short tenure of Didius Julianus (March to June), Septimius Severus staging the delayed funeral as part of consolidating his own power.

Pertinax's mortal remains were not the subject of the ceremony, rather a wax effigy formed the 'body' which was the focus of the rite.

> All the rest of us [senators], now, marched ahead of the bier, some beating our breasts and others playing a dirge on the flute, but the emperor [Severus] followed behind all the rest; and in this order we arrived at the Campus Martius. There a pyre had been built in the form of a tower, having three storeys and adorned with ivory and gold as well as a number of statues, while on its very summit was placed a gilded chariot in which Pertinax had been

> wont to drive. Inside this pyre the funeral offerings were cast and the bier was placed on it, and then Severus and the relatives of Pertinax kissed the [wax] effigy. The emperor then ascended a tribunal, while we, the senate, except the magistrates, took our places on wooden stands in order to view the ceremonies both safely and conveniently. The magistrates and the equestrian order, arrayed in a manner befitting their station, and likewise the cavalry and the infantry, passed in and out around the pyre performing intricate evolutions, both those of peace and those of war. Then at last the consuls applied fire to the structure, and when this had been done, an eagle flew aloft from it. Thus was Pertinax made immortal (75.4–5).

The role of the succeeding emperor in the ritual, as Marcus will have performed for Antoninus, and as Septimius did for Pertinax, was evidently a major one. This suggests that Commodus will have taken a leading part in the frontier obsequies for Marcus, seemingly confirmed by his banal and simple-minded comment, as reported by Herodian:

> Assuredly, my father has gone up to heaven, where he is already companion and counsellor of the gods. But it is our task to devote ourselves to human affairs and administer the world (Herodian 1.5.6).

For its part, the *Historia Augusta* mentions Marcus' funeral, but fails to confirm where it took place, although a location at Rome ('the senate and people'), doubtless the Campus Martius, is strongly implied:

> Such love for [Marcus] was manifested on the day of the imperial funeral that no one thought he should be mourned, since all were sure he had been lent by the gods and had now returned to them. Finally (*denique*), before his funeral was held, many say, the senate and people hailed him as a propitious god, not in separate places but sitting together, which had never been done before and was never done again afterward (*HA MA* 18.2–3).

Was the actual cremation undertaken at the frontier, while a ceremony involving a wax effigy – and an eagle, seemingly a clinching feature – was staged at Rome, so that the senate and the people could witness Marcus' deification? The case of Pertinax's funeral suggests that a lapse of time was seen as no insuperable obstacle, so perhaps a trimmed-down 'military-style' cremation on base was followed, after an interval of months, with the lavish production reserved for Rome. For his part, Herodian gives this kind of account of Severus' cremation (in Britain), with the interment of his ashes some time later in Rome (3.15.7–8).

Evidence is also surprisingly limited about Marcus' final resting place. Beckmann, surprisingly in a work devoted to his column, and treating in some detail the known information about Antonine funerals, does not address it. For his part, Kovács cites what he calls 'the fragmentary funerary inscription of Marcus Aurelius concerning his cremation in October 180,' which at first glance would refute any suggestion that the cremation might have occurred earlier.[32]

This inscription, found near the Montecitorio (as we have seen, a location key to the Antonine memorials), is indeed fragmentary, so much so that the only surviving letters are the final three of the word AVGVSTVS. The inscription has been reconstructed as follows (the only surviving letters are shown in bold):

> IMP CAESAR MARCVS ANTONINVS AVGVS**TVS** HIC CREMATVS EST

'Emperor Caesar Marcus Antoninus Augustus was cremated here.'[33] Note that no date is included or implied, yet the record as given in the relevant online database (with a date of 2012) is that of Marcus' death, 17 March 180. Well attested as the death date is, it is implausible as a date for cremation, funeral, or interment.[34]

As explained in a note earlier in this chapter, several inscriptions from Hadrian's Mausoleum, recorded in early surveys of Rome such as the Einsiedeln MS (eighth or ninth century), subsequently disappeared. These included records of the interment of Antoninus Pius and the elder Faustina, their three children who died in childhood, and the three first-born children of Marcus and Faustina II (T. Aurelius Antoninus, T. Aelius Aurelius, and Domitia Faustina).[35] Some of these inscriptions are preserved in the ILS collection, and can be viewed online.

As it happens, the one confirmation about Marcus' own interment comes, in passing, from Herodian. In 211, Septimius Severus died in Britain. As noted earlier, Herodian tells us that:

> The body of Severus had been cremated and the ashes with perfumes consigned to an alabaster urn. This [his sons Caracalla and Geta] now escorted to Rome to be placed in the sacred imperial mausoleum (3.15.7–8).

Once in Rome,

> Then a procession went ahead escorting the urn and laid it in the temple where the sacred memorials of Marcus and his imperial predecessors were displayed (*deiknutai*, 4.1.4).

The Lost Arch

That we are lucky to have Marcus' column and equestrian statue is highlighted not only by the fate of Antoninus' column, but by that of Marcus' triumphal arch.

On the corner of the Via del Corso and the Via della Vite, just a few blocks from the Piazza Colonna, high up, is a plaque bearing a Latin inscription. This records the removal, by Pope Alexander VII in 1665, of some structures which were in the way (*impeditam*). The space, we are told, was restored to public use. His Holiness seems proud of the action, as it no doubt improved the safety of participants in festival horse-racing along the thoroughfare. But we have reason to regret it, because in all probability, the structure which was removed was the triumphal arch of Marcus.

By this time, it will not surprise the reader to learn that there remains confusion about whose arch it was. It seems to have been known, by the fifteenth century, as the Arch of Portugal (Arco di Portogallo), as the diplomatic quarters of Portugal were close by. It may also have been known as Hadrian's Arch, because Hadrian and his wife Sabina featured on some panels. In any event, part of it had already been destroyed by medieval times.[36]

We can be thankful that Pope Alexander seems to have ordered the removal and preservation of several relief panels, prior to the final destruction of the arch. Eight of these were re-used as part of the restoration of the Arch of Constantine near the Colosseum, while three others were removed in the sixteenth century to the Stairway of the Conservators, which now forms part of the Capitoline Museums.[37] There, they can still be seen, far more readily than the partially deteriorated reliefs encircling Marcus' column.

In fact, they force themselves on the viewer: larger than life, in high relief, and depicting Marcus in a range of important roles. As would befit a triumphal arch, the scenes are relevant to his campaigns. In one, he prepares to perform a sacrifice: his head is veiled, there are assistants and musicians, soldiers with their standard, and a nervous-looking bull at the rear.

In another panel, strongly recalling the equestrian statue, Marcus extends his right hand, in a gesture which we have learned to recognise as that of a pacifier, towards a group of defeated barbarians. A similar scene, we noted, formed one side of the pedestal of his column (which did not survive restoration in the sixteenth century). It was evidently an iconic tableau representing his campaigns and his reign. Just as the relief series on Marcus' column highlighted his role as military commander, in the tradition of Trajan, the arch reliefs underscore his dutiful conduct (*Pietas*), his justice (*Iustitia*), and his mercy (*Clementia*).[38]

Walking With Marcus IV: Carnuntum-Vienna

Vienna is such a busy capital that it has several 'central' rail stations, and it is from Wien Mitte-Landstraße, to the south-east, that the traveller will go next. To follow Marcus and the legions to the eastern extent of the Danube frontier, we take the train to Petronell-Carnuntum, on the Wolfsthal line.

Past the airport, and heavy and light industries, we come within half an hour to villages with names such as Wildungsmauer: mauer, 'walls,' can refer in place names to the remnants of Roman structures, mysterious as they were for centuries after the departure of the legions. And before long the train arrives at Petronell-Carnuntum.

We got off the train on a bright, though windy, Sunday in March, the only tourists to do so. As we walked through the town of Petronell, the locals – fixing their cars, or gardening – called a friendly greeting. Signs direct the visitor towards the archaeological site at the north of the town.

Evidently a great deal of European and global money has been, at different times, poured into the partial restoration of the settlement at Carnuntum; the site has UNESCO credentials. The tourist approaches through a small visitor centre and museum, featuring a short film about the Roman occupation of the area. In the film, an actor playing Marcus Aurelius dictates his Meditations to a secretary. Is this how the work was written? We tend to imagine Marcus himself wielding his pen in total privacy, but this may well be a misapprehension.

Out into the sunshine again to explore the town. This is the civilian settlement; the legionary camp proper was located some way to the east. The entire area was occupied from the first to the fifth centuries CE. *Reconstructions have been carried out using local materials and largely traditional methods.*

Notably, the bath-house facilities are heated using wood fires, just as would have occurred in antiquity. Interior decorations are authentic and beautifully executed. This really feels like a living town, of which the human inhabitants – the oil merchant, the cloth dealer, the pub proprietor, and all their families – have just stepped out, or taken a brief vacation, leaving us to enjoy their amenities.

From a nearly-clear sky a sudden hailstorm struck (lending credibility, perhaps, to the story of the Rain Miracle not too far from these parts). It seemed entirely fitting to head to the restaurant for lunch. We shared a lentil stew, and a beef casserole, simple and tasty fare straight from Roman times.

The hail having passed as quickly as it came, we walked to the civilian amphitheatre, erected perhaps within Marcus' own reign. A vast complex, it could seat 13,000 spectators. Only in 2011 was an adjoining gladiator school discovered, featuring a 100 square-metre training facility with underfloor heating, and its own bathing facilities. In keeping with recent archaeological practice, these discoveries have been filled in, requiring the visitor to use their imagination; an underwhelming wooden 'training' structure has been erected instead. March hares raced about the fields, as no doubt they had done for millennia.

By now we were keen to return to the station in order to catch the next Vienna train, but first we hurried to the Heidentor, the 'pagans' gate,' to the south of the Carnuntum civilian town. Later than Marcus' day, it was probably erected under Constantius II in the fourth century. Its scale and grandeur, even as a ruin, have made it a recognisable symbol for the region.

As we saw earlier, there remains uncertainty as to where Marcus died; possibly here, possibly in Vienna (Vindobona) proper, and possibly at Sirmium. If here, these wide skies and green fields may have been among the last sights that he saw. Unfortunately, both are now largely disfigured by wind turbines (which naturally do not feature in promotional photographs of the area).

Returning to Vienna, the visitor may enjoy the Römermuseum (Hohen Markt, opposite Marc-Aurel Straße), which has been developed directly above two officers' quarters, excavated and exposed to view. The ancient camp housed Legio X Gemina, around 6,000 men, and associated facilities. The Roman square street plan formed the basis for central Vienna, its traces evident today in such streets as the Tiefer Graben, 'deep trench,' which formed the western boundary of the original settlement.

As the centre of the Austro-Hungarian empire, Vienna never forgot its inheritance from its great Roman predecessors. It is therefore no surprise to find several equestrian statues. In the Josefsplatz, the Habsburg emperor Joseph II (1741–1790) is depicted on horseback; the inspiration from Marcus' statue is evident, but equally the later work seems stiff and lacks the off-centre grandeur of the original. Both more flamboyant and more evocative is a late sample of the genre, the 1899 statue of Archduke Albrecht, Duke of Teschen (1817–1895), in front of the Albertina.

Our final stop in Vienna will be the Ephesus Museum, Hofburg. Between 1895 and 1906, Austrian archaeologists removed quantities of antiquities from the ancient city of Ephesus, now in Turkey; excavations continue to this day (as Wikipedia blandly states, 'interrupted only by the two world wars'). Among these is a remarkable relief depicting four emperors: Hadrian, Antoninus Pius, a youthful Marcus Aurelius, and the even younger Lucius Verus. This formed a section of the Parthian Monument, a massive series of reliefs celebrating Verus' victory during the 160s over the Parthians. Visitors who have been to Ephesus will recall the marvellous Library of Celsus, where the reliefs may originally have been displayed.

Chapter Nine

Marcus Magus

Marcus and magicians – The Chaldeans – Non-Roman cults – Divine powers – The Rain Miracle – The Antonine Questions – The Ephesian Letters – The Ryedale Hoard

When Elagabalus was making plans to take up the war against the Marcomanni [c. 220 CE], which Marcus Antoninus had fought with great glory, he was told by certain persons that it was by the help of astrologers and magicians that Marcus had made the Marcomanni forever the liegemen and friends of the Roman people, and that it had been done by means of magic rites and a magic spell (*carminibus et consecratione*). But when he inquired about what this was or where it could be obtained, he could get no response.

Historia Augusta Elagabali 9.1

Was Marcus Aurelius perceived by at least some of his people as a worker of magic?

Some traditions depict him as at least ready to consult magicians. One story in the *Historia Augusta* life tells us that Faustina confessed to him that she was in love with a gladiator. Marcus confided in the 'Chaldeans,' the Zoroastrian believers who were considered to be skilled practitioners of magic in ancient Rome. They advised that Faustina should bathe in the blood of a deceased gladiator, and then sleep with Marcus. The result of this dubious proceeding, on the account, was the conception of Commodus, but in any event Faustina was cured of her deadly passion (*HA Marc.* 19.1–4). Evidently, part of the impetus for this story was an endeavour to account for the unvirtuous Commodus' birth to his virtuous father, but such a tale would only have effect if Marcus were known to be open-minded about magic practices.

The tale from the reign of Elagabalus, at the top of this chapter, may, it has been suggested, imply that the Chaldeans, or their successors, were in a position to try to thwart the unvirtuous Elagabalus' desire to locate Marcus' magic inscription.[1] This may mean that they formed a quasi-official body, one which had not only been tolerated under Marcus but even protected or promoted.

This would be consistent with Marcus' undoubted reputation as a powerful proponent of 'foreign religions.' During the anxious times in the mid-160s, as the Marcomanni were attacking the northern frontier, Marcus 'summoned priests from all over, performed foreign religious ceremonies and purified the city in every way.' In addition, Marcus and Verus delayed their expedition to the front in order to celebrate the 'feast of the gods' (*lectisternia*) for seven days. Further consternation arose with a fresh phase of the Antonine Plague (*HA* 13.1–3). In such an uncertain and threatening situation, it made perfect sense for Marcus to spend time and resources in conciliating any non-Roman deities, as well as the familiar pantheon. At least any disasters could not then be attributed to a failure in proper observance.

At the same time, Marcus demonstrated that he was not the dupe of any stray pretender to prophetic powers. A 'foolish fellow' gave speeches from the famous fig tree in the Campus Martius, declaring that the end of the world would come if he should fall from the tree and be turned into a stork. Eventually he did fall, releasing a stork from his cloak. Marcus' response was to pardon the man, an instance of his kindness (*clementia*, *HA* 13.6).

Also entirely relevant to this is the practice of deification, which Marcus undertook for his predecessors, and which would be undertaken for him upon his death. As the *Historia* tells us:

> Finally, before his funeral was held, many say, the senate and people hailed him as a propitious god (*propitium deum*), not in separate places but sitting together, which had never been done before and was never done again afterward (18.3).

As we have seen, there was (and continues to be) confusion around the location and timings of Marcus' death and funeral. Nonetheless, the upshot is clear: Marcus was considered to be qualified in a unique degree for the status of divinity. This – if it meant anything – meant that he was considered to have supernatural powers, and not only posthumously: he was 'an associate of the gods both in life and in death' (*talis ac diis vita et morte*, 18.4).

Indeed, his cult – not simply a public institution – became virtually obligatory for private home worship, in the coming years:

> It was not enough, indeed, that people of every age, sex, degree and rank in life gave him all honours given to the gods, but also whoever failed to keep the emperor's image in his home, if his fortune were such that he could or should have done so, was held guilty of sacrilege (*sacrilegus iudicatus est*, 18.5).

Some people pointed out that Marcus had predicted certain events because of dreams, and that they themselves had a similar agency (18.7).

Against this background, it becomes increasingly implausible to maintain, as many do, that there are no miracles in Stoicism.[2] On such a view – reminiscent of A.D. Nock's inter-war account emphasising the 'rational' and 'irrational' – Marcus was engaging in empty charades, in which he himself had no confidence, when he made observances to both traditional and non-Roman gods. An account more sensitive to the *Meditations* would suggest that in Marcus' Stoicism, *everything* is a miracle, evidence of divine ordination of the cosmos, the conventional pantheon representing different aspects of this order; and we have every reason to believe that Marcus' own piety was heartfelt.

The 'supernatural' event most associated with Marcus and his reign, famously depicted on his column, is the Rain Miracle: the saving of a Roman army during the Marcomannic War through a sudden downpour. The events, of which Cassius Dio gives a version, are most likely to have taken place towards the end of the campaign, in 172 or 174. During one confrontation with the Quadi, a Roman contingent was surrounded. The weather was very hot, and the Romans were on the brink of surrender through thirst. Suddenly, Dio writes, 'not without divine intervention,' a rainstorm burst forth, and the desperate Romans caught the water in their shields for themselves and their horses. Hail fell upon the enemy, and the momentum of battle reverted to the Romans.[3]

There is an unusual degree of consensus about what occurred from literary, numismatic, and archaeological evidence.[4] Where consensus fails is in attributing the cause of the extraordinary meteorological events. Cassius Dio mentions an Egyptian magician in Marcus' entourage; the Christian writer Tertullian, noting that most observers ascribed it to Jupiter, instead maintains that the miracle was a Christian one. Yet Tertullian's language is curious; he suggests that Marcus brought about the miracle, through the means of Christian soldiers in his army appealing to their God:

> Moreover, Marcus Aurelius, while warring with the Germans, obtained (*inpetravit*) plentiful rain during a great drought, through the supplications which the Christian soldiers in his army made to God (*Ad Scapulam* IV.6).

Where one would have expected Tertullian to ascribe the agency to God, the subject of the verb *inpetravit* – to bring about, obtain, procure – is Marcus. If even a Christian writer could view the emperor as intimately involved in bringing about a miracle, then surely many a pagan will have attributed to him supernatural agency.

Marcus Aurelius equestrian statue, Capitoline Museums, Rome, March 2024. (© *Stuart Wilson*)

Caelian Hill, March 2024, Judith Stove. (© *Stuart Wilson*)

Antonine Pedestal, Vatican Museums, Rome, 2010. (*Wikimedia Commons*)

Panel from Marcus arch, Marcus preparing to sacrifice, Capitoline Museums, Rome, March 2024. (© *Stuart Wilson*)

Panel from Marcus arch, Marcus extending clemency, Capitoline Museums, Rome, March 2024. (© *Stuart Wilson*)

Plaque indicating removal of arch, Via del Corso, Rome, March 2024. (© *Stuart Wilson*)

Marcus Aurelius aureus (145–160 CE) obverse. (*RIC III Antoninus Pius 432B, American Numismatic Society*)

Marcus Aurelius aureus (145–160 CE) *Hilaritas* reverse. (*RIC III Antoninus Pius 432B, American Numismatic Society*)

Via Appia, March 2024. (© *Stuart Wilson*)

Carnuntum amphitheatre, March 2024. (© *Stuart Wilson*)

Francis Hutcheson (c. 1745), by Allan Ramsay, Hunterian Museum and Art Gallery. (*Wikimedia Commons*)

David Bailie Warden, c. 1805. (*Wikimedia Commons*)

Last Words of the Emperor Marcus Aurelius, by Eugène Delacroix. (*Salon of 1845; Museum of Fine Arts of Lyon, via Wikimedia Commons*)

George Long. (*Wikimedia Commons, reported as 1825 but probably c. 1860s*)

Matthew Arnold, 1869. (*Hills & Saunders, via Wikimedia Commons*)

CM The British Museum's Portable Antiquities Scheme: YORYM

Ryedale Hoard, Yorkshire Museum. (*2020, Portable Antiquities Scheme, Amy Downes, via Wikimedia Commons*)

Trimontium, Newstead, Scotland, site of Roman camp, April 2024. (© *Stuart Wilson*)

Marcus Aurelius, Stirling Heads, Stirling Castle, April 2024. (© *Stuart Wilson*)

Villa Adriana, Canopus, Tivoli, Rome, April 2022. (© *Stuart Wilson*)

Villa Adriana, Pecile, Tivoli, Rome, April 2022. (© *Stuart Wilson*)

Villa Adriana, poppies, Tivoli, Rome, April 2022. (© *Stuart Wilson*)

Fish Catalogue mosaic, c. 100 BCE, Pompeii. (*n. 120177, Naples National Archaeological Museum, Adobe Stock*)

Marcus' ambiguous standing with regard to Christianity is well enough known. A far lesser known body of Marcus lore comes from the Jewish tradition. 'The Antoninus Questions' are a set of anecdotes and reported conversations between (probably) Rabbi Judah I (c. 135–217 CE), a key leader of the Jewish community in Roman Judaea, and 'Antoninus,' an emperor who has at times been variously identified as Antoninus Pius, Caracalla, Lucius Verus, or – for our purposes – Marcus Aurelius.[5] The surviving fragments are, it is conjectured, only a fraction of the original corpus.

The stories broadly follow a formula of a great king (Antoninus) seeking the counsel of a foreign sage (the rabbi), a genre probably derived from stories of Alexander the Great meeting sages such as Diogenes and even, on campaign, the 'naked intellectuals' (*gymnosophistai*) of India.[6] Alexander, we may also note, was the prototype of the earthly king whose great feats justified claims to divinity.

The general form of the fragments suggests that 'Antoninus' asked the rabbi to interpret some Biblical verses; Antoninus is permitted a kind of rhetorical win, but ultimately acknowledges the wisdom of the Jewish tradition, which he wishes to understand. Considering Antoninus as a willing proselyte might offer scope for him to share in a future world, otherwise denied to him as a gentile.[7]

The Stoic flavour of several of the themes has led scholars to identify 'Antoninus' with Marcus Aurelius.[8] In fact, it has been suggested that the Jewish author of the Questions was familiar with the *Meditations*. If so, this would be evidence of wide dissemination – perhaps even in Hebrew translation – of the work in the generations following Marcus' death (the date of the work has been estimated as the first half of the third century).[9]

> This recourse which the Jewish author of the apocryphon had to the [*Meditations*] represents the oldest reliable instance of the popularity Marcus Aurelius' book must have enjoyed.[10]

Some of the 'questions' are, in fact, related to physical processes or the soul, and as such may plausibly have been inspired by Marcus' actual words. These include:

> 3. Antoninus said to Rabbi (Judah the Prince): At what time is the soul placed within the person? Is it at the moment of conception or the moment of formation (of the embryo)? Answer: (Rabbi) answered: From the moment of the formation. (Antoninus) replied: Is it possible for a piece of unsalted meat to last even three days without rotting? Rather, considering this it must be from the moment of conception (*peqidah*). Rabbi (Judah) said: This is what Antoninus taught me, and a verse of scripture supports it, for it says: 'Your providence (*pequdah*) preserved my spirit' (Job 10:12).[11]

Here we see Marcus scoring a debating win acknowledged by the Rabbi, who even adduces a verse of Job in confirmation. The concept of providence is of course, as we have observed, one of Marcus' central concerns, as are also the natural processes of physical dissolution and reassembly.

The following question takes a similar form: Marcus raises a thorny matter, is unconvinced by the Rabbi's account, and offers his own, which the Rabbi accepts and once again supports with a scriptural verse:

> 4. Antoninus said to Rabbi (Judah the Prince): From what time does the evil impulse prevail within the person, the moment of formation or the moment of emergence (from the womb)? Answer: Rabbi (Judah) answered: From the moment of the formation (of the embryo). But Antoninus replied: If that were so, wouldn't the foetus kick the mother's insides in order to emerge from the womb? Rabbi (Judah) said: Antoninus taught me this, and a verse of scripture supports him, as it is said: 'Sin crouches at the entrance' (Gen. 4:7).[12]

The Genesis verse, God's warning to Cain, indeed refers to an 'evil impulse.' While Marcus was certainly an observer of the less savoury sides of human character, it is difficult to see any Stoic link here: Stoicism, rather, maintained the innate goodness of all creation, including humanity. What we may be seeing, though, is the kind of argument which Marcus, throughout the *Meditations*, repeatedly undertook with himself.

Several persons mentioned in the Questions have been identified as members of Marcus' family, although such identifications must remain uncertain. The overall significance of the texts must be to underline the great standing of Marcus as a wise ruler, highlighted perhaps in the wide influence of his *Meditations*. Indeed, we may consider the Questions as yet another instance – perhaps the very earliest, and in a language neither Greek nor Latin – of Marcus fan-fiction.

It was no doubt, in part, Marcus' reputation as open to a range of approaches to the divine, that has caused his name to have been linked with a famous magical formula from antiquity: the *Ephesia grammata* or 'Ephesian Letters.' This was a 'spell,' a set of words which appear to be nonsensical, but hold a significance in part because of this unintelligibility. The formula, which in varying versions was known from the sixth century BCE, ran in one form: *aski(on) kataski(on) lix tetrax damnameneus aision (aisia).*[13] These words are in the main not standard Greek, and there have been a range of interpretations, including that Lix Tetrax may be a folk name for one of the prevailing winds.

A recent article on the popular *Classical Wisdom* website specifically states:

> Marcus Aurelius, the great Philosopher and Emperor, was also known to recite the *Ephesia Grammata* to keep fear and harm away.[14]

Such a practice would seem rather on the superstitious end of the supernatural spectrum, even for as open-minded a philosopher as Marcus, and indeed we may here be dealing with a confusion, in part textual. Another aspect may be a dim recollection of the tradition reported at the start of this chapter, that Marcus had had access to secret magical resources.

The only evidence for Marcus knowing the Ephesian letters was found by some earlier scholars in *Meditations* 11.26.[15] Yet a recent translation gives for this passage:

> In the writings of the Epicureans there was a maxim to always think of some person of times gone by, who practised virtue (11.26).[16]

Recent scholarship, at least since Farquharson, prefers the reading of 'Epicurean' over 'Ephesian,' with the support of a passage in Seneca (perhaps refuting the often-repeated view that Marcus made no reference to Seneca).[17] Marcus, on this view, was appealing to two perfectly respectable philosophical texts, from Epicurus and Seneca, not to the mysterious magical formula. The mix-up shows the importance of carefully sifting the evidence, always mindful of the textual difficulties involved.

One final legacy of Marcus as a magical figure emerged as recently as 2020. The Ryedale Hoard is a set of four objects found by metal-detectorists near Ampleforth in North Yorkshire. All made from copper alloy, they comprise a plumb-bob; a broken key with a horse-head handle, the horse modelled with care; a small figure of a horseman; and a head instantly recognisable as that of Marcus, with exaggeratedly huge eyes and parted beard. The portrait, in the manner of a cartoon, preserves key features to convey the likeness. In the words of a recent scholar: 'The stylization of the portrait is remarkable.'[18]

Because the discovery is recent, scholarship is only in early stages. The Yorkshire Museum, location of the items, has prepared some videos about the hoard and its significance; other information, on which the following is based, appears in the hoard's entry in the formal database of UK archaeological finds.

The horse-and-rider figurine has tentatively been identified as a local version of the Roman god Mars. Over twenty such figurines have been found in Britain, this being the most northerly. The head of Marcus is thought to have been used atop a sceptre in relation to the imperial cult. Not only the original use, but the deposit itself, is thought to have had a votive function, preserving items from priestly regalia. For its part, the plumb-bob was a tool used in Roman surveying (as well as building and carpentry), and one theory is that it denoted an approach to the demarcation of sacred spaces.[19]

It is not hard to imagine that the exquisite head of Marcus – only thirteen centimetres tall – with its extraordinary eyes, could be seen to have possessed some sacred or enduring power. We recall that while he never visited Britain, Marcus was directly responsible for sending the Sarmatian horsemen to Britain, which became a known centre for the formidable cavalry of the Roman army. Numerous sites, including from the northernmost frontier in Scotland, the Antonine Wall, have yielded cavalry regalia such as helmets used in displays and training. The Ryedale Hoard underscores deep connections between cult and culture, the enduring Roman influence in northern Britain, and the greatest of the Antonines.

Chapter Ten

Julian the Apostate's Marcus Fan Fiction

Dividing the empire – Constantine's family and Christianity – Julian the Apostate – His education and 'conversion' to paganism – His 'Caesars,' a Platonist pastiche – Julian satirizes his predecessors – An Olympian contest for the emperors – Marcus wins – Constantine the Christian loses

There was a time when I believed that I ought to try to rival men who have been most distinguished for excellence, Alexander, for instance, or Marcus; but I shivered at the thought and was seized with terror lest I should fail entirely to come up to the courage of the former, and should not make even the least approach to the latter's perfect virtue (*teleias aretēs*).

Julian, *Letter to Themistius the Philosopher* 253B

Some 150 years after Marcus' death, Flavius Claudius Iulianus was born, probably at Constantinople (Istanbul), into the family of the reigning emperor Constantine I. Julian the Apostate, as he is best known today, was a deep admirer of Marcus Aurelius as an imperial role model, and this chapter will examine his relationship with his long-dead mentor.

Much had changed since Marcus' death on Rome's northern frontiers. Diocletian's careful arrangements did not survive the death of Constantius in 306, when the Roman army – always a key player in allocating power – proclaimed his son Constantine as emperor, at York. Civil war began afresh, with rivals competing once again. Constantine started to favour Christianity in 312, the year he defeated Maxentius (Maximian's son) at the Battle of the Milvian Bridge north of Rome, and by 324 he emerged as the successful sole ruler, establishing his own sons as heirs.

The dynastic struggles involving the next generation, however, seemed like a throwback to the excesses of Nero's court. In 326, Constantine had his eldest son Crispus executed, along with his stepmother, Constantine's own wife Fausta, for reasons which remain obscure. Constantine sought baptism as a Christian late in life, sometime before his death in 337. His next eldest son, Constantine II, succeeded jointly with his brothers Constantius II and Constans.

Their bloody rivalries culminated in Constans' troops killing Constantine II, and Constantius II, in his turn, ordering the murders of his father-in-law, cousins, and other potential rivals.

That father-in-law was Julius Constantius, father of young Julian (b. 331). Julian and his half-brother Gallus personally survived the mass murders ordered by their cousin Constantius II, and were kept in obscurity in remote parts of Bithynia (now part of Turkey), although Julian was given good teachers. At eighteen, he was brought to Constantinople and Nicomedia, becoming a *lector*, 'reader' (a minor official) in the Christian church. For the imperial house was officially Christian: these latest massacres and blood rivalries occurred in the most powerful Christian family in the empire.

To state uncomfortable truths, becoming Christian had not imparted moral restraint to holders of absolute power. In fact, it might have done the opposite, in giving a sense of ultimate justification to one or another participant. Constantius II was an adherent of the Arian variety of Christianity; other Western leaders favoured Nicene Christianity. Sectarian difference was now added to personal, political, and military conflict.

When he was about twenty, Julian turned against the faith in which he had been brought up, and made a personal commitment to the religion of the old gods. He had several teachers who belonged to the Platonist schools of the time. The subsequent historical tradition about this period of Platonism suggests a focus on mysticism, indeed on 'theurgy,' complete with implications of what would later become known as 'the occult': magic, ritual, and invocation.[1] There is certainly within Plato's own works a strand of this kind, most visible in the dialogue *Symposium*, in which the priestess Diotima outlines a process by which humans may aspire to the divine. But this is far from the only or main preoccupation of Plato, presented in his works largely through the character of Socrates: just as important, or perhaps more important, was a focus on leading everyday life in pursuit of virtue.

That both these strands of Platonism influenced Christianity at certain points is clear. On the other hand, in polemical contexts – such as the later Christian assessments of Julian's life and reign – writers were often at pains to identify the theurgic beliefs and practices as 'novel,' 'superstitious' or 'profane.' On such an assessment, Julian was less a philosopher than a would-be magic-worker; less a champion of the old ways than a trifling pretender to ancient wisdom.[2]

Fortunately, we are not forced to rely solely on such hostile readings. Julian was a prolific writer, producing speeches, letters, religious and philosophical treatises, and – most important for our purposes here – satires.[3] One of his preoccupations was the nature of imperial power, understandably for one raised in the purple, and it is clear that his imperial role model was Marcus Aurelius. Let us examine in detail Julian's satire, *Caesars*.

Julian recalls classical literary models, in particular Plato's: the work is a dialogue, and from the outset appeals to several aspects of the master: humour, myth, and serious messaging within the merriment.

> 'It is the season of the Kronia, during which the god allows us to make merry. But, my dear friend, as I have no talent for amusing or entertaining I must, it seems, take care not to talk mere nonsense.'
>
> 'But Caesar, can there be anyone so dull and stupid (*pachus esti kai archaios*) as to overthink jokes? …'
>
> 'Yes … for I'm not naturally inventive about making fun, or parody, or comedy. But since I must obey the god's rules, would you like me to share with you a myth in which, maybe, there is a lot of worthwhile content?'
>
> 'I'll listen with great pleasure, since I also am far from disregarding myths, and I certainly don't rule out ones which have a good message. In fact I agree with you and your beloved, or rather everyone's beloved, Plato – he often gave a serious lesson in his myths' (306 A-C).[4]

So what follows is satire, but Julian wishes us to note that it will contain some important themes. The narrator sets the scene: a banquet of the gods, again recalling Plato's most famous banquet-themed work, *Symposium*. 'Never indeed will there be or appear an orator so gifted that he could describe such surpassing beauty as shines forth on the countenances of the gods' (308 A). References to Homer also feature. We read that Silenus helps to entertain Zeus, and this recalls Socrates, whose appearance was often likened to that of Silenus.[5]

To this banquet were invited the Roman emperors, and Octavian – later Augustus – is shown as changing colour and manner in a bizarre fashion. Zeus' response is to hand him over to Zeno, founder of the Stoic school:

> Zeno obeyed, and thereupon, by reciting over Octavian a few of his doctrines (*mikra tōn dogmatōn*), in the fashion of those who mutter the incantations of Zalmoxis, he made him wise and self-controlled (*apephēnen andra emphrona kai sōphrona*, 309 C).

Here we see Julian imagining Augustus converted into a virtuous man simply through hearing Stoic principles; as we saw in another chapter, wisdom and self-control were two of the key Platonic and Stoic cardinal virtues. It is known that Augustus had at least two Stoic advisers, Arius and Athenodorus, but Augustus himself was known rather for political expediency than personal virtue. Plato had referred to the legendary magician-king Zalmoxis, worshipped in Thrace (north of Greece), in his dialogue *Charmides*, an important intertext for understanding Plato's views on the virtue of self-control. Julian, then, is creating a complex fabric of Roman imperial history, interwoven with classical Platonic and Stoic ideas.

Indeed, there is a sense that, one by one, Rome's greatest leaders are found wanting against the standards of the traditional gods. Tiberius is punished for his crimes; Claudius looks ridiculous; and as for Nero's pretensions to being an artist:

> While Silenus was speaking, Nero entered, lyre in hand and wearing a wreath of laurel. Whereupon Silenus turned to Apollo and said, 'You see, he models himself on you.' 'I will soon take off that wreath,' replied Apollo, 'for he does not imitate me in all things, and even when he does he does it badly.' Then his wreath was taken off and Cocytus [one of the legendary rivers of the Underworld] instantly swept him away (310 C).

For their parts, Nerva and Trajan are treated mildly. Hadrian's most famous relationship features:

> Silenus when he saw him said, 'What do you think of this sophist (*sophistēs*)? Can he be looking here for Antinous?' (311 C-D).

Antoninus Pius gets short shrift as an old fuss-pot ('This old man seems to me the sort of person who would split cumin seed,' 312 A), but then come Marcus Aurelius and Verus, here, confusingly, known by their original names: Verus (Marcus) and Lucius.

> Silenus scowled horribly because he could not make fun of them, especially not of [Marcus]; but he would not ignore his errors of judgement in the case of his son [Commodus] and his wife [Faustina], in that he mourned the latter beyond what was becoming, considering that she was not even a virtuous woman (*oude kosmian ousan*) … and that though [Marcus] had an excellent son-in-law [Pompeianus, second husband of Lucilla] who would have administered the state better, and besides would have managed the youth better than he could manage himself. But though [Silenus] refused

> to ignore these errors, he reverenced the exalted virtue of [Marcus], (*to megethos autou tēs aretēs*), 312 B).

Even here, in Julian's satirical context, the issue of succession is considered relevant to Marcus' ultimate legacy.

A parade of lesser lights follows: Pertinax, Macrinus, Heliogabalus, Aurelian, Probus. Finally appear Diocletian and his court, bringing us to recent history: 'Next Diocletian advanced in style, bringing with him the two Maximians and my grandfather Constantius [Chlorus]' (315 A).

The gods hold a contest to establish the greatest leader of all, and first summon the military specialists: Alexander the Great, Julius Caesar, Augustus, Trajan. But Kronos says that philosophers are no less dear to him than military emperors: 'So tell Marcus to come in too.'

> Accordingly Marcus was summoned and came in looking excessively majestic (*semnos agan*), showing the effect of his studies in the expression of his eyes and his lined brows. His aspect was beautiful in that he was plainly attired and unbeautified; he had a very long beard, simple and sensible (*lita kai sōphrona*) clothing, and from lack of nourishment his body was shining and transparent, like the purest and most revealing light (317 C-D).

Several aspects of this description are significant. First, being 'excessively majestic' is curious, because key to all of Greek culture was one of the proverbs inscribed at the temple of Apollo at Delphi: 'Nothing too much,' *mēden agan*. Yet here, Marcus seems to exceed the norm of imperial majesty. Secondly, the reference to Marcus' eyes is striking: the heavy lids and thoughtful expression so familiar to us from portraiture must have been recognized as distinctive.

There is another reference to traditional virtue: even Marcus' attire manifests the virtue of self-control, one key meaning of the adjective *sōphrōn*. And finally, Marcus' habitual fasting – of which we know from the historical sources, which claim that even on campaign he only ate one meal, in the evening – results in his remarkable holy appearance.[6] We may conjecture that Julian is presenting his role model as equal, or superior, in mortification of the flesh to any Christian ascetic. In fact – and here of course Julian is also challenging the Christian worldview – Marcus is being held up as quasi-divine, as indeed the Roman imperial cult had maintained that he was.

Seeing himself, like his role model, as a philosopher, Julian appropriately now raises a deeply philosophical question, in the mouth of Dionysus, god of wine: 'King Kronos and King Zeus, can any incompleteness exist among the gods?' (317 D). The word used to mean 'incompleteness,' *ateles*, is cognate with *telos*, the standard word in Aristotelian and Stoic philosophy to mean the ultimate aim of life. *En theois*, 'among the gods,' could mean in their general timeless divine existence, or it could mean actually present among them, here and now, at the banquet. Taking this latter meaning, Dionysus commands that any leader given to pleasure should now be tried at the entrance: 'Let Constantine come as far as the door' (318 A). Provocatively, then, Julian introduces his uncle – the great sponsor of Christianity – as a devotee of pleasure, and unworthy of presence among the pagan gods.

Hermes introduces the contest of the great leaders in a pastiche of the verses pronounced at the opening of the Olympic games, Julian having the opportunity to show off his versifying. Julius Caesar declaims his superiority to Alexander the Great, nominating the number of his campaigns and rivals as markers of greater skill, and his clemency to defeated foes as far greater than the Macedonian's. Alexander responds in kind.

For his part, Octavian/Augustus, with his usual keen sense of how the wind is blowing, endeavours to position himself as a friend of philosophy:

> I showed myself so gentle to the guidance of philosophy that I even put up with the plain speaking (*parrhesia*) of Athenodorus, and instead of resenting it I was delighted with it, and revered the man as my preceptor, or rather as though he were my own father. Areius I counted my friend and close companion, and in short I was never guilty of any offence against philosophy (326 A-B).

For his part, Trajan defends himself against the charge of laziness and fondness for drink, conciliating the gods in the end because of his gentleness, *praotēs*, which was 'particularly pleasing to them.' And now it is Marcus' turn: compared to those of his predecessors, his *apologia* is brevity itself:

> When Marcus Aurelius began to speak, Silenus whispered to Dionysus, 'Let us hear which one of his paradoxes and extraordinary doctrines this Stoic will come out with.' But Marcus turned to Zeus and the other gods and said, 'It seems to me, O Zeus, and you other gods, that I have no need to make a speech or compete. If you did not know all that concerns me, it would indeed be appropriate for me to inform you. But since you know all and nothing is hidden from you, do you of your own accord assign me what honour I deserve.'
>
> Thus Marcus showed that, admirable as he was in other respects, he was wise also beyond the rest, because he knew 'When it is time to speak and when to be silent' (328 B-D).

It is striking that the Greek which Julian puts in Marcus' mouth here is artfully, elegantly, brief, and indeed recalls the aphoristic, abrupt style of Marcus' own writing in the *Meditations* (it is very difficult in English translation to convey just how concisely Marcus wrote). It is surely not a coincidence that the earliest direct reference to *Meditations* which survives today occurs in the work of Themistius (317–388), philosopher, polymath, and older contemporary and correspondent of Julian. Themistius is known as an interpreter of Aristotle, but the scope of his learning was broad, and he mentions the exhortations (*parangelmata*) of Marcus (Orations 6.81c).[7]

Silenus' quip references the reputation Stoicism had of maintaining 'paradoxes,' doctrines (such as that virtue is the only good), which were at variance with common belief, in passing underlining Marcus' adherence to the Stoic school. Finally, the quote ending the passage is from the playwright Euripides, providing a link with classical (non-Stoic) wisdom tradition.

All the contestants are then cross-examined by the gods, and all are found to have been ambitious, self-serving, or otherwise flawed – except for one.

> 'Look out' [says Dionysus to Silenus], 'how you can find any fault with Marcus, for he seems to me a man, to quote Simonides, "four-square and built without a flaw."' Then Hermes addressed Marcus and said, 'And you, Verus, what did you consider the most beautiful aim of life (*biou telos*)? In a low voice and simply he said, 'To imitate the gods.' This answer they agreed was not unworthy – in fact it was the most worthwhile of all.

Marcus' simplicity stands in contrast with Constantine's boastfulness, and Alexander's attempts to deploy the logical arguments of his teacher Aristotle (330 C-331 A). But Silenus finds one fault, a strange one to be sure: 'Why did you eat bread and drink wine, and not ambrosia and nectar like us?' Marcus responds:

> It was not in the style of my diet that I thought to imitate the gods. But I nourished my body because I believed, perhaps falsely, that even your [the gods'] bodies have to be fed by the fumes of sacrifice. And not that I supposed I ought to imitate you in that respect, but rather as regards the mind (*tēn dianoian*, 333 D).

For a moment Silenus is silent 'as if struck by a good boxer' (a reference to Plato's dialogue *Protagoras*). Marcus explains – again, in the brief style familiar to us from his writings – that by imitating the gods, he meant having few needs, and doing good to as many people as possible.[8]

Here, Julian even mimics Marcus' habit of using diminutives to denote insignificance: 'I [Julian's Marcus says] had no needs, but my silly body (literally, my little body, *isōs de to sōmation mou mikrōn*) maybe had a few' (334A). As we have seen, this verbal habit had been evident as early as Marcus' correspondence with Fronto. The usage may have been inspired by that of Epictetus, who also deployed it in the mouth of Zeus: 'If it had been possible, I would have made your little body (*sōmation*) and mini-property free and unhindered' (*Disc.*I.1.10–12).

In this short but rich exchange, Julian has his Marcus gesture to Socrates' insistence, notably in the dialogue *Phaedo*, that he, Socrates, will not be in the body which will exist after his death – that he is not co-extensive with his body – as well as to Marcus' restraint about corporeal essentials.

But then Silenus comes up with a more substantial objection to Marcus' record: his indulgence to his wife Faustina, in deifying her after her death, and in entrusting the empire to his son Commodus, as 'neither right nor according to reason' (*ouk orthōs oude kata logon*). Again, Julian is pitch-perfect: for the Stoics, behaving 'unreasonably' was something unnatural for humans; Silenus lands a telling blow.

Once again, however, Marcus presents a compelling riposte: here, too, he had been imitating the gods. In the *Iliad*, Homer had had Achilles, son of a goddess, declare 'Whoever is a true man and sound of mind, loves and cherishes his wife' (9.341–2). As for indulging his son, Marcus cites, again, Homer, where Zeus rebukes his son the war-god Ares: 'Long ago I should have smitten you with a thunderbolt, had I not loved you because you are my son' (a paraphrase of *Iliad* 5.897). Further:

> Besides, I never thought my son would prove so wicked. Youth ever vacillates between the extremes of vice and virtue, and if in the end he inclined to vice, still he was not vicious when I entrusted the empire to him; it was only after receiving it that he became corrupted (334 C).

Marcus had introduced no novelty: succession by male son was the norm, and earlier emperors had decreed divine honours for their wives. But, he concludes, 'I forget myself when I make this lengthy explanation (*apologoumenos*) to you, O Zeus and other gods; for you know all things. Forgive me this rashness' (334 D-335 A).

Julian's readers will have been reminded of the *apologia* of Socrates at his trial, as reported by Plato. Yet we recall that the court was not persuaded by Socrates; will Marcus persuade the gods?

Hermes questions Constantine on his motive, receiving the answer: 'To amass great wealth and then to spend it liberally so as to gratify my own desires and the desires of my friends' (335 B). This unvirtuous response recalls the attitudes of the sophist Callicles in Plato's *Gorgias*, and the familiar practices of Greek tyrants of history. A secret ballot cast by the gods ensues, with Marcus receiving most of the votes.

Zeus announces: 'Depart then wherever you please, and in future live every one of you under the guidance of the gods. Let every man choose his own guardian and guide' (335 D). Marcus 'stuck fast' to Zeus and Kronos. Constantine caught sight of Pleasure, ran up to her, was received with caresses, and led over to Self-Indulgence (*Asōtia*):

> There too he found Jesus, who had taken up his abode with her and cried aloud to all comers: 'He that is a seducer, he that is a murderer, he that is sacrilegious and infamous, let him approach without fear! For with this water will I wash him and will straightway make him clean. And though he should be guilty of those same sins a second time, let him but smite his breast and beat his head and I will make him clean again' (336 A-B).

We see that Julian makes explicit a pagan argument against the Christian doctrine of radical forgiveness of sinners, such as that represented in the parables in the Gospel of Luke (the lost coin, the lost sheep, and the Prodigal Son). We need to recall that this is not an argument from ignorance or misunderstanding: Julian had been brought up in the church. Whether it amounts to a fair representation of Christian attitudes to unvirtuous behaviour will probably be up to each reader to determine. In any event, Jesus does not save Constantine from the gods' divine punishment for the murders of family members, but Zeus remits these for the sake of Julian's own relatives (336 B), Claudius and Constantius Chlorus. Hermes tells Julian to follow the commandments of the deity Mithras, as his guardian god, and here the satire ends (336 C).

The *Caesars* is a sparkling work, full of resonances from earlier Greek literature and philosophy, and exhibiting Julian's command of various traditions. It is also a finely drawn tribute to Marcus as the greatest of past Greek and Roman leaders.

Chapter Eleven

A Superior Genius: Marcus Among the Anglicans

Stoicism and Christianity: key divergences – Many gods – Body, death, the soul – Virtue and grace – Suicide – Jeremy Collier, Marcus admirer – 'Natural religion' – Edmund Gibson co-opts (pagans) Julian and Marcus

> As to the *Stoicks* notwithstanding their Advantage of other *Sects;* They were not without their Mistakes. For Instance; They Believe'd a Plurality of Gods, that the Soul was a part of the Deity, and that their Wise Man might dispose of himself, and make his Life as short as he pleas'd … [1]
>
> Jeremy Collier *Antoninus Conversation with Himself,* Preface

We have seen in 'A Knight Called Marcus' that from the fifteenth century onwards, Marcus' reputation steadily increased. In this chapter, we will discover that the thoroughly pagan Marcus would be deployed as a weapon during the bitter ideological debates within the Church of England during the eighteenth century.

But before considering the ways in which Marcus' legacy was celebrated and claimed by rival groups in the period, we need to explore in greater detail some of the key areas of conflict between Stoicism and Christianity.

Plurality of Gods

The Romans, like the Greeks before them, had worshipped a large number of gods and goddesses. Centred on the triad of Jupiter (Jove), Juno, and Minerva, the pantheon also featured Venus, considered the ancestress of the Roman people. Lesser deities included the household spirits, the Lares and Penates. There were also the *Di Manes*, the 'good gods,' to whom deceased people were commended on many a Roman tombstone with the inscription *Dis Manibus* ('to the good gods,' often abbreviated to D.M.). The Stoics accepted these as cultural givens, while also – without, in their view, inconsistency – also conceiving God as eternal reason, immanent throughout the cosmos.

In contrast, like its predecessor Judaism, Christianity involved the worship only of one God. In times of national stress, such as the Antonine Plague and the Marcomannic Wars, when divine support was repeatedly sought, Christians fell afoul of both Roman and regional authorities because they refused to offer sacrifice to the pagan gods, or to the deified emperors.

During Marcus' reign, while the Parthian war was in progress, the Christian writer Justin, originally from Palestine, was tried at Rome, along with several companions. Justin (b.c. 100) had explored the pagan philosophical schools before converting to Christianity. In 155 he had appealed to Antoninus Pius and his heirs: 'to [Pius'] son Verissimus the Philosopher, and to Lucius [Verus] the Philosopher … a lover of learning.'[2] Justin's aim was to dissuade the emperors from sanctioning the targeting of Christians. A decade on, Justin himself came before Junius Rusticus, formerly one of Marcus' teachers and now prefect of the city of Rome. Ordered to sacrifice to the gods, Justin and the others refused, and were executed (c. 165).[3]

Later in Marcus' reign, a severe persecution of local Christians is said to have taken place at Lyons, in Gaul (France). The date usually given is 177, once more a time of stress when northern disturbances again seemed imminent, but some scholars consider that the events may have taken place (a) in a different location altogether, and/or (b) some years later (possibly not in Marcus' reign at all).[4]

These two episodes, taken together, contributed to the reputation of Marcus as having, if not encouraged the persecution of Christians, presided over its prevalence. (The only supposed mention of Christians in the *Meditations*, often understood as a criticism of their 'contrariness,' is textually doubtful.[5]) During the cultural recriminations which followed the sack of Rome in 410, Augustine, the most influential of Christian writers, named Marcus as the fourth persecuting ruler, after Nero, Domitian, and Trajan. This was despite Trajan, famously, having endeavoured to discourage zealous local persecutors; Augustine's account of Marcus is likely to be similarly suspect.[6]

As we have seen in an earlier chapter, accounts of the Rain Miracle, commemorated on Marcus' column as a key event during the Marcomannic War, and attested in a range of sources, seem to provide strong evidence of Christians serving in the Roman army. This is evidence which is hard to reconcile with a view either of Marcus as a persecutor, or of Christians as a body being unwilling to take part in standard military observances.

Body, Death, and the Soul

The Athenian philosopher Plato, an inspiration for all the later schools of antiquity, had suggested, in dialogues such as the *Phaedo*, that the soul was of a non-material kind, and likely to survive the death of the body. The souls of the virtuous would gather in a beautiful location, while those of wrong-doers might be reincarnated as animals (*Phaedo* 81e) or wander as unpurified souls in Hades (108b-c).

This Platonic scheme (apart from the reincarnation part) proved broadly suitable to early Christian theorists.[7] The resurrection of Jesus, the key event in Christianity, could only be accepted if there were some kind of survival after death; while the prospect of an eternal and better life provided motivational fuel for ordinary church members to endure the difficulties present in the earthly context.

By complete contrast, the Stoics maintained that there was no immaterial stuff in the cosmos: there was only matter, formed and shaped in a multitude of different ways, and maintained in a state of tension through active and passive principles.[8] This meant that on a person's death, his or her being would cease, the body dissolving into other bodies.

This belief is expressed by Marcus Aurelius in several instances.

> What, then, can guide one safely? Only philosophy: this consists in keeping one's guardian spirit free from violence and unharmed, stronger than pleasures and troubles, doing nothing without purpose, nor dishonestly or with hypocrisy, not requiring anyone else to do or not do something; accepting everything which occurs and is allotted as coming from the place (wherever it is) from which he himself came; and finally, awaiting death with a cheerful mind, as nothing other than the dispersal of elements, from which all forms of life are composed. If there is nothing terrible for the elements constantly being converted into something else, why should someone have any anxiety about the changes and dispersals? For it's according to nature, and nothing according to nature is bad (2.17.2).[9]

Some Christians around the same time, such as Tertullian, followed the Stoics in conceiving that the soul was material but surviving death (partly in order to receive punishment where appropriate).[10] Doctrine was surprisingly various on the issue, but by the time of St Thomas Aquinas over a thousand years later, standard Christian doctrine had accepted that while body and soul formed the human person, the soul might have a separate existence after death.[11]

Virtue and Grace

Platonism, Aristotelianism and Stoicism had all emphasized the importance of virtue in living the best kind of life, one of well-being (*eudaimonia* in Greek). As we saw in Chapter One, the key individual virtues were wisdom, courage, self-control, and justice; the best kind of life, according to philosophers of these schools, was one spent in pursuit of these virtues. Again, a passage from Plato's *Phaedo* is key, in which Socrates describes his own life's work in the pursuit of virtue and wisdom (69a-d).

In Christianity, the emphasis was far less on human achievement than on human failings. The doctrine of Original Sin taught that through Adam and Eve's having eaten the apple in the Garden of Eden, evil came into the world. Through this action, on some early views, humans lost their conformity to the image of God; Adam and his descendants were reduced to 'their natural condition' (*eis to kata phusin*).[12]

Now as we saw, the Stoics considered that 'nothing is evil which is according to nature'; yet for Christianity, humanity's 'natural condition' remains one of evil. The Stoics argued for the possibility and obligation of pursuing virtue; the Christians, the certainty of human failing and insufficiency. Augustine (354–430 CE) taught, again most influentially, that all humans deserved damnation, but that God might exercise grace – that is, supernatural help – or He might not.[13]

Against this background, there had long been a concern within Christian thought as to the status of pagans who had been celebrated for their virtue. Were there indeed virtuous pagans, and if so, how were they to be regarded? In his epic poems, Dante Alighieri (c. 1265-c. 1321) was to place the emperor Trajan in Paradise, the poet Virgil in limbo, and the Stoic role-model Cato the Younger in Purgatory (as he had committed suicide, see below).[14]

The Wise Man

In Stoic theory, although the life of virtue is to be pursued, in fact hardly anyone would achieve the status of a truly virtuous person, the sage or wise man (or woman), although some in ancient times considered that Socrates or, later, Laelius the Wise, and Cato the Younger approached sage-like status. This extreme rarity laid Stoicism open to the allegation that its ideal was effectively unachievable and unrealistic for human capacity, a charge regularly made by Christians throughout history.

Suicide

Of the ancient Stoics, Epictetus, in particular, emphasized that if conditions of life proved unbearable, the philosopher always had the option of suicide.[15] Seneca had taken his own life, on instructions from Nero. Roman history and legend included many men and women who had taken their own lives rather than act dishonourably, and such a death was regarded as heroic rather than disgraceful.

By contrast, while several Old Testament characters are recorded as having committed suicide (e.g. King Saul), this was regarded in Christianity as a terrible sin: after all, only God is to dispose of human lives. Once again, the influence of Augustine was key: he argued that the commandment 'Thou shalt not kill' applied to suicide as well.[16]

We thus see a number of fundamental disagreements between Christianity and Stoicism. Nonetheless, in the sixteenth and seventeenth centuries, many scholars sought to minimize the incompatibilities. The most famous such attempt was by Justus Lipsius (1547–1606), whose selective reworking of aspects of Stoicism, generally called Neo-Stoicism, achieved popularity.[17]

Around the same time, there was a further impetus to accommodation with Stoicism as Marcus' biography and his own *Meditations* became widely read. It was implausible to argue that he had nothing to offer as a moral exemplar, particularly in an age during which the responsibilities of princes and leaders were the subject of debate. Meric Casaubon's first English translation appeared in 1634, his Greek-Latin edition appeared in 1643, and Thomas Gataker's in 1652, these works consolidating the book's status as a key source for Stoicism.[18]

By the end of the century, it was time for a new English version. Jeremy Collier (1650–1726) was a 'non-juror,' a clergyman who had protested against the so-called Glorious Revolution of 1688–9 – the departure of Catholic James II and ascent to the throne of his Protestant daughter Mary and her Dutch husband William – and its accompanying legislation, which ensured that from then on, only Protestants would hold the British throne. Collier served time in prison for his protests against the church's stand; indeed, for his support of two would-be assassins of William III, he was outlawed, and officially remained so for the rest of his life.[19]

Collier maintained that his view about the church's role in the political saga was consistent with 'the primitive church,' that is, early Christian doctrine and practice. He was also very concerned about the moral decline of his day, one factor in which he identified in the state of the English theatre, then in one of its most vigorous phases. If Collier is known at all today, it is as an opponent of theatrical performances. As he was engaged in this debate at the same time as translating Marcus, perhaps this, too, was undertaken in order to effect moral improvement in English society at large.

We have seen in the epigraph to this chapter that Collier briefly noted 'mistakes' in Stoic theory, but having ticked that box, he moved quickly to lavish praise on the Stoic emperor's work, seeming rather star-struck. Collier used a colloquial style, no doubt to appeal to the widest possible readership.

> [Marcus'] Thoughts then are Noble, and Uncommon, and his *Logick* very true and exact. He generally flies his Game home, seldom leaves his Argument till he brings it to a Demonstration, and has pursued it to its first Principles ... as for the Emperor he charges thorough and thorough, and no Difficulty can stand before him. His Reason is no less irresistible than his Arms, and he loves to Conquer in his *Closet,* as well as in the *Field.* There's a peculiar Air of Greatness and Gravity in his Discourses: He seems to think up to his *Station,* and writes with that Magnificence of Notion; as if he believ'd himself oblig'd, to exceed other Authors as much in the Vigour of his Mind, as in the Lustre of his Fortune.
>
> He appears to have thought to the bottom of his Argument, and to have had a Comprehensive View of the World, of the Interest and Relations of *Society.* Hence it is that his Morality is so particularly Serviceable and Convincing, that his Sentences are so Weighty, and his Reasoning so very just. By thus digging to the Foundation, He's in a Condition to assign every thing its true Grounds, and set every Duty upon its proper Basis. Farther, the great Probity of this Prince, his Fortitude, and the Nobleness of his Mind, gave Freedom and Spirit to his Thoughts, and made him exert for the Service of Principle and Truth. Besides he seems to have been born with a Prerogative of Nature, bless'd with a superiour Genius, and made up of richer Materials for Sense and Virtue, than other People.[20]

There is quite a lot more of this praise, concluding: 'In short; Abating for some of the Errors [of Stoicism] above-mention'd, [Marcus] seems to have drawn up an Admirable Scheme of Natural Religion.' This last expression was a significant term for the age, and undoubtedly used consciously by Collier.

'Natural religion' was understood to cover the project of using all the faculties 'natural' to humans – reason, sense-perception, introspection – to investigate religious or theological matters.[21] At the time, it stood in contrast to 'revealed religion,' which meant the specific claims of the Bible and other Church doctrine about Christ's miracles and resurrection, and men's salvation. 'Natural religion' was considered to be theology at which, it was thought, people could reasonably arrive, even without any particular acquaintance with Scriptural texts. In parallel with developments in scientific practice, natural religion endorsed the use of individual reason, maintaining that this would inevitably lead people to a notion of God.

Theologians such as the influential Samuel Clarke (1675–1729) had openly endorsed 'natural religion' as a support and preliminary to Christian commitment, writing in one of his many published sermons:

> No man can effectually believe in *Christ,* except he first believes in God. *Natural* Religion, is the best Preparation for the reception of the Christian [religion].[22]

Critics, however, worried that endorsement of natural religion meant downplaying of the Scriptures (Clarke himself also maintained the importance of 'revealed religion'). There was also a risk to public morals, it was feared, in de-emphasising the Christian rewards and punishments in the afterlife. Yet evidently Collier, whether he shared these concerns and however dimly he may have regarded 'natural religionists' in general, felt that there was much to be gained in promoting Marcus' broad moral appeal.

We clearly see such misgivings about morality in the writings of Collier's contemporary Edmund Gibson (1669–1748). A young man during the Glorious Revolution, he took the opposite side of the debate from Collier. At first his interests were antiquarian: he prepared a new edition of the *Britannia,* the topographical and historical survey published in Latin in 1586 by William Camden (the first English edition had appeared in 1610). Entering the church early in the 1700s, Gibson became an active spokesman for Whig and anti-Catholic causes. Promotions followed, and in 1715 Gibson was appointed Bishop of Lincoln – the largest diocese in the land – and eventually of London. His power was such that he gained the nickname 'the Pope,' a highly ironic one given his strong opposition to Catholicism.[23]

Gibson was conscious of problems facing the church in this time of great change. On the one hand, as noted, he opposed those sympathetic to Catholics; but on the other, he saw just as great a threat in the growth of so-called 'free-thinking,' a term which covered a spectrum from 'natural religionists' through to 'infidelity,' i.e. effective atheism (though this charge was more often made as a polemical thrust – frequently in a confused way – than justified by the targets' actual writings[24]). Indeed, Gibson reacted with horror to the proposal, by Queen Caroline (the wife of King George II) that Samuel Clarke, of whom she was a patroness, be promoted to a bishopric.[25]

Gibson wrote pamphlets and public essays aimed at combating the rise of this general tendency. He could not honestly claim that well-known men on that side were immoral themselves, but he could, and did, suggest that their claims would have a bad influence on others:

> And tho' we should grant our *Free-thinkers* to be a set of refined spirits, capable only of being enamoured of virtue, yet what would become of the bulk of mankind who have gross understandings, but lively senses and strong passions? What a deluge of lust, and fraud, and violence would in

> a little time overflow the whole nation, if these wise advocates for morality were universally hearkened to?[26]

'Natural religion' recalled, to educated readers, in its aspect of postulating a good creator and a benevolent cosmos, the ancient philosophical systems of Platonism and Stoicism themselves. In the circumstances, Gibson made a startling move: an appeal to the authority of these ancient pagans.

> The Christian religion requires, that, after having framed the best Idea, we are able, of the Divine Nature, it should be our next care to conform our selves to it, as far as our imperfections will permit. I might mention several passages in the Sacred Writings on this head, to which I might add many maxims and wise sayings of moral Authors among the *Greeks* and *Romans*.[27]

Gibson's source proved no less bold. It was none other than the famously pagan emperor Julian, 'the Apostate,' who, as we have seen, two centuries after Marcus, had tried to turn the Roman empire away from Christianity back to paganism. Gibson summarized Julian's *Caesars*, which we have already explored in detail:

> The Emperor [Julian] having represented all the *Roman* Emperors, with *Alexander* the Great, as passing in review before the Gods, and striving for the superiority, lets them all drop, excepting *Alexander, Julius Caesar, Augustus Caesar, Trajan, Marcus Aurelius,* and *Constantine*. Each of these great heroes of antiquity lays in his claim for the upper place; and, in order to it, sets forth his actions after the most advantageous manner. But the Gods, instead of being dazzled with the lustre of their actions, enquire, by *Mercury,* into the proper motive and governing principle that influenced them throughout the whole series of their lives and exploits.
>
> *Alexander* tells them, That his aim was to conquer; *Julius Caesar*, That his was to gain the highest post in his country; *Augustus,* To govern well; *Trajan*, That his was the same as that of *Alexander*, namely, to conquer. The question, at length, was put to *Marcus Aurelius*, who replied, with great modesty, That *it had always been his care to imitate the Gods.* This conduct seems to have gained him the most votes and best place in the whole assembly. *Marcus Aurelius* being afterwards asked to explain himself, declares, That, by imitating the Gods, he endeavoured to imitate them in the use of his understanding, and of all other faculties; and in particular, That it was always his study to have as few wants as possible in himself, and to do all the good he could to others.[28]

Gibson goes on to explain that 'revealed religion' has given people a better idea, than the ancient pagans could have had, of the divine Being (singular, of course) 'whom every reasonable creature ought to imitate.' There is an argument from the comparison: if Marcus, in his time and culture, could act virtuously in imitation of his gods, surely people in Gibson's time were much better placed to do so, as the Christian God – understood through Scriptural texts - offered a far better role-model than the pagan Jupiter and the rest of the Olympian pantheon.

Thus Gibson adroitly turned his free-thinking opponents' 'natural religion' back upon themselves, daringly using a pagan model and an anti-Christian source to demonstrate the superiority of 'revealed,' that is Scriptural, religion. Gibson's decision to co-opt the greatest 'hero of antiquity' onto the Whig, low-church side, was nothing less than inspired. It robbed the natural-religion party to his left – not to mention Collier, a high-church moralist on his right – of their Exhibit A, not just *a* virtuous pagan, but *the most* virtuous leader in all of Greek and Roman history.

Gibson's essays were widely read and highly influential, partly as a result of his publishing them under the banner of the popular writer Joseph Addison's *Evidences of the Christian Religion*, in which it is difficult to determine where Addison ends and Gibson begins. The volume, first appearing in 1730, was republished in London well into the nineteenth century (the second, 1733 version is the one referenced here).[29]

For his part, Collier's translation of *Meditations* remained the standard English version until George Long's in 1862. While Collier's quixotic campaigns against the Orange regime and the English theatre had their brief day, his colloquial translation continued to bring Marcus to generation after generation of readers.

Chapter Twelve

Marcus Incognito: The Strange Case of Defoe's *Dumb Philosopher*[1]

The versatile Daniel Defoe – Father of the English novel – A minor work – Moral advice – Reproduces Marcus' Meditations (Collier translation) – Was the ethical background to the English novel Stoic, rather than Protestant? – Marcus' pervasive influence

'When thou risest from sleep with reluctance, remember that it is according to thy constitution and according to human nature to perform social acts …'
Marcus Aurelius, *Meditations* Book 8.12[2]

We have seen how Marcus Aurelius was deployed as a weapon in the Anglican controversies of the early-eighteenth century. Let us now turn to an even more surprising development, courtesy of a short work by Daniel Defoe, *The Dumb Philosopher*. Defoe is best known as the author of the first modern novel, *Robinson Crusoe* (April 1719), and *The Dumb Philosopher* appeared some six months later.[3]

Defoe (1660–1731) was at times a journalist, a political activist – for which he served time in prison – a businessman, and an intelligence agent. He wrote dozens of pamphlets, travel guides, political tracts, historical works, and books of moral guidance, written under a range of pseudonyms, in addition to his famous novels, *Robinson Crusoe, Moll Flanders* (1722), and *Roxana* (1724). Defoe's very versatility has made it difficult for critics to assess his overall literary achievement.

Writing in the mid-twentieth century, however, the British scholar Ian Watt, in his ground-breaking *The Rise of the Novel: Studies in Defoe, Richardson and Fielding* (1957 and numerous later editions), thought he had found the key. Watt sought to demonstrate that Defoe's family background and education in the English Puritan tradition were critical for understanding his writing. Hard work and productivity are highly valued qualities in Defoe; his character Robinson Crusoe exhibits practical ingenuity in overcoming the challenges of life alone on an island. Watt wrote:

> Defoe clearly belongs to the tradition of Ascetic Protestantism … in Dickory Cronke's aphorism, for example: 'When you find yourself sleepy in a morning, rouse yourself, and consider that you are born to business, and that in doing good in your generation, you answer your character and act like a man.'[4]

This aphorism, however, had not arisen from any English or Christian source, but was a paraphrase of Marcus Aurelius' *Meditations* 8.12, given above as the epigraph to this chapter. We now need to take a closer look at Defoe's enigmatic text.

A Project Gutenberg version of *Dickory Cronke: The Dumb Philosopher, or, Great Britain's Wonder*, by Daniel Defoe, is readily available. It purports to be (I) a factual account of a certain Dickory Cronke,

> a Tinner's son, in the county of Cornwall, [who] was born Dumb, and continued so for Fifty-eight years; and how, some days before he died, he came to his Speech; with Memoirs of his Life, and the Manner of his Death. II. A Declaration of his Faith and Principles in Religion; with a Collection of Select Meditations, composed in his Retirement. III. His Prophetical Observations upon the Affairs of Europe, more particularly of Great Britain, from 1720 to 1729. (loc. 11)

The author's preface vouches for the authenticity of his work by claiming that his sources are extant 'in the custody of a person of unquestionable reputation.' He adds, cryptically, that what the reader:

> has now before him was collected from a large bundle of papers, most of which were writ in shorthand, and very ill-digested. However, this may be relied upon, that though the language is something altered, and now and then a word thrown in to help the expression, yet strict care has been taken to speak the author's mind … Here is a dumb philosopher introduced to a wicked and degenerate generation, as a proper emblem of virtue and morality; and if the world could be persuaded to look upon him with candour and impartiality, and then to copy after him, the editor has gained his end … (loc. 27).

The supposedly biographical account, then, says that Dickory Cronke was born in 1660 (also the year of Defoe's birth). His inability to speak was identified after he turned three. As he grew older, his health did not permit him to work in the Cornwall tin mines, but he lived first with his mother and later as a private servant with several employers. He saved enough money to live independently for some years, eventually discovering that his whole family, in the interim, had died, except for a widowed sister.

> This doleful news ... must be extremely shocking, and add a new sting to his former affliction; and here it was that he began to exercise the philosopher, and to demonstrate himself both a wise and a good man. All these things, thinks he, are the will of Providence, and must not be disputed ... (loc. 89).

Cronke went to live with his surviving sister, until his death, which we are told took place in 1718. Defoe writes that he made walking a constant habit; ate sparingly; never complained; and 'was a person of great wisdom and sagacity. He understood nature beyond the ordinary capacity, and, if he had had a competency of learning suitable to his genius, neither this nor the former ages would have produced a better philosopher or a greater man' (loc. 114).

Strangely, just before his death, Cronke regained the power of speech. He advised his sister:

> Do but look seriously and impartially upon the astonishing notion of time and eternity, what an immense deal has run out already, and how infinite it is still in the future ... (loc. 155)[5]

Part II of the work consists of Cronke's written reflections. The first batch sets out conventional beliefs about the Scriptures, the Trinity, and eternal salvation through Christ's resurrection, including endorsement of the Anglican system as 'one of the most excellent branches of the Church Universal' (loc. 251). Then, however, things take a very Stoic turn.

Cronke appends 'a few [in fact, forty numbered] meditations and observations relating to the Conduct of Human Life in general.' These turn out, very largely, to be selections from Marcus Aurelius' *Meditations*, probably in the 1701 translation by Jeremy Collier which we have already encountered, in places lightly altered.

The table below gives eleven representative examples, chosen from at least twenty-five probable Marcus excerpts among the forty meditations attributed to Cronke (these include the one taken from 8.12 which, as we saw above, misled Watt). I have emphasized the closest verbal similarities with bold type; but even where the wording of Defoe varies from that of Collier, it will be clear that the sentiment is identical.

	Cronke Meditations	Defoe Text (1719)	Marcus Meditations	Collier Text (1701)
1	1	**Remember how often you have** neglected the great duties of religion and virtue, and slighted the opportunities that Providence has put into your hands.	2.4	**Remember how often you have** postpon'd the minding your Interest, and slip'd those Opportunities the Gods have given you.
2	2	**Let an unaffected gravity, freedom, justice and sincerity shine through** all your actions, and let no fancies and chimeras give the least check to those excellent qualities. This is an easy task, **if you will but suppose everything you do to be your last**, and if you can keep your passions and appetites from crossing your reason. **Stand clear of rashness, and have nothing of insincerity or self-love to infect you.**	2.5	**Let unaffected Gravity, Humanity, Freedom, and Justice shine through it** [your action]. And be sure you entertain no Fancys, which may give check to these Qualities. This Task is very practicable **if you will but suppose every thing you are upon your Last;** if your Appetites and Passions don't cross upon your Reason; If you **stand clear of Rashness,** and don't complain of your Destiny, and **have nothing of Insincerity, and Self-Love to infect you.**
3	5	Among your principal observations upon human life, let it be always one to take **notice what a great deal both of time and ease that man gains who is not troubled with the spirit of curiosity, who lets his neighbours' affairs alone, and confines his inspections to himself, and only takes care of honesty and a good conscience.**	4.18	**What a great deal of Time and Ease that Man gains who is not troubled with the Spirit of Curiosity: Who lets his Neighbours Thoughts and Behaviour alone, confines his Inspections to himself; And takes care of the Points of Honesty and Conscience.**
4	6	**If you would live at your ease,** and as much as possible be free from the incumbrances of life, manage but a few things at once, and let those, too, be such as are absolutely necessary. By this rule you **will draw the bulk of your business into a narrow compass, and have the double pleasure of making your actions good, and few into the bargain.**	4.24	**If you would live at your ease,** says *Democritus, Manage but a few Things.* I think it had been better, if He had said, do nothing but what is necessary; and what becomes one made for Society; Nothing but what Reason prescribes, and in the Order too she prescribes it. For by this Rule a Man may both secure the Quality, and **draw in the Bulk of his Business; And have the double Pleasure of making his Actions Good, and Few, into the Bargain.**

	Cronke Meditations	Defoe Text (1719)	Marcus Meditations	Collier Text (1701)
5	10	**When you happen to be ruffled and put out of humour by any cross accident, retire immediately into your reason,** and do not suffer your passion to overrule you a moment; for the sooner you recover yourself now, the better you will be able to guard yourself for the future.	6.11	**When you happen to be ruffled a little, and thrown off your Temper by any cross Accident, retire immediately into your Reason;** And don't move out of Rule any longer than needs must: For the sooner you recover a False Step, the more you will be Master of your Practice.
6	16	**When you have a mind to entertain yourself in your retirements, let it be with the good qualifications of your friends and acquaintance.** Think with pleasure and satisfaction upon the honour and bravery of one, the modesty of another, the generosity of a third, and so on; **there being nothing more pleasant and diverting than the lively images and the advantages of those we love and converse with.**	6.48	**When you have a mind to divert your Fancy, consider the good Qualities of your Acquaintance.** As the enterprising Vigour of this Man, the Modesty of another, the Liberality of a Third, and so on. For **there's nothing so Entertaining as a Lively Image of the Virtues, and Advantages of those we Converse with.**
7	17	**As nothing can deprive you of the privileges of your nature, or compel you to act counter to your reason, so nothing can happen to you but what comes from Providence, and consists with the interest of the Universe.**	6.58	**As no body can rob you of the privileges of your Nature, or force you to live Counter to your Reason, so nothing can happen to you but what comes from Providence, and consists with the Interest of the Universe.**
8	21	**When you hear a discourse, let your understanding, as far as possible, keep pace with it,** and lead you forward to those things which fall most within the compass of **your own observations.**	7.31 [NB: appears as 7.30 in Long and Hays versions]	**When you hear a Discourse, make your Understanding keep pace with it,** and reach as far as you can into those Things which fall under **your Observation.**
9	26	It is a very ancient observation, and a very true one, that **people generally despise where they flatter, and cringe to those they design to betray; so that truth and ceremony are, and always will be, two distinct things.**	11.14	**People generally Despise, where they Flatter; And cringe to those they would gladly overtop, so that Truth, and Ceremony, are two Things.**

	Cronke Meditations	Defoe Text (1719)	Marcus Meditations	Collier Text (1701)
10	29	**Gentleness and good humour are invincible, provided they are without hypocrisy** and design; they disarm the most barbarous and savage tempers, and **make even malice ashamed of itself.**	11.18	[Ninthly] **that Gentleness and Good Humour are invincible, provided they are of the right Stamp, without any thing of Hypocrisy,** or Grimace. This is the way to Disarm the most Barbarous, and Savage: A constancy in Obliging Behaviour will make the most Outragious [sic] **Person ashamed of his Malice.**
11	30	In all the actions of life let it be your first and principal care to **guard against anger on the one hand, and flattery on the other, for they are both unserviceable qualities, and do a great deal of mischief in the government of human life.**	11.18	And here you must take care to **Guard against Flattery, as well as Anger; For these are both unserviceable Qualities, and do a great deal of Mischief in the World.**

Remarkably, it would appear that no scholar to date has been moved to determine the source of Defoe/Cronke's meditations. Writing in 1940, John Robert Moore called them 'colorless,' finding the only significant part of the entire work to be Part III, Cronke's prophecies for the ensuing years (which lie outside the scope of this chapter). 'Everything,' wrote Moore, 'that precedes the concluding prophecies is innocuous enough,' that is to say, to him uninteresting. Moore reported that some earlier writers had believed Cronke to have been a real person, but concluded that the apparent 'true story' of Cronke's life was offered simply to lend verisimilitude to the prophecies, which Moore regarded as politically motivated. 'The religious meditations are merely a part of the realistic groundwork.'[6]

For his part, Watt regarded Defoe's attitude as displaying:

> a confusion of religious and material values to which the Puritan gospel of the dignity of labour was peculiarly liable: once the highest spiritual values had been attached to the performance of the daily task, the next step was for the autonomous individual to regard his achievements as a quasi-divine mastering of the environment. It is likely that this secularization of the Calvinist conception of stewardship was of considerable importance for the rise of the novel ... It is ... likely that the Puritan conception of the dignity of labour helped to bring into being the novel's general premise

> that the individual's daily life is of sufficient importance and interest to be the proper subject of literature.[7]

But the 'dumb philosopher' was no Puritan. Rather, he was the Stoic, Marcus Aurelius, the 'person of unquestionable reputation,' who, disguised as Dickory Cronke, regained the power of speaking to a 'wicked and degenerate generation' through Defoe's text. As Defoe in this period was preaching the moral framework set out by the Stoic emperor, perhaps the individual's 'performance of the daily task,' tending towards 'quasi-divine' standing, involved not a 'confusion,' but a coherent Stoic purpose. Further, if as critics after Watt have agreed, the English realist novel of Defoe and his successors represented, in certain aspects, an incorporation of British empiricist philosophy, then Stoicism's insistence on the self-preserving agent working productively within his or her community may also have contributed, as it were, upstream, through the works of Locke and Shaftesbury.[8]

It is worth noting that in his sequel to the novel, *Serious Reflections During the Life and Surprising Adventures of Robinson Crusoe* (1720), responding to critics on themes raised in the novel, Defoe insisted that true solitude – that is to say, meditation – was as practicable among crowds as anywhere else:

> … among the Hurries of Conversation, and Gallantry of a Court, or the Noise and Business of a Camp … (17).

Knowing, as we now do, that Marcus' *Meditations* had recently been in Defoe's mind, it is likely that here we see a reference to the Emperor's own court and camp.

We can also see Marcus' influence in the appended essay *A Vision of the Angelick World*. In this fantasy work, Defoe's narrator takes an imaginary journey into space. This recalls Marcus' injunction to 'Look round at the courses of the stars, as if you were going along with them' (7.47). Here, Marcus was instructing himself to employ the Stoic practice known as the 'view from above,' aimed at reframing our view of life and events. Recognising this practice, if not its classical Stoic origins, one recent scholar observes: 'Crusoe's spectacular view of the planets allows him to ignore the pettiness of ordinary human life in the name of a seemingly timeless, disembodied state of being.'[9]

It remains to offer a suggestion about the English version of Marcus from which Defoe so freely plagiarized. Introducing his fresh and colloquial English version of *Meditations*, Collier included a translation of the comprehensive biographical essay by André Dacier (which had appeared in French in 1697), as well as appending a portion of Gataker's own comparison of Stoic and

Epicurean philosophies. On the basis of the strong verbal echoes shown in the table, I estimate that Defoe used a Collier text rather than a Gataker, noting of course that Collier is likely to have preserved some phrasing of Gataker's.

A clue confirming Collier as the origin appears in the preface to *The Dumb Philosopher*, in which, as we noted, Defoe describes his source as 'writ in shorthand.' This may well recall Collier's insightful preface, in which the translator describes Marcus' way of writing Greek:

> One Word more of the Emperour's Stile, and I have done: Now his way of expressing himself is extraordinarily Brief: His Words are sometimes over-burthen'd with Thought, and have almost more Sense than they can carry. Indeed, 'twas part of his Character to write in this Concise manner; for neither the Emperour, nor the *Stoick* would allow of any length of Expression. Besides, he wrote chiefly for himself, which makes him still more sparing in his Language; He sometimes draws in little, writes his Meaning, as it were, in Short-Hand, and does not beat out his Notions to their full Proportion ...

Shorthand writing was an innovation developed during the seventeenth century, and its metaphorical appeal fits Collier's up-to-the-minute style. Indeed, the *OED* advises that Collier himself, in an article from 1695, had been the first to use the image in this figurative sense.[10]

In the circumstances, it is ironic – but not, given his multiple identities and allegiances, surprising – that Defoe maintains a reputation as a 'modernist,' impatient with the ancient writers in part because of their (supposed) tendency to plagiarize. Watt quoted Defoe as writing in 1725:

> A Merry Fellow of my Acquaintance assures me, that our cousin *Homer* himself was guilty of the same *Plagiarism* ... the *Poet* never did much himself, only published and sold his Ballads still, in his own Name, as if they had been his own; and by that, got great Subscriptions, and a high Price for them.[11]

Citing scornful remarks by Defoe concerning Virgil, Watt concluded: 'This note of hardly concealed impatience at the irrational and immoral idolatry of the ancients is a suitable one on which to leave Defoe.'[12] As we have seen, however, Defoe paid the sincerest tribute to the morality of Marcus Aurelius, the greatest of the Roman Stoics, in passing it off – successfully, for over three hundred years, until now – as his own.

Chapter Thirteen

Saint Antoninus: Enlightenment and Revolution

Hutcheson and Moor translate Meditations – Elizabeth Carter translates Epictetus – The French philosophers co-opt Stoicism – Antoine-Léonard Thomas' 'Eulogium on Marcus' – A revolutionary Irish translator – Thomas Jefferson 'the Marcus of the United States' – German illuminati read Stoicism; German Lutherans reject it

We observed in an earlier chapter that Marcus, and Stoicism, were deployed as weapons in the ideological rivalries between different wings of the Anglican church during the culture wars of the early Enlightenment. This trend was to continue, even spreading across the Channel, the Irish Sea, and the Atlantic; this chapter will attempt to cover some of these voyages over the course of the eighteenth and early-nineteenth centuries.

Hutcheson and Moor's *Meditations* (1742)

As we saw, Jeremy Collier's translation of the *Meditations* remained widely read. But as we also saw, Collier's choice of style – emblematic of his approach more generally – was idiosyncratic if not eccentric. In 1742, a new English translation of the *Meditations* appeared, with a fresh introduction and notes, prepared by two authors who were both at pains to remain anonymous.

The authors were Francis Hutcheson (1694–1746), professor of moral philosophy at Glasgow University, and his student and friend James Moor (1712–1779), classicist and librarian. Originally from County Down, Ireland, Hutcheson studied, taught and wrote several key works while living in Dublin, including essays on beauty, order, and moral matters (combating the work, among others, of Thomas Hobbes). His moral philosophy is a complex matter, with some scholars seeing him as a proto-Utilitarian long before Jeremy Bentham – Hutcheson's open use of algorithms to express ethical content is a factor here – while others consider more important his theory of a 'moral sense.'[1]

For our purposes, certain aspects of Hutcheson's worldview are relevant. As a liberal thinker and teacher, Hutcheson, while a minister of the church, faced difficulties against the backdrop of the extremely strict Calvinist church politics which prevailed in Scotland at the time. He took up the Glasgow appointment in 1730. During the following years, various attacks were made upon Hutcheson on the grounds of his teaching.

In 1738, an anonymous pamphlet listed several grounds on which Hutcheson might be charged with heresy.[2] We can see some of the details in a response which was produced by a group of Hutcheson's students and friends in his defence: 'A Vindication of Mr Hutcheson from the Calumnious Aspersions of a Late Pamphlet.'

One of the supposedly heretical teachings was: 'Tendency to promote the Happiness of Others is the "Standard of Moral Goodness."' The allegation was that Hutcheson, in suggesting this, was discounting God as the ultimate authority of moral goodness. The students indignantly retort:

> Mr Hutcheson ever maintains, That the Observation of the Divine Laws tends to the greatest Good of Mankind; tho' 'tis disingenuously alledged [sic], that he speaks only of Tendency to external Good … (p. 9).

Another problematic teaching was alleged: 'Selfmurder is in some Cases lawful.' As we saw in an earlier chapter, the sin involved in suicide was a central principle in Christianity, and in accusing Hutcheson of excusing the act, his anonymous critic had hit a sensitive cultural nerve.

The students, however, were having none of it.

> We assert, He never approved of any, even, the most celebrated Instances of Suicide among [the ancients], which Christians have since looked on as the most excusable: For Example, he condemn'd those of Lucretia, [the Stoic] Cato, and Brutus … He told us, at great length, the plausible Arguments of a great Number of Writers, in Defence of the Doctrine and Practice of many Ancients: and the Arguments on the other Side, in the most plausible Cases. But we never heard him decide, as our Author alledges [sic] (pp. 8–9).
>
> Never did any Man of Gravity say *Selfmurder* was lawful in any Case. But our Author knew this was an odious Word, always importing Guilt … he knew the Word *Selfmurther* [sic] was fit to raise a *Popular Odium and Clamour* (p. 10).

Through his students' diligent defence, Hutcheson comes across as a careful and balanced teacher, not afraid to tackle issues which were sensitive in the

Christian context generally, and particularly so in the charged atmosphere of Glasgow Calvinism.

James Moor was one of the loyal signatories to the *Vindication*, and just a few years later would join Hutcheson in the project of translating Marcus' *Meditations*.[3] Hutcheson's attitude towards the 'pagan moralists' was complex, and was not by any means entirely supportive, but it is no coincidence – whatever the students claimed – that the 'tendency to promote the happiness of others,' and a relatively tolerant attitude to suicide, were both features of classical Stoicism.

Not, as noted above, that either author was willing to be named. Hutcheson sent copies to Thomas Drennan in Belfast with a cryptic note:

> I don't let my name appear in it, nor indeed have I told it to any here but the Man concerned. I hope that you'll like it; the rest was done by a very ingenious lad one Moore [sic].[4]

Publishing anonymously permitted Hutcheson and Moor to express sentiments which would undoubtedly have attracted controversy, if not actual censure.

Scholars consider that the first two books were translated by Moor, and the rest by Hutcheson.[5] The authors claimed that the more recent English version by Collier was unsatisfactory: 'the late translation seems not to preserve sufficiently the grand simplicity of the original.'[6] Overall, then, the reason for their project was to spread the moral writings of Marcus Aurelius to a wide public of English readers, and their introduction stressed that even a pagan was a great, and could be an accessible, teacher of goodness:

> The authors ... judging ... that these divine sentiments of Antoninus, may be of some advantage to many who have not access to them, while they are kept in the learned languages, undertook to make them as plain as the subjects would admit. Some of these meditations cannot well be apprehended without a considerable acquaintance with the philosophy and stile [sic] of the Stoics ... [but] there are many of [the Meditations] obvious to every capacity; which contain some of the plainest, and yet most striking considerations, to affect the hearts of those who have any sense of goodness, and warm them with the noblest emotions, of piety, gratitude, and resignation to GOD; contempt of sensual pleasure, wealth, worldly grandeur, and fame; and a constant inflexible charity, and good-will and compassion toward our fellows, superior to all the force of anger or envy, or our little interfering worldly interests.[7]

The 'little interfering worldly interests' was just a warning shot. Hutcheson and Moor's biographical introduction culminated in a powerful peroration reminding the reader how poorly placed many modern Christians were to dismiss Marcus Aurelius on the grounds of his alleged persecution of Christianity:

> Let none make this objection to Antoninus, but those who, from their hearts, abhor all Christian persecutions, who cannot hate their neighbours, or deem them excluded from the divine favour, either for neglecting certain ceremonies, and pieces of outward pageantry, or for exceeding in them; for different opinions, or forms of words, about some metaphysical attributes or modes of existence, which all sides own to be quite incomprehensible by us; for the different opinions about human liberty; about which the best men who ever lived have had opposite sentiments; for different opinions about the manner in which the Deity may think fit to exercise his mercy to a guilty world, either in pardoning of their sins, or renewing them in piety and virtue...[8]

This, then, was a statement asserting Enlightenment tolerance, with Marcus providing the occasion. No doubt, Hutcheson and Moor continued, Marcus should have acquainted himself better with Christianity. But how much leisure had the emperor had for making the time to explore a sect which was widely despised for immorality? Rather, they argued:

> We see with what a just contempt of ease, pleasure, and luxury, he keenly embraced the scheme of philosophy [Stoicism] most remarkable for piety, austerity, and disinterested goodness; and how long Christian magistrates, spirited up by the pretended embassadors [sic] of the meek Jesus, have been persecuting their fellow-Christians with fire and sword; and that for very honourable tenets; often much better than those of the persecutors.[9]

Finally, Hutcheson and Moor appealed to the early Christians as having accepted the worth of virtuous pagans:

> Nay, the early Christians believed the spirit of Christ operated in Socrates, Plato, and other virtuous heathens; and that they were Christians in heart, without the historical knowledge: And, sure, we may charitably judge the same of this Emperor, who plainly depended on God for such sanctifying influences ... [10]

Evidently, Hutcheson's championing of Marcus left a lasting impression in Calvinist Glasgow. In 1753, some years after Hutcheson's death, his followers were ridiculed for their adherence to the 'saintship of Marcus Antoninus.'[11]

One of these followers may well have been the youthful Adam Smith. Born in 1723, he began his studies in moral philosophy at Glasgow, under Hutcheson, at the age of fourteen. Smith would in his turn, after the intervening tenure of Thomas Craigie, become Professor at Glasgow. In his first published book, *The Theory of Moral Sentiments* (1759), Smith discussed ancient and modern moral systems.

The extent to which Smith's own moral theory was himself influenced by Stoic views has been the subject of debate.[12] At any rate, his section discussing Stoicism is thorough, sensitive, and largely accurate, even if tending to underplay its prosocial aspects (although some modern commentators consider that he adopts the important Stoic principle of *oikeiōsis*[13]). Smith quotes at length from Marcus – 'the mild, the humane, the benevolent Antoninus' – to illustrate Stoicism's principle of submission to the order of Providence:

> The good-natured emperor, the absolute sovereign of the whole civilized part of the world, who certainly had no peculiar reason to complain of his own allotment, delights in expressing his contentment with the ordinary course of things, and in pointing out beauties even in those parts of it where vulgar observers are not apt to see any.[14]

We might query Smith's statement that Marcus had nothing to complain of in his lot, but must be glad that he included lengthy quotations from the *Meditations*. These include a paraphrase of 5.8:

> As we frequently say … that the physician has ordered to such a man to ride on horseback, or to use the cold bath, or to walk barefooted; so ought we to say that nature, the great conductor and physician of the universe, has ordered to such a man a disease, or the amputation of a limb, or the loss of a child … [15]

Another passage quoted is 4.23:

> O World … all things are suitable to me which are suitable to thee. Nothing is too early or too late to me which is seasonable for thee. All is fruit to me which thy seasons bring forth. From thee are all things; in thee are all things; for thee are all things. One man says, O beloved city of Cecrops [Athens]. Wilt thou not say, O beloved city of God?[16]

Smith does not, as we might have expected, use Hutcheson's translations here: they are likely to have been his own. In his biographical essay on Smith, first delivered in 1793, Edinburgh philosopher Dugald Stewart – who had himself been strongly influenced by Hutcheson – remarked on Smith's practice of translation as a way of improving his own style. Stewart also reports that a Mr Dalzel, Professor of Greek, had commented on:

> Mr Smith's memory on philological subjects, and the acuteness and skill he displayed … on some of the *minutiae* of Greek grammar.[17]

Through Hutcheson and through Smith, the thoughts of Marcus will have found thousands of new readers: *The Theory of Moral Sentiments* went through six editions, the last – featuring the most thorough treatment of Stoicism – appearing in 1790.[18]

Carter's Epictetus (1758)

Around the very same time as Smith's *Moral Sentiments* first appeared, Stoicism was reaching a far wider readership in the English-speaking world. The seminal event was the translation of Epictetus' *Discourses* and *Handbook* (drafted over many years and published in 1758) by the daughter of an Anglican clergyman, Elizabeth Carter. This work had been encouraged and sponsored by Thomas Secker, at the time Bishop of Oxford. Early in the project, the Bishop urged Carter to present Epictetus' teaching in plain and straightforward English. He wrote:

> [Florid and persuasive speeches] were the methods in vogue when Epictetus lived; and they had brought philosophy into disregard and disgrace. He saw it with grief; and reproved Messieurs les Philosophes with an honest zeal. Surely then we should be very careful to do nothing that may but seem to approach towards transforming him into one of these gentlemen.[19]

In other words, the good Bishop was concerned about the co-opting of Epictetus, and of Stoicism in general, by the *philosophes*, the radical writers of the French salons, whom he thus identified with the sophists of ancient times. As it turned out, Carter's version proved to be scholarly while achieving the effect of plain, direct 'preaching,' and went into numerous editions; Carter never had to write for money again, and her popular version remained the standard English translation until the mid-twentieth century. The Bishop's anxiety was perhaps unreasonable, considering, as we have seen, that already, for decades, Anglican factions had not hesitated to parade Marcus Aurelius as a moral mascot, on one side or another during theological and ecclesiastical debate.

In any event, the Stoic horse had, on the Continent, well and truly bolted. To take only a few samples of Stoicism's appearances in the writings of the *philosophes*: Montesquieu's reverence for Stoic-inspired moral works was on view in his ground-breaking *L'esprit des lois* (*The Spirit of Laws*, 1748). He wrote:

> Never were any principles more worthy of human nature, and more proper to form the good man, than those of the Stoics: and if I could for a moment cease to think that I am a Christian, I should not be able to hinder myself from ranking the destruction of the sect of Zeno among the misfortunes that have befallen the human race … Laying aside for a moment revealed truths, let us search through all nature, and we shall not find a nobler object than the Antoninus's.[20]

For his part, Voltaire regularly contrasted Christian persecution with the greater toleration of the pagan age: he wrote that 'the moral reflections of Marcus Aurelius … struck me as the masterpiece of antiquity.'[21] Finally, one of the historical novels of the period, Marmontel's *Bélisaire* (1767), a thinly disguised critique of Louis XV's regime, turned out to have a prominent sub-plot and numerous footnotes promoting the 'virtuous pagans' over the Christian emperors, even featuring a Stoic 'view from above' within the story proper. For years, the novel was a best-seller in a range of European languages, inspiring 'spin-offs' throughout popular culture.[22]

Thomas' and Warden's Marcus Fan-Fiction

Thomas Secker – by then the Archbishop of Canterbury – died in 1768. He would surely have been horrified by the political ends to which Marcus Aurelius would in time be put, by an actual revolutionary: David Bailie Warden (1772–1845), an Irishman, and translator of the *Eulogium on Marcus Aurelius*, by Antoine-Léonard Thomas. It is this work which may have provided the inspiration for Frank McLynn's version of Marcus' death, the confusion around which, as we observed, offered space for a range of speculations.

Antoine-Léonard Thomas (1732–1785) was not so much a *philosophe* as a critic and populariser, most famous in his own day for his fictionalised tributes for historical figures. His *éloge* for René Descartes had appeared to acclaim in 1765. Today he is best known, if known at all, for his *Essai sur les femmes* (1772), a contribution to the perennial question of the roles of women.

Thomas' *Éloge*, an important work of Marcus fan-fiction, also appeared in the 1770s. It was delivered publicly, but then was censored from appearing in print:

> This Eulogium, which had been read at a public sitting of the French Academy, on the day appointed for the reception of the Archbishop of Toulouse, made a very deep impression. The great truths it contains, and which then appeared so much the more bold, as they seemed an indirect satire upon a ministry who openly hated all truth and all virtue ... THOMAS was prohibited from printing the Eulogium on MARCUS AURELIUS ... When it was permitted to praise virtue, the Eulogium on Marcus Aurelius reappeared with splendor: it is, without dispute, the best production of the author.[23]

Warden's Ireland

Before exploring the text of the Eulogium, it is worth recounting the life of its translator, David Bailie Warden. In 1772, Warden was born, like Hutcheson, in County Down, and also, later to attend the University of Glasgow, graduating MA in 1797; perhaps the followers of 'Saint Antoninus' were still present at this time.

Returning to Ireland, he became a popular preacher, joining the Society of United Irishmen, of which Theobald Wolfe Tone is perhaps the best-known member. The Society was composed largely of dissenters from the ruling Anglican regime. During the 1790s, it looked to America and France for inspiration in attempting to bring about a more equal polity, including the removal of restrictions on Catholics from participation in politics.

There were indeed links between the legacies of Hutcheson among the new generation of Irish activists. The Belfast friend to whom Hutcheson had written, enclosing copies of his translation of Marcus, was Thomas Drennan, the father of William Drennan (1754–1820). The younger Drennan in his turn had studied at Edinburgh under Dugald Stewart. It was William who in 1791 drafted the membership 'test' of the United Irishmen:

> I ... in the presence of God, do pledge myself to my country, that I will use all my abilities and influence in the attainment of an impartial and adequate representation of the Irish nation in parliament: and as a means of absolute and immediate necessity ... I shall do whatever lies in my power to forward a brotherhood of affection, an identity of interests, a communion of rights, and a union of power among Irishmen of every religious persuasion ...

Drennan employed the Hutcheson formula, 'the greatest happiness of the greatest numbers,' as a grand aim of the organisation.[24] We may also, perhaps, see some Stoic influence in the assertion of a 'brotherhood' of all, beyond the sectarian rivalries so persistently prominent in Irish life.

The Republic of Newtownards

In the first half of 1798, sporadic, violent uprisings took place across Ireland, largely organised by the United Irishmen. A French fleet had been despatched in December 1796 to the west coast of Ireland, accompanied by Wolfe Tone, but had been prevented from landing by bad weather. Another French intervention was launched in 1798, only to be intercepted by the Royal Navy.

The British authorities and their local representatives, on high alert, met the disorganised actions of the rebels with great severity. One quixotic confrontation took place at Newtownards, east of Belfast. Here, in June, the young Presbyterian minister David Bailie Warden, a 'colonel' in the United Irish forces, led a small group of rebels to take over the town. They were met with musket fire from the Market House, but the government troops withdrew, and a small 'Committee of Public Safety' was established on the French revolutionary model. This little Republic survived only two days, when the main rebel force, of about 4000 men, was crushed by the British commander, George Nugent, with a force of about 2000, at Ballynahinch.

As other battles took place in an isolated way across Ireland, British government reprisals against the United Irish leaders were swift, brutal, and persistent. Several were court-martialled and hanged, the heads of some being paraded in public. Wolfe Tone committed suicide in prison in Dublin, aged only 35.

Some Irish rebel leaders were permitted to negotiate terms, including exile to France or the United States, in exchange for the cessation of judicial reprisals. In this group was David Bailie Warden. He was imprisoned in Belfast, then transferred to the prison ship *Postlethwaite* anchored in Belfast Lough. In preparation for a new life in the United States, Warden applied for credentials from the local Belfast Presbytery, which would have allowed him to be received by a US presbytery, but these were denied. In May 1799 Warden sailed for New York from Belfast, with over a hundred other United Irishmen.

Warden had influential friends, among them Matilda Tone, Wolfe's widow, and Eliza Custis, the step-granddaughter of George Washington. Working first as a physician, then as a teacher, Warden joined the already considerable Irish community which supported Thomas Jefferson, by then serving as the third President. Warden's students included the children of Senator John Armstrong, and when Armstrong was named the American Minister to France, Warden accompanied him. In 1808, Jefferson appointed Warden as US Consul in Paris.[25]

Warden would forward to Jefferson many articles, translations and periodicals, and it is from this period (December 1808) that his translation of Thomas' *éloge* dates. The dedication reads:

> To THOMAS JEFFERSON, the MARCUS AURELIUS of the UNITED STATES.

Thomas depicts the Stoic philosopher Apollonius, one of Marcus' teachers and friends, delivering an impassioned speech over the emperor's coffin, which, he writes, had been accompanied on its journey to Rome by Pertinax. (Thomas thus short-circuited what we now know to be some of the obscurities involved around Marcus' death and funeral.) Both historical information (from the *Historia Augusta* and Cassius Dio), and the text of Marcus' own *Meditations*, are paraphrased at times.

Apollonius' monologue focuses on aspects of particular interest: the emperor's role; issues of freedom; virtue in power. All of these, naturally, could be refracted through the lens of contemporary concerns in a France, and United States, both undergoing political and social upheaval.

On Marcus' adoption by Antoninus, Apollonius remarks, hitting keynotes such as 'rights of men':

> From that time, Antoninus became to him a new master, who instructed him concerning the great virtues. The rights of men respected, the laws flourishing, Rome tranquil, the world happy; such were the new lessons which Marcus Aurelius received during twenty years.[26]

Another topical reflection follows, this time on censorship and political repression:

> Romans! Dare I praise philosophy in Rome, where philosophers have so often been calumniated, and from which they have been so often banished? It is hence, it is from these sacred walls, we were exiled to rocks and desert isles: here, our books were committed to the flames: here, our blood has streamed by the poignard. Europe, Asia, and Africa have seen us wandering and proscribed, seeking an asylum in the dens of ferocious beasts, or condemned to work in chains with robbers and assassins.

A footnote here mentions the exile of the Stoic Musonius Rufus to forced labour in Corinth.[27] No doubt this passage had resonance for Warden and the political exiles of 1798. In addition to the more distinguished exiles in France and America, hundreds of 1798 prisoners had been transported to the penal colony of New South Wales, where it is estimated that at this time they formed a third of the immigrant population.[28]

Thomas' text skilfully weaves Marcus' actual reflections into the dramatic monologue of Apollonius, interspersed with clumsy and ominous interruptions from Commodus. Honest work comes in for favourable mention, in a passage which contrives to capture some of Marcus' tone:

> I shall almost live as if I were poor: though a prince, I have only the wants of a man. I shall give to sleep the time of which I cannot deprive it: I shall say to myself every morning: this is the hour when crimes awake, when passions and vices take possession of the universe, when the unhappy awake to the sentiment of their evils; when the oppressed, moving in his prison, again feels the weight of his chains ... If study and business occupy all my hours, pleasure will find no void of which she can take possession.
>
> Here Commodus, with a troubled voice, again interrupted Apollonius: What! Are all pleasures denied a prince?
>
> Thy father made the same question, replied the philosopher, and here is his answer.
>
> No, Marcus Aurelius, thou shalt not be deprived of all pleasures; the gods have reserved thee the most exquisite and pure. Thy pleasures are to soften pain, to console the unfortunate, to be able, by a word, to relieve provinces, and to render every day two hundred nations happy.[29]

Here, once again, the Roman empire served as a ready metaphor for the colonial powers of France and Britain. The contrast was all the more effective, as Marcus had wielded an absolute power, while his modern successors had far less excuse for arbitrary or unlawful acts:

> O gods, must two hundred nations be unfortunate, if it happen that a single individual is without virtue? Marcus Aurelius, armed with all the force of despotism, voluntarily throws it off. Not to abuse his power, he sets limits to it on all sides. He augments the authority of laws, which too many Emperors wished to destroy: he strengthens that of magistrates, who often were but phantoms or slaves.[30]

Another sensitive issue was taxation, a perennial grievance in France as it had been for the American colonies. Here, once again, Marcus was held up as a contrasting model:

> [Marcus'] moderation extended to the public treasury. You have seen him, under the most pressing wants, give back all that was due, when he thought the tax too burdensome.[31]

There follows the tale we have already encountered, of Marcus selling the treasures of the imperial house rather than impose fresh taxes on the people to fund his wars. Not only this, but the Marcus celebrated by Thomas and Warden turns out to be a promoter of human equality, sounding reminiscent of Rousseau:

> Romans, I confess to you, said he, there is an idea which overwhelms me, and which has more than once excited sorrow: it is the immense inequality which pride has placed between men. Nature always beneficent, had created beings equal and free: tyranny came, and made them weak and unfortunate.[32]

Marcus' promotions of Pompeianus, married to Lucilla, and Pertinax, son of a freedman, are given as examples of his liberal attitude. The work concludes abruptly after Apollonius recounts the death of Marcus: Commodus shakes his spear at the speaker, and: '[The people] then felt that Marcus Aurelius was *indeed no more*.'[33]

As noted, this translation dates from early in Warden's posting to Paris. His tenure came constantly under threat from attacks by rivals and journalists, largely opposed to the Jefferson and later James Madison administrations. Warden was dismissed in 1813, remaining in France until his death in 1845. Alexis de Tocqueville visited Warden prior to his famous travels in the United States, and his observations may owe something to Warden's points of view.[34]

German Perspectives

In the meantime, German liberals – somewhat late to the Stoic party – were experiencing the tail-end of 'Greek mania.' Towering polymaths and cultural authorities, Johann Joachim Winckelmann and Johann Wolfgang von Goethe had led the way in familiarising the German public with the art and ideas of ancient Greece. Rome's influence was also celebrated, and the final decades of the eighteenth century saw an explosion of translations of classical works into German.

In 1779 Marcus' *Meditations* was translated into German by Johann Schulthess.[35] In the same period, the secret group known as *Illuminati* were active in several centres, and the organisation insisted that members should endeavour to educate themselves through reading, including the works of classic Stoic writers. 'Read the ancients' was the injunction, and the list of mandatory readings included Seneca's philosophical works, Epictetus, and Marcus' *Meditations*.[36] Notable members of the movement in Bonn included the composer Ludwig van Beethoven's teacher Christian Gottlob Neefe. The aim of such reading was to educate men with a view to the improvement of society, but naturally this goal could be, and was, represented as revolutionary, and the Bavaria and Bonn groups were banned in the mid-1780s.[37]

While the *Illuminati* reading list is unlikely to have been top of mind for the authorities, it is worth noting in this connection that the German association of the Stoic writers with atheism and other suspect tendencies had begun early in the eighteenth century, with the influential anti-Stoic works by Johann Franz Buddeus (1667–1729) of Halle and Jena. Christopher Brooke has shown that it was Buddeus, above all other critics, who managed to change the ancient Stoics, in the mind of the literate public, from proto-Christians into Spinozists *avant la lettre*, and hence into dangerous atheists.[38] As we have also seen, however, by contrast, in Britain all levels of the established church, and in France progressive elements, continued throughout the century to be happy to invite Marcus and Epictetus on board as practical allies and exemplars. Indeed, Buddeus' own anti-Stoic work had not prevented him from issuing a scholarly edition of Marcus' *Meditations* (1729).

Buddeus' work was continued by his student Johann Jakob Brucker (1696–1770), Lutheran pastor and historian of philosophy. Brucker dismissed the Stoics essentially as eclectic quibblers with nothing to offer the modern seeker after truth.

> The idle quibbles, jejune reasonings, and imposing sophisms, which so justly exposed the schools of the dialectic philosophers to ridicule, found their way into the Porch [Stoa], where much time was wasted, and much ingenuity thrown away, upon questions of no importance ... Their doctrine of moral wisdom was an ostentatious display of words, in which little regard was paid to nature and reason.[39]

Brucker's word choice here must have been deliberate: 'nature' and 'reason' were of course Stoic keywords, so Brucker was contesting the very core of Stoic tenets. Ironically, as Brooke has concluded, it would be Brucker's dismissive account which would influence Denis Diderot's *Encyclopédie* article, 'Stoicisme': for his part, and in the starkest of contrasts with his German sources, Diderot saw no problem with materialism or atheism.[40]

Chapter Fourteen

Decline and Fall: Marcus and His Heirs

Devastating fire of 192 – Gibbon's account of decline – Marcus not the ultimate cause – Decline a theme for Delacroix – 1845 Salon exhibition – Marcus 'culpable or ineffectual'? – the facts about the imperial succession – a striking counter-factual – Cicero's archer

As has been confirmed in recent years with the rediscovery of certain works by Galen, a devastating fire took place in Rome during March 192, bringing the destruction of several libraries, archives and storehouses.[1] One influential medieval writer explicitly described the catastrophe, involving a major loss of Rome's culture, as an act of God in punishment for the crimes of Commodus (who would be assassinated in the December of that year). John of Salisbury (d. 1180) claimed that the destruction was a 'punishment of the city [which] followed upon the crimes of its king.'[2] On such a view, the 'sins' in pagan culture had invited downfall, neglect, and deliberate erasure; and for such tragic outcomes, Marcus Aurelius sat squarely in the frame.

As we have seen, more positive readings dominated Marcus' reception from the fifteenth to the mid-eighteenth centuries. From the later 1770s onwards, however, one work above all others set the tone for the popular reception of Marcus. The first volume of Edward Gibbon's *The History of the Decline and Fall of the Roman Empire* appeared in 1776, to an instant sensation. In a passage which has justly become famous, Gibbon wrote:

> If a man were called to fix the period in the history of the world, during which the condition of the human race was most happy and prosperous, he would, without hesitation, name that which elapsed from the death of Domitian to the accession of Commodus. The vast extent of the Roman empire was governed by absolute power, under the guidance of virtue and wisdom. The armies were restrained by the firm but gentle hand of four successive emperors, whose characters and authority commanded involuntary respect …

> The labours of [Trajan, Hadrian, Antoninus, Marcus] were overpaid by the immense reward that inseparably waited on their success; by the honest pride of virtue, and by the exquisite delight of beholding the general happiness of which they were the authors. A just, but melancholy reflection embittered, however, the noblest of human enjoyments. They must often have recollected the instability of a happiness which depended on the character of a single man. The fatal moment was perhaps approaching, when some licentious youth, or some jealous tyrant, would abuse, to the destruction, that absolute power, which they had exerted for the benefit of their people. The ideal restraints of the senate and the laws might serve to display the virtues, but could never correct the vices, of the emperor.[3]

The corollary of such a eulogy to the period ending with Marcus' death is naturally a judgment on the arrangements made by Marcus during his life. Gibbon rehearses the criticisms – familiar from Julian, if no earlier – that the emperor was overly indulgent to the supposedly unfaithful Faustina, and to Commodus.

> The monstrous vices of the son have cast a shade on the purity of the father's virtues. It has been objected to Marcus, that he sacrificed the happiness of millions to a fond partiality for a worthless boy; and that he chose a successor in his own family, rather than in the republic.[4]

Yet Gibbon is fair in his treatment. He notes the evidence, which we have seen in an earlier chapter, that Commodus was simple and incapable to begin with: 'Nature had formed him of a weak, rather than a wicked disposition. His simplicity and timidity rendered him the slave of his attendants, who gradually corrupted his mind.'[5] So far, so broadly consistent with the ancient sources. Gibbon chooses to consider that it was the assassination attempt of 182, fostered by Lucilla, along with her husband Pompeianus and other associates, which turned Commodus into a paranoid butcher.[6] In this way, Gibbon adroitly deflects blame away from Marcus himself; rather, for Gibbon, the essential problems lay within the very structures of Roman imperial power.

J.G. Pocock has argued that Gibbon was following a tradition, deriving ultimately from Machiavelli, in conceiving the growth of refinement and commerce as a move away from Republican virtue and civic pride, with a resulting decline in both. 'In so paradoxical a vision of history, there were no golden ages, but only golden moments at which the creative had not yet begun to destroy. Gibbon's age of the Antonines is a silver moment of this kind, a moment of relaxation in the downward swing of a civilisation.'[7] Indeed, Gibbon was explicit about the latent disaster nestled in the very bosom of imperial prosperity:

> It was scarcely possible that the eyes of contemporaries should discover in the public felicity the latent causes of decay and corruption. This long [Antonine] peace [prior to Marcus' reign], and the uniform government of the Romans, introduced a slow and secret poison into the vitals of the empire ... Spain, Gaul, Britain and Illyricum, supplied the legions with excellent soldiers, and constituted the real strength of the monarchy. Their personal valour remained, but they no longer possessed that public courage which is nourished by the love of independence, the sense of national honour, the presence of danger, and the habit of command.[8]

On such a basis, once again, Marcus can hardly be considered more to blame than any of the other Antonines for the events which took place after his death. Nonetheless, in the early decades of the nineteenth century, superficial readings of Gibbon contributed to the development of more negative views of Marcus and his legacy than we saw had been current during the mid-1700s. There were aspects both aesthetic and political to this shift. We can infer the changing assessment from the circumstances around Eugène Delacroix's painting, *The Death of Marcus Aurelius*.

By the mid-1840s, Delacroix (1798–1863) had been a successful and popular painter for two decades, having enjoyed considerable success with large-scale historical subjects. He had been strongly inspired by the action canvasses of Théodore Géricault, such as *The Raft of the Medusa* (1818–9, in which Delacroix himself had been included, as a walk-on model). Delacroix's *The Massacre at Chios* (1824) likewise confronted contemporary events, the enslavement of the Greeks of Chios by the Ottoman Turks. In the works of both painters there is evidently a trend for drama, and for dynamic, if not chaotic, arrangements of figures in a scene. His *Liberty Leading the People*, celebrating the revolution of 1830, remains readily recognised today.

Delacroix seems to have read the *Meditations* and been broadly acquainted with Stoicism. In his journal we find the reflection in February 1847, two years after the painting was exhibited:

> The moralists and philosophers, I mean the real ones, like Marcus Aurelius and Jesus, never talked politics, since they did not consider it save from the standpoint of humanity. Equal rights, and twenty other chimeras, did not concern them; all they recommended to men was resignation to fate, not to that obscure *fatum* of the ancients, but to that eternal necessity which no

> one can deny, and against which the philanthropists will not prevail when they try to escape from the severe laws of nature. To follow those laws, and to play his part in the place assigned him amidst a general harmony, is all that the philosophers have demanded of the wise man. Sickness, death, poverty, the torments of the soul, all are eternal, and will torture humanity under every kind of government; the form, democratic or monarchical, has nothing to do with the case.[9]

Here we see that, so far from persisting as a progressive exemplar, Marcus is seen as offering no guidance for the 'philanthropists,' or political reformers, of the modern age. Delacroix frequently offers similar reflections in his journal, impatient if not cynical about the political and social trends of his day.

He seems, however, to have considered that Marcus' writings could offer consolation to the suffering. In March of the same year:

> I went to call on Viellard, who is ill. We talked a great deal about the eternal question of progress, which we understand in such diverse fashion. I spoke to him about *Marcus Aurelius* [italics in original], it is the only book from which he has drawn any consolation since his misfortune ... I told him that, all things considered, religion, better than all the systems, explains the destiny of man, which is to say, resignation. *Marcus Aurelius* says nothing else.[10]

Over the period, the Greco-Roman, the classical, and the imperial had fallen out of favour as cultural trends; the modern, the national, and exotic had come in. Against this background, Marcus was a surprising choice of subject. The star painting of the Salon for 1845 was *The Taking of the Smala* by Horace Vernet, a panoramic depiction of the battle between French and Algerian forces two years prior (the *smala* was the camp of the Algerian leader). The work was highly topical, nationally inspiring, and action-packed, featuring horses as well as human fighters.

In contrast, Delacroix's painting of Marcus' deathbed is unwontedly static. Théophile Gautier, making a name as a journalist and art critic, described it for his readers with rather faint praise:

> The emperor, on his deathbed, recommends his son Commodus to wise men, to Stoic philosophers like himself. These serious characters, with uncultivated hair, sullen faces, elbow on knee, hand buried in a stream of white or gray beard, cast worried and pensive glances at the young Commodus, who patiently listens to the remonstrances and advice from

> his father, from whom he would have already escaped if he were not held by an arm that he vainly tries to free from his father's hands. The head, chest and purple dress of the young Caesar are of a beauty of color to make the Flemings and the Venetians envious. The figure of Marcus Aurelius, ill it is true and almost dying, seems to us to have decomposed too early; the green and yellow tones marring his face give him a completely cadaverous appearance. Some draperies are perhaps too rumpled, especially for antique draperies; some attitudes lack nobility; but everywhere shines a firm and masterful touch, a solid and powerful locality which makes *Marcus Aurelius* one of the good pieces of the exhibition, although we would prefer to see Mr Eugène Delacroix treat the themes of the Middle Ages and the Orient.[11]

Delacroix himself seems to have absorbed such criticism, retaining mixed feelings about the work. In 1849 he wrote:

> Coming home after seeing the figure by [fashionable portraitist Édouard] Dubufe, the paintings in my studio and, among others, my poor *Marcus Aurelius*, which I have accustomed myself to disdain, looked to me like masterpieces. What does that impression come from? From the fact, assuredly, noted in the presence of Meissonier's drawing, that the impression produced by my painting is infinitely superior to one produced by studies from nature.[12]

In a laudatory survey of the painter's life and work, Charles Baudelaire wrote that *Marcus* was 'a picture that is splendid, magnificent, sublime, and not understood.'[13] Gautier's reaction – impatience with the Stoic old men, including Marcus himself – confirms that Delacroix's message was out of step with the times.

Yet as Michèle Hannoosh has recently explained in a sensitive study, *Marcus Aurelius* expresses one of Delacroix's most deeply felt concerns: the potential for degeneration emerging from within civilisation. As we saw, a similar view had been expressed by Gibbon in such a way as largely to exonerate Marcus himself.

Delacroix's own political sympathies, as indicated in his journal, seem to have been the reverse of revolutionary. He had little confidence in the stability of even the most exquisite or sophisticated culture, to prevent corruption if not violent overthrow. Many historical events, Delacroix showed, were, as seen at ground level, occasions for confusion, destruction, and bloodshed. One of his own major historical works, *Richelieu Saying Mass,* had been destroyed in the attack on the Palais Royal during the 1848 revolution.[14]

In the light of these reflections, the previous generation's co-opting of Marcus in the cause of revolution must have seemed naïve at best. In the case of Delacroix's *Marcus*, Hannoosh writes:

> Not only is virtue powerless to prevent the destruction of civilisation; it is seemingly blind to it as well ... Delacroix's Marcus Aurelius seems helpless, bearing some responsibility for the disastrous future that awaits the empire, and the collapse of the civilized values that he has himself embodied.[15]

Gautier's stated preference for a Middle Ages or Oriental theme underscores the sense of Marcus Aurelius as disappointing; a failure, and culpable, where not simply irrelevant.

This negative school of Marcus' reception would persist over the remainder of the nineteenth century, alongside other, more positive readings. As recently as the twentieth century, others have gone a great deal further in ascribing to Marcus personal responsibility for 'decline and fall.' The great Russian emigré historian, Mikhail Rostovtzeff (1870–1952) declared, in his 1926 classic on the Roman empire: 'In making his son his partner in power and in leaving him as his successor, Marcus broke a tradition which now, after nearly a century of observance, was firmly rooted.'[16]

Yet the facts do not support such a reading. Trajan's links with Hadrian were familial and dynastic as much as they were a 'choice of the best.' In his turn, Hadrian's arrangements for the succession seem to have been far from optimal at first: his initial choice, Lucius Ceionius Commodus, had no obvious personal qualifications for the role, before predeceasing Hadrian.[17] We have noted that Antoninus Pius and Faustina I had no son who survived childhood; if they had, it is almost certain that this son would have succeeded, not his cousin Marcus Aurelius. Nor could anyone have predicted how long Antoninus would live after his accession (over twenty years, as it turned out). In other words, the Antonine peace, in many of its aspects, had largely been a matter of particularly good luck rather than, or as much as, sound planning.

If Marcus had bypassed Commodus and selected a non-relative as his heir, there might well have been instant revolt by partisans of Commodus, including among the legions, up to and including general civil war. The rising of Avidius Cassius showed that even the merciful Marcus was not exempt from rivals prepared to go to any length, even dividing the empire, in pursuit of power.[18] As we have seen, the unity of the imperial family, as depicted on coinage and on artworks such as the Antonine pedestal, represented a powerful and positive message; to have publicly side-lined Commodus would have undermined this approach, with potentially catastrophic results.

Another counter-factual scenario occurs. Marcus and Faustina's youngest daughter, Vibia Sabina, born around 170, may cause us most poignantly to reflect on what might have been. Prior to Marcus' death, no doubt to afford the child princess, about to be orphaned, some legal and physical protection, she was engaged to Lucius Antistius Burrus at probably not yet ten years old, while he was about thirty. Burrus was a Senator originally from Thibilis in North Africa, and it was here that they returned on their eventual marriage. Burrus was to hold the consulship in 181. Thibilis was a thriving community (now part of Algeria) which had already provided one consul in Burrus' father, in 167. No doubt a family connection with the imperial house had been forged at that time, if not earlier.

Vibia and Burrus are likely to have stayed largely at Thibilis and avoided seeing first-hand at Rome the horrors of Commodus' early reign, including the exile and murder of Lucilla and other relatives. But in 188, Burrus seems to have taken part in another conspiracy to murder Commodus. The plot failed, and Burrus was executed.

Vibia, now well established in Africa, married for a second time, Lucius Aurelius Agaclytus, the son of Agaclytus I, a freed slave who had been influential in the imperial household during Marcus' lifetime. Agaclytus I had in fact been married, with the permission of Lucius Verus during his co-reign with Marcus, to a relative from the extended Annius clan, a move apparently disapproved by Marcus himself.[19] In any event, perhaps Vibia was now of an age and experience to choose for herself: with Commodus' assassination in 192, the last vestige of central control or harassment from Rome, it is to be hoped, had vanished.

She became a respected, responsible leader in her North African community. We know this because of an inscription from the community of Calama (Guelma, north-eastern Algeria). It reads:

> Vibiae Au/relliae di/vi M.f., divi / Severi sor. / Sabinae, / patronae / municipii / decurio [*n. / decreto p. p.*][20]

> 'To Vibia Aurelia Sabina, daughter of the deified Marcus, sister of the deified Severus, patron of the community, by decree of the local officials.'[21]

Commodus' memory had undergone *damnatio memoriae* in early 193, a process of rooting his name and image out of official records, but this was overturned (unusually) by emperor Septimius Severus in 197. Severus also insisted on Commodus' being accorded divine honours, so this inscription must date from after that time.[22] (Curiously, and undoubtedly in an attempt to improve his own credentials for imperial power, Severus formally adopted himself into Marcus' family, as if he himself were Marcus' son, so *Severi soror* may have this double valence.)

Scholars have explored what the role of a local *patrona* (feminine form) involved. Women, from this very period (late-second and early-third century CE), seem to have assumed a range of official roles, recognised for their service in inscriptions. In Italy and North Africa, thirteen such texts, mentioning women as local patrons, have been found, most of these in Africa. Most of the women listed are mentioned with their husbands, although not Vibia (while her 'divine' father and brother do feature); one scholar suggests that this was surprising, noting that Vibia's (first) husband had been local to the area. But perhaps the answer is that her second husband, the son of a freedman, was considered her distinct inferior in rank.[23] Vibia does not appear to have had children from either marriage.

Accession to *patrona* status does not necessarily seem to reflect monetary benefaction to the community, although it is recorded in some cases. No doubt Vibia's family connections formed part of the background to the status. She must have been a trusted, respected, and prominent member of the community: perhaps she had even taken part in decision-making at the local level. We can imagine the chatty toddler, fluent in Greek as well as Latin, and observer of her father's careful judicial practice from an early age, developing the sound judgment required in every public situation, from the local to the imperial.

In a number of measures, such as taking a co-emperor, Marcus had shown himself prepared to make constructive innovations; perhaps such a radical step might have slowed the trajectory, considered so inevitable by Gibbon, of 'decline and fall.' And perhaps, had it been possible for a woman to succeed to imperial power, if Vibia Sabina had succeeded, the kingdom of gold might have been preserved.

Or perhaps it might also have led to civil war. Marcus' dilemma was profound. In Stoic doctrine, stated in several places in Epictetus, it is futile to speculate on the motivations which prompt people to certain actions. As Marcus himself wrote:

> Do not waste the remainder of your life in thoughts about others … For you lose the opportunity of doing something else when you have such thoughts as these: 'What is such a person doing? And why? And what is he saying? And what is he contriving? (3.4, Long, modified)

Ultimately, we are only responsible for our own thoughts, decisions, and actions.

Marcus and his advisers made every effort to educate Commodus, as he himself had been educated, into a virtuous man and leader. The attempts did not succeed. But in his final days, Marcus may well have recalled the famous metaphor, put by Cicero in the mouth of the great Stoic Cato: an archer can train, aim, and shoot to the very best of his ability: yet he or she has no control over whether or not the arrow will hit the target.[24]

Chapter Fifteen

Marcus for the Modern Age

George Long, Virginia slave-owner and later Marcus translator – partisan of the Southern states – Matthew Arnold, interpreter of Marcus and Christianity – Walter Pater's original Marcus fan-fiction – Leo Tolstoy and the influence of Marcus: making things strange

As we have seen, by the 1840s, Marcus was *passé*: an ineffectual old man on his deathbed. But, as always seems to occur, within a few years, he was restored to life again, like Plato's hero of the Myth of Er, from his very funeral pyre.

In the English-speaking world, this was almost entirely due to one man: George Long (1800–1879), whose translation of *Meditations* appeared in 1862. Even today, over one hundred and sixty years later, this remains the translation which many readers first encounter, as it is freely available online.

A successful student of classics at Cambridge, Long was in 1824 appointed as professor of ancient languages at the new University of Virginia, where Thomas Jefferson – whom we last met as the 'Marcus Aurelius of the United States' – was rector. Jefferson befriended the young Long, who developed a love for his new country.

The University opened in 1825 on the basis that staff and students would be supported by African-American slaves, through household help, classroom assistance, maintenance, and gardening. Gayle M. Schulman has conducted a detailed study of the arrangements involving slaves from the early decades of the University to the Civil War period, distilling information about their lives from University records. Regularly called 'servants,' these people were of course not voluntary labourers: they were human property, belonging to individuals from Jefferson down.

According to these records, George Long, not long after his arrival from England, acquired a slave, 'Jacob.'[1] We know from later records that Jacob's surname was Walker. Regular sales took place at which professors and other staff purchased slaves, whose duties over time extended to cleaning the boots of students each day.[2] There were instances of students physically abusing slaves both male and female. Notwithstanding the close relationships which developed within some University families, the fact remained that slaves were property to be 'punished, hired away, or sold as their owners wished.'[3]

In 1827, George Long married Harriet, the widow of Joseph Selden, a former major in the US Army and then judge in the Arkansas Superior Court. Three years prior, Selden and another judge had been involved in a quarrel during a card game, and a pistol duel ensued, with Selden shot through the heart.[4] He left Harriet with one young daughter and a second yet to be born.

In the year after the marriage, Lord Brougham invited Long to return to London as professor of Greek in the new University of London. As there were no slaves in Great Britain, Walker was considered as the Longs' servant.

We know this specifically because of information on the tombstone which George Long erected in 1841 for his wife and for Jacob, in St Marys parish church, Hornsey. The grave was among a number accorded Grade II heritage listing in 2007, the two-hundredth anniversary of the abolition of the slave trade in Great Britain.[5]

Long was bereaved of his wife and his servant within two months of each other.

HARRIET LONG
A NATIVE OF VIRGINIA
THE WIDOW OF JOSEPH SELDEN
LIEUTENANT COLONEL IN THE ARMY
OF THE UNITED STATES
AND THE WIFE OF GEORGE LONG
DIED AT HIGHGATE
ON THE 18TH DAY OF JUNE 1841
IN THE 40TH YEAR OF HER AGE
LUX OCULIS RIDENS MAJESTAS FRONTE SERENA
FULGERAT TOTO SUAVIS AB ORE DECOR
PAR ANIMUS FORMAE GRANDES IN PECTORE VIRES
CASTE FIDES PIETAS INGENIUMQUE SIMUL
JACOB WALKER
A NATIVE OF VIRGINIA
IN AMERICA THE FAITHFUL SLAVE
IN ENGLAND THE FAITHFUL SERVANT
OF HARRIET AND GEORGE LONG
AND AN HONEST MAN
DIED AT HIGHGATE
ON THE 12TH AUGUST 1841
IN THE 40TH YEAR OF HIS AGE

In the English inscription, George Long has created careful parallels to underline the equal consideration of his wife and his servant: each is described as 'a native of Virginia'; each died at Highgate (probably the Longs' home in Jacksons Lane), at about the same age. The Latin lines, of Long's own composition, indicate Harriet's beauty and virtues: 'purity, piety, and talent.' For Jacob, the descriptors are 'faithful' and 'honest.'

By this time Long had left the university, whose early years were marked by administrative disputes. He had resigned in protest at the dismissal of another professor.[6] Long then became editor of a radical journal, *Quarterly Journal of Education*, which sought far-reaching reform in British schools. In the 1841 census, he is described as 'barrister,' evidently having undertaken study in the law. Not long after the census, Harriet had died from a form of cancer, and Jacob's death was put down to 'smallpox after vaccination.'[7]

The census entry also shows a number of children, including Elizabeth Selden, 18 years old, and Josephine Selden, 16, no doubt the daughters from Harriet's first marriage. There were four younger boys, George, 13, James, 11, William, 7, and Charles, 3.[8] On his wife's death, then, Long was left with a large family to support in any way he could. During this time Long was also preparing textbooks and important works of reference, including atlases of classical geography and specialist works on Roman law.

After a period as a law lecturer at the Middle Temple in London, he returned to teaching at Brighton College in 1849. He was considered an inspiring teacher, even 'establish[ing] for the infant school a formidable reputation in classical scholarship.'[9] It was during the lengthy Brighton phase, after preparing editions of other classical writers such as Cicero, that Long undertook to translate Marcus. Translations had appeared in French, German, Italian and Spanish, as well as English, by the time Long undertook his own.[10]

As a parent and teacher, he must have been especially interested in Marcus' upbringing, as he writes in his introduction:

> Young men who are destined for high places are not often fortunate in those who are about them, their companions and teachers; and I do not know any example of a young prince having had an education which can be compared with that of M. Antoninus. Such a body of teachers distinguished by their acquirements and their character will hardly be collected again; and as to the pupil, we have not had one like him since.[11]

Long's plain and direct English is noticeable here, as well as his elevation of Marcus beyond all his successors.

In his introduction Long gives a comprehensive treatment of the vexed question of Marcus' dealings with the Christians of the empire. Noting that much of the surviving evidence is unreliable, including many documents which, while purporting to be official letters, speeches, or decrees, are evidently forgeries (often with the intention of making Marcus appear generous or tolerant towards the Christians), Long concludes:

> Our extant ecclesiastical histories are manifestly falsified, and what truth they contain is grossly exaggerated; but the fact is certain that in the time of M. Antoninus the heathen populations were in open hostility to the Christians, and that under Antoninus' rule men were put to death because they were Christians ... We cannot admit that such a man was an active persecutor, for there is no evidence that he was, though it is certain that he had no good opinion of the Christians, as appears from his own words. But he knew nothing of them except their hostility to the Roman religion, and he probably thought that they were dangerous to the state, notwithstanding the professions false or true of some of the Apologists.[12]

Long decided, he writes, to prepare a translation of *Meditations* 'after having used the book for many years.' He dismissed Jeremy Collier's 1701 version: 'a most coarse and vulgar copy of the original.' (Interestingly, the version by Hutcheson and Moor, and several subsequent translations, seem to have lapsed into obscurity during the intervening years.) Long writes:

> I made this translation for my own use, because I found that it was worth the labour; but it may be useful to others also and therefore I determined to print it ... I could have made the language more easy and flowing, but I have preferred a ruder style as being better suited to express the character of the original ... [13]

The introduction concludes with a statement about one of the great men influenced by Marcus: Captain John Smith (bap. 1580–1631). Long writes that Machiavelli's and Marcus' books were read by Smith as a young man; Smith's travels on the continent are likely to have exposed him to a range of works and authors.

> Smith is almost unknown and forgotten in England his native country, but not in America where he saved the young colony of Virginia ... For a man's greatness lies not in wealth and station, as the vulgar believe, nor yet in his intellectual capacity, which is often associated with the meanest moral

> character, the most abject servility to those in high places and arrogance to the poor and lowly; but a man's true greatness lies in the consciousness of an honest purpose in life, founded on a just estimate of himself and everything else, on frequent self-examination, and a steady obedience to the rule which he knows to be right, without troubling himself, as the emperor says he should not, about what others may think or say, or whether they do or do not do that which he thinks and says and does.[14]

Here we see Long's affection for his adopted Virginia – the birthplace of Harriet and Jacob – and the fruits of his often negative experiences with people in academic life. (Today, despite evident misgivings about John Smith's dealings with the native inhabitants of Virginia, he seems to be still remembered with respect in that state, in recognition of his efforts to establish the colony.[15])

Long appended a chapter on Marcus' philosophy which highlighted the influence from Epictetus, giving a full account of Stoic doctrine while showing Marcus' consistency with the Greek Stoic tradition. Here, Long discusses Nature, and what his readers might consider 'laws of nature,' but which are in fact, he argues, simply phenomena which occur in regular progressions. The 'Nature of Things,' he concludes, 'is an everlasting continuity.'[16] This statement endorses Marcus' Stoic view. Notably, Long avoids any Christian terminology or concepts in his account, except for some references to Scriptural echoes of pagan thought which he includes in footnotes, and some references to the works of Bishop Joseph Butler (1692–1752). In Long's view, Butler was expressing the very same sentiments as the Stoic emperor, in writing of 'the natural supremacy of reflection or conscience … [the faculty] which surveys, approves or disapproves the several affections of our mind and actions of our lives.'[17] This was the Stoic *hegemonikon*, revived in classical Anglican theology; we have already seen how useful Marcus and Epictetus had both proven to be in Anglophone theological controversies.

We have seen that Long wrote, of his translation, that he employed 'a ruder style,' and this turns out – when we reach the actual text – to mean a consciously old-fashioned one. Perhaps the most famous passage in the whole of the *Meditations* is 2.1:

> Begin the morning by saying to thyself, I shall meet with the busybody, the ungrateful, arrogant, deceitful, envious, unsocial … (2.1)

> Throw away thy books: no longer distract thyself; it is not allowed … (2.2)[18]

Long's choice of 'thyself,' which, considering that Marcus is addressing himself, appears very often, rather than 'yourself,' may have been a concession to the increasingly antiquarian taste of the Victorian public: this was, after all, the age of the Gothic Revival and 'medievalism' as an aesthetic. It is also likely to have been a deliberate antithesis to Collier's now-dated version. Finally, it will have recalled the style of the King James Bible, thus laying claim to both moral authority and cultural *gravitas*. It strikes the modern reader as anything but modern, yet, paradoxically, this seems to have suited the taste of its early readership.

Long's Marcus was received as both timely and relevant. This is evident from Matthew Arnold's (1822–1888) justly famous 'Essay on Marcus Aurelius' which first appeared in the *Victoria Magazine* in 1863, an appreciation of Long's translation, in which Arnold describes Marcus as 'this truly modern striver and thinker.' Marcus, Arnold insists, lived in an age comparable to the mid-nineteenth century:

> Marcus Aurelius has, for us moderns, this great superiority in interest over Saint Louis or [King] Alfred, that he lived and acted in a state of society modern by its essential characteristics, in an epoch akin to our own, in a brilliant centre of civilisation. Trajan talks of 'our enlightened age' just as glibly as the *Times* talks of it. Marcus Aurelius thus becomes for us a man like ourselves, a man in all things tempted as we are.[19]

At the time of writing this essay, Arnold was a published poet of note, and was branching out into literary criticism. His day job, for thirty-five years, was as an inspector of schools, a profession involving much travel on the railways across much of England, and no doubt much tedium; literature remained his passion, although his poetic side found little outlet in his later life.[20]

Arnold's assessment, while positive and clearly committed to asserting Marcus' relevance to the modern reader, is eccentric. One can only wonder at sentences such as these: 'The record of the outward life of this admirable man has in it little of striking incident' and 'Of the outward life and circumstances of Marcus Aurelius, beyond these notices which he has himself supplied [the *Meditations*], there are few of much interest and importance.'[21]

What of the Antonine Plague? The fifteen years of campaigning in the Parthian, Marcomannic and Sarmatian wars? The Avidian revolt? It is hard to believe that Arnold had failed to read Long's thorough introduction to the translation, or any other biographical account. Even Jeremy Collier's much-maligned version (which Arnold suggests had been his first introduction to Marcus) had included a comprehensive biography.

Such a cavalier handling tends to undermine Arnold's overall message. Here, too, we see that a version of the 'ineffectual Marcus' view retained some currency:

> It remains true that this sage, who made perfection his aim and reason his law, did Christianity an immense injustice and rested in an idea of State-attributes which was illusive. And this is, in truth, characteristic of Marcus Aurelius, that he is blameless, yet, in a certain sense, unfortunate; in his character, beautiful as it is, there is something melancholy, circumscribed, and ineffectual.[22]

Arnold's reasoning for such an opinion cannot simply allude to the 'decline and fall' trope: as we have seen, he did not consider the actual events of Marcus' life to have been significant. Rather, it relates to Marcus' unfortunate relationship with Christianity.

Arnold is perhaps best known today for his poem 'Dover Beach,' drafted in the 1850s (before the Darwinian revolution) but not published until 1867. This piece – surprisingly slight in view of its fame and subsequent influence – expresses a regretful mood about the ongoing decline of Christian faith:

> The Sea of Faith
> Was once, too, at the full, and round earth's shore,
> Lay like the folds of a bright girdle furl'd;
> But now I only hear
> Its melancholy, long, withdrawing roar...(lines 21–5).

It is the regretful yearning of 'Dover Beach' which Arnold has projected onto a very different (and far greater) writer in Marcus, who, in Arnold's view, was haunted by the missed opportunity of his failure to engage productively with Christianity:

> What an affinity for Christianity had this persecutor of the Christians! The effusion of Christianity, its relieving tears, its happy self-sacrifice, were the very element, one feels, for which his soul longed ... We see him wise, just, self-governed, tender, thankful, blameless; yet, with all this, agitated, stretching out his arms for something beyond, – *tendentemque manus ripae ulterioris amore* ['reaching out his hands with longing for the farther shore,' from Virgil, *Aeneid* 6.314].[23]

The reference to the *Aeneid* is to the souls of the unburied dead reaching hopelessly towards the boatman of the Underworld, Charon, pleading to be taken to a permanent home, denied to them until their bones receive proper burial: Aeneas, visiting the Underworld, is much moved by the sight. Arnold's image, then, of Marcus is of a restless and tormented soul, the very reverse of the calm and decisive persona which most readers discover in the *Meditations*.

Meanwhile, as Long's translation and Arnold's essay reached their first readers, the United States itself was undergoing the most profound crisis in its history. The second edition of Long's translation of *Meditations* would feature a blunt and combative prefatory 'Note':

> I have been informed that an American publisher has printed the first edition of this translation of M. Antoninus … If the American politicians, as they are called, would read [Marcus' thoughts] also, I should be much pleased, but I do not think the emperor's morality would suit their taste …
>
> I have never dedicated a book to any man, and if I dedicated this, I should choose the man whose name seemed to me most worthy to be joined to that of the Roman soldier and philosopher. I might dedicate the book to the successful general who is now the President of the United States, with the hope that his integrity and justice will restore peace and happiness, so far as he can, to those unhappy States which have suffered so much from war and the unrelenting hostility of wicked men.
>
> But, as the Roman poet said,
>
> *Victrix causa Deis placuit, sed victa Catoni* ['the winning side pleased the gods, but the losing side pleased Cato']
>
> And if I dedicated this little book to any man, I would dedicate it to him who led the Confederate armies against the powerful invader, and retired from an unequal contest defeated, but not dishonoured; to the noble Virginian soldier, whose talents and virtues place him by the side of the best and wisest man who sat on the throne of the Imperial Caesars.[24]

The Latin tag is from the epic poem *Pharsalia* (1.128) by Lucan, the nephew of Seneca and a Stoic himself, forced in 65 CE, aged just twenty-five, by Nero to commit suicide. The 'winning side' in Lucan's epic was that of Julius Caesar: the Stoic Cato, hero of Lucan's poem, had taken the side of Pompey, and on the defeat, took his own life.

It is ironic that George Long, the man who above all others reintroduced Marcus Aurelius to the English reading public, considered General Robert E. Lee the man best qualified to stand as Marcus' heir: better even than the leader of 'integrity and justice,' Abraham Lincoln. The Stoic worldview considered all men and women as equal participants in the divine, and justice is one of the key Stoic virtues: yet Long supported that side in the US Civil War which sought to preserve the injustice of the enslavement of Africans and their American descendants.

For his part, in another twist, Matthew Arnold had found nothing of interest or importance in the events of Marcus' life, yet – in a poignant parallel with his subject – Arnold would know the grief of having several sons die in their youth, while in later life he was forced to undertake lecture tours in order to repay the gambling debts contracted by his surviving son Richard.[25] The situation lends a sting to his musing: 'Still one cannot help wishing that the example of Marcus Aurelius could have availed more with his only [surviving] son.'[26]

* * *

The most important work of Marcus fan-fiction in the English tradition is the ground-breaking novel *Marius the Epicurean: His Sensations and Ideas* (1885), by Walter Pater (1839–1894). Pater was a lecturer in classics at Oxford and a writer of miscellaneous criticism, who for some years had been subject to the covert censorship and exclusion of men suspected of homosexual activity or even of same-sex attraction. For many such men, the more sexually liberal (at least for male same-sex relationships) ancient Greek society inspired a kind of cultural nostalgia.

Today, Pater's broad and sensitive erudition, on themes from the Renaissance to Coleridge and Charles Lamb, seems far more noticeable than any 'advocacy' around the cause, however delicately expressed, of greater tolerance for same-sex relationships.[27] At the time, controversy ensued around Pater's relationships; there was a real risk of Pater being expelled from his Oxford position, and in response to official disquiet, Pater retired for several years into self-censorship, while working on his novel.

By the time Pater came to draft *Marius the Epicurean*, he had thought and written for many years about art and literature. He considered that classical and the Romantic had been as two intertwining strands in art since Greek times, each with elements of the other: the Romantic, shorn of its excrescences, reverts to the Classical; the Classical adopts a strange twist or two, and shades into the Romantic.[28]

In seeing this essential unity in alternation, with its origins in Greece, Pater was well placed to appreciate Marcus' legacy. For what could be more classical than Stoicism, with its emphasis on order, discipline, and virtue? And yet what could be more strange, more jolting, more exhilarating, than Marcus Aurelius' unique, abrupt, prose, and his technique of 'stripping-back' of complex phenomena into everyday elements?

After the quixotic archaism of Long and the post-Christian anxieties of Arnold, Pater's treatment of the age of Marcus Aurelius brings a gust of fresh air. The reader of *Marius* who comes from Marcus' own writing can see its influence throughout. Pater's novel seems very modern in its accumulation, lightly sketched, of scenes and impressions, minutely described. The *Meditations* has many such scenes; even in the letters to Fronto, we have seen Marcus' ability to convey a whole scene in miniature. The current moment, in Stoicism, is all we have, and Marcus was a pioneer of condensing the various into a single view. Pater also embeds myths, that of Cupid and Psyche, and a cameo of its author, Apuleius, creator of *The Golden Ass*, one of the great books of Marcus' period and of all periods. *Marius the Epicurean*, appropriately then, is both classical and radical in conception and structure.

As suggested by the novel's subtitle, all is seen through the eyes of Marius, a young Roman with a profound love of the beauty to be found in both nature and in local traditions.

> And now what relieved in part this over-tension of soul was the lad's pleasure in the country and the open air; above all, the ramble to the coast, over the marsh with its dwarf roses and wild lavender, and delightful signs, one after another – the abandoned boat, the ruined flood-gates, the flock of wild birds – that one was approaching the sea; the long summer-day of idleness among its vague scents and sounds.[29]

Marius develops a personal programme for an aesthetic and visual way of life:

> To keep the eye clear by a sort of exquisite personal alacrity and cleanliness, extending even to his dwelling-place; to discriminate, ever more and more fastidiously, select form and colour in things from what was less select; to meditate much on beautiful visible objects, on objects, more especially, connected with the period of youth – on children at play in the morning, the trees in early spring, on young animals, on the fashions and amusements of young men; to keep ever by him if it were but a single choice flower, a graceful animal or sea-shell ... [30]

As is evident from the book's title, Marius rejects the Stoic way of life for the Epicurean. But he comes to work as a secretary for Marcus Aurelius, and reads the *Meditations* in draft. In a brilliant tribute, several of Pater's scenes of Marcus Aurelius resemble the master's own vivid and memorable snapshots. Marius has his first glimpse of the emperor during the triumph with Lucius Verus after the Parthian campaign:

> Marius beheld a man of about five-and-forty years of age, with prominent eyes – eyes, which although demurely downcast during this essentially religious ceremony, were by nature broadly and benignly observant. He was still, in the main, as we see him in the busts which represent his gracious and courtly youth, when Hadrian had playfully called him, not Verus, after the name of his father, but Verissimus, for his candour of gaze, and the bland capacity of the brow, which, below the brown hair, clustering thickly as of old, shone out low, broad, and clear, and still without a trace of the trouble of his lips. You saw the brow of one who, amid the blindness or perplexity of the people about him, saw all things clearly; the dilemma, to which his experience so far had brought him, between Chance with meek resignation, and a Providence with boundless possibilities and hope, being for him at least distinctly defined.[31]

This is an explicit reference to a number of passages in the *Meditations* (e.g. 4.3, 10.6) in which Marcus contrasts 'providence or atoms' as competing accounts of the cosmos. Pater's narratorial use of 'we' as viewers of ancient portrait busts shifts us briefly to the modern age, but straightaway the second person ('you saw') brings the reader back as a co-observer with Marius, dwelling reverently on Marcus' face in a way which recalls Julian's *Caesars*. These temporal lurches once again recall the cosmic perspective of Marcus himself.

Unlike so many previous interpreters, Pater understands the significance of the disaster that was the surgery and death of little Marcus Verus during the preparations for the [second] northern campaign in 169. What many might prefer to avoid, Pater imagines as a film director might do today, creating an unforgettably moving cameo:

> Lights burned at the windows. It seemed that numerous visitors were within, for the courtyard was crowded with litters and horses in waiting. For the moment, indeed, all larger cares, even the cares of war, of late so heavy a pressure, had been forgotten in what was passing with the little Annius Verus; who for his part had forgotten his toys, lying all day across the knees of his mother, as a mere child's ear-ache grew rapidly to alarming sickness with great and manifest agony, only suspended a little, from time to time, when from very weariness he passed into a few moments of unconsciousness. The country surgeon called in, had removed the imposthume with the knife. There had been a great effort to bear this operation, for the terrified child, hardly persuaded to submit himself, when his pain was at its worst, and even more for the parents. At length … the eminent Galen had arrived,

only to pronounce the thing done visibly useless, the patient falling now into longer intervals of delirium.

And thus, thrust on one side by the crowd of departing visitors, Marius was forced into the privacy of a grief, the desolate face of which went deep into his memory, as he saw the emperor carry the child away – quite conscious at last, but with a touching expression upon it of weakness and defeat – pressed close to his bosom, as if he yearned just then for one thing only, to be united, to be absolutely one with it, in its obscure distress.[32]

Here, Pater, not a father himself, has brilliantly expressed the grief which we know Marcus had regularly to remind himself to manage.[33]

Marius the Epicurean was influential on a generation of writers, from Oscar Wilde to Virginia Woolf. By the 1920s, literary impressionism was no longer fresh and startling, and Pater's contribution would largely be overlooked where not actively disparaged. It would take reassessments from the mid-twentieth century onwards to restore a sense of what he had achieved. One of the most nuanced was by fellow classicist C.M. Bowra in 1949:

> Pater was able to do this [illuminate aspects of his historical subjects] because his sensibility was such that he had almost a clairvoyant insight into the minds of those whose works he admired. Sometimes perhaps he failed … But usually he wrote only about those men with whom he had an imaginative affinity or who had so absorbed his attention that he understood them by an effortless sympathy.[34]

Pater's imaginative tribute to Marcus Aurelius was, we may be sure, very far from effortless, but Bowra's point remains.

Alongside Pater's fictional exploration, Marcus continued to offer a moral exemplar, and not only to those who had separated from conventional Christian faith. Dean Frederic William Farrar (1831–1903) was a prominent churchman of liberal approach. Along with works on the church fathers and religious books for children, Farrar's *Seekers After God* (dating from between 1876 and 1883) outlined the lives and thought of Seneca, Epictetus, and Marcus Aurelius.

Farrar's prose was purple, but his appreciation for Marcus seems to have been genuine.

> Their [Epictetus' and Marcus'] glory shines the purer and brighter from the midst of a corrupt and deplorable society. Epictetus showed that a Phrygian slave could live a life of the loftiest exaltation. Aurelius proved that a Roman Emperor could live a life of the deepest humility … a Roman,

> a patrician, strong, of heavenly beauty, of noble ancestors, almost born to the purple, the favourite of Emperors, the greatest conqueror, the greatest philosopher, the greatest ruler of his time – proved for ever that it is possible to be virtuous, and tender, and holy, and contented in the midst of sadness, even on an irresponsible and imperial throne. Strange that, of the two, the Emperor is even sweeter, more simple, more admirable, more humbly and touchingly resigned, than the slave. In him, Stoicism loses all its haughty self-assertion, all its impracticable paradox, for a manly melancholy which at once troubles and charms the heart.[35]

At the same time, Marcus' artistic practice and effects were receiving attention in several European quarters. No longer considered primarily as an adjunct to, or replacement for, Christian morality, Marcus' *Meditations* could stand as a work unique in the surviving ancient literary corpus, although opinions differed on its value. Hungarian composer Franz Liszt would write from Rome, in 1881, to his friend Olga von Meyendorff, objecting to Marcus' practice of 'stripping-back':

> The gentle and wise Marcus Aurelius seems to have uttered a truly imperial stupidity in counselling us to *divide* up each thing in our thoughts so as to become imbued with the emptiness of everything. To reduce music to single sounds, to isolate the features of a beloved person, is this to philosophize? Away with this method; let us look for the whole, the harmony.[36]

It is likely that the particular passage to which Liszt refers is this one:

> You will learn to disregard dance moves, musical performances, and contact sports, if you separate the notes and interrogate each by itself, as to whether you are overpowered by *that*. That will put you off (*Meditations* 11.2).[37]

Evidently this was Marcus at his most stringent, but no doubt he offers an effective strategy against succumbing to sentimental or thoughtless responses to random stimuli. More broadly, however, *contra* Liszt, Marcus has not attempted to do away with harmony within the cosmos: rather, as a true Platonist, he repeatedly celebrates it:

> Everything harmonises with me which is harmonious with you, O Cosmos (4.23).
>
> This is what we mean in saying that things are suitable to us, as craftsmen say dressed stones in walls and in pyramids are suitable, fitting well with each other and in a sound combination. For there is one harmony overall (5.8.2).[38]

While Liszt seems to have seen 'stripping-back' as purely reductive, to consider a complex phenomenon in its elements may allow us to adjust our impressions, rendering ourselves more in harmony with the whole as it unfolds. It is his own transformation which Marcus always seeks.

Meanwhile, Russian writer Leo Tolstoy (1828–1910), a successful and highly prolific writer over decades, experimented with different narrative approaches. In a striking 1996 paper, literary scholar Carlo Ginzburg has traced a precursor to Tolstoy's short story *Kholstomer* (1886), told from the viewpoint of a working horse, in Marcus Aurelius' practice of 'stripping back.' Ginzburg quotes Marcus' famous exhortation:

> When you are seated before delicacies and choice foods, to impress upon your imagination [*phantasian*] that this is the dead body of a fish, that the dead body of a bird or a pig; and again, that the Falernian wine is grape juice and that robe of purple a lamb's fleece dipped in a shellfish's blood … (6.13)[39]

'This extraordinary passage,' Ginzburg writes, 'inevitably strikes the twentieth-century reader as an early example of estrangement.' Ginzburg goes further:

> I would like to suggest that even Tolstoy's uncompromising approaches to law, ambition, war and love were deeply indebted to Marcus Aurelius. Like a horse, like a child, Tolstoy looked at human conventions and institutions as strange, opaque phenomena, thereby stripping them bare of their conventional meanings. Things unveiled themselves to his passionate and detached gaze 'as they really are,' to use Marcus Aurelius' phrase.[40]

In turn, Tolstoy's *Kholstomer* exerted a key influence on the early twentieth-century writers who became known as Formalists (although they rejected the status of a 'movement') such as Viktor Shklovsky (1893–1984). In a programmatic statement from 1917, 'Art as Device,' Shklovsky wrote of the numbing and blinding effect of habit and routine on our powers of perception, and suggested that the purpose of art is to break through and force us to see once again:

> This is how life becomes nothing and disappears. Automatization eats things, clothes, furniture, your wife, and the fear of war … And so this thing we call art exists in order to restore the sensation of life, in order to make us feel things, in order to make a stone stony. The goal of art is to create the sensation of seeing, and not merely recognizing, things; the device of art is the 'enstrangement' of things … [41]

This had been precisely a goal of Stoic endeavours to approach and observe the cosmos, as Seneca wrote:

> I gaze upon [wisdom] with bewilderment (*obstupefactus*), just as I sometimes gaze upon the world itself, which I often behold as if I saw it for the first time (*tamquam spectator novus video*, Letter 64.6).

Ginzburg goes on to identify another stream of influence upon Tolstoy's practice of estrangement: the Enlightenment tradition familiar from Montaigne and perfected in the age of Voltaire. For Voltaire, viewing familiar European sights as if through the eyes of a foreigner – or, as in the case of his most famous hero, Candide (1759), with the innocence of a child – lent force, new perspectives, an ironic thrust. Ginzburg speculates that this stream, also, may have derived in part from the fifteenth-century work of Marcus fan-fiction, Antonio de Guevara's *Dial of Princes*, in combination with the 'barbarians' voiced in popular works by Roman historian Tacitus, the *Germania* and *Agricola*; but this must remain uncertain.[42]

Tolstoy included sayings from Marcus Aurelius in his vast compendium *Wise Thoughts for Every Day*, collected during the first decade of the twentieth century, and as it turned out his final work. In a sense, Marcus diluted in this fashion ceases to exert the impact of the *Meditations* in full. Yet even in these final years, Tolstoy did not neglect the whole book. Ginzburg writes:

> Aleksandra, one of Tolstoy's daughters, tells a revealing anecdote. One day, she said to an old peasant woman, who worked at her house as a housemaid, that she was sad.
>
> 'If you read Marcus Aurelius,' the old woman replied, 'all your sadness would disappear.'
>
> 'Marcus Aurelius? Who? Why Marcus Aurelius?' Aleksandra Lvovna inquired.
>
> 'Yes,' the woman explained, 'it's a book the Count gave me. In the book there is written that all of us will die. And if death is facing us, our sadness is nothing. As soon as you think about death, you feel a sense of lightness. When I feel some grief, I always say: "Children, read me Marcus Aurelius!"'[43]

Chapter Sixteen

Nadir and Renewal

G.K. Chesterton finds Marcus intolerable – World War I – Anglophone indifference – 'psychological' readings – American misunderstandings – A.S.L. Farquharson's monumental version – Marcus' 'spiritual' writings, taken up by Pierre Hadot – a revival of Stoicism

If the final decades of the nineteenth century were a time of appreciation for the Stoic emperor, the inevitable setback was not long in coming. One thread of this reversal came, perhaps unsurprisingly, from a militant Christianity competing against more recent systems, or against atheism and materialism.

Stoicism, as a corporeal framework, was indeed 'materialist,' even while promoting an ethical approach, and this alone rendered it suspect. In addition, growing political enfranchisement meant that Stoicism could be portrayed as undesirably 'elitist,' particularly by comparison with Christianity.

The writer and critic G.K. Chesterton (1874–1936) declared in 1908:

> Only the other day I saw in an excellent weekly paper of Puritan tone this remark, that Christianity when stripped of its armour of dogma (as who should speak of a man stripped of his armour of bones), turned out to be nothing but the Quaker doctrine of the Inner Light. Now, if I were to say that Christianity came into the world specially to destroy the doctrine of the Inner Light, that would be an exaggeration. But it would be very much nearer to the truth. The last Stoics, like Marcus Aurelius, were exactly the people who did believe in the Inner Light. Their dignity, their weariness, their sad external care for others, their incurable internal care for themselves, were all due to the Inner Light, and existed only by that dismal illumination. Notice that Marcus Aurelius insists, as such introspective moralists always do, upon small things done or undone; it is because he has not hate or love enough to make a moral revolution. He gets up early in the morning, just as our own aristocrats living the Simple Life get up early in the morning; because such altruism is much easier than stopping the games of the amphitheatre or giving the English people back their land.[1]

Chesterton went further:

> Marcus Aurelius is the most intolerable of human types. He is an unselfish egoist. An unselfish egoist is a man who has pride without the excuse of passion. Of all conceivable forms of enlightenment the worst is what these people call the Inner Light. Of all horrible religions the most horrible is the worship of the god within. Any one who knows any body knows how it would work; any one who knows any one from the Higher Thought Centre knows how it does work. That Jones shall worship the god within him turns out ultimately to mean that Jones shall worship Jones. Let Jones worship the sun or moon, anything rather than the Inner Light; let Jones worship cats or crocodiles, if he can find any in his street, but not the god within. Christianity came into the world firstly in order to assert with violence that a man had not only to look inwards, but to look outwards, to behold with astonishment and enthusiasm a divine company and a divine captain. The only fun of being a Christian was that a man was not left alone with the Inner Light, but definitely recognized an outer light, fair as the sun, clear as the moon, terrible as an army with banners.[2]
>
> [...] On the other side our idealist pessimists were represented by the old remnant of the Stoics. Marcus Aurelius and his friends had really given up the idea of any god in the universe and looked only to the god within. They had no hope of any virtue in nature, and hardly any hope of any virtue in society. They had not enough interest in the outer world really to wreck or revolutionise it. They did not love the city enough to set fire to it.[3]

Where the Christians of the second century, identifying their system as another philosophical school, addressed Marcus as a fellow philosopher; where the Renaissance popes and princes had seen him as a role model; where the Anglicans of the early eighteenth century had held him up as a moral exemplar: now, he was classed as a pernicious threat and deadly rival, 'intolerable,' 'horrible.'

Chesterton's polemic is a caricature, both of Stoicism and of Marcus himself, trading on the fact that it was increasingly unlikely that his readers would be familiar with the writings of either. It retains the 'sad Marcus' and the now-familiar 'ineffectual Marcus' themes (although it is unlikely that a more cheerful Marcus would have pleased Chesterton). The sideswipe at Quakerism is also surprising. Did Chesterton really think that most Quakers worship themselves? Perhaps the most startling angle here are the wishful gestures to cathartic violence: Christianity's 'army with banners' is meant as a threat, and Chesterton seemed to think it would have been better if the Stoics had burned down Rome (instead of peacefully resisting Nero to the death, as many did). Or is Chesterton making an oblique reference to the fire of 192? Once again, the contrast with ancient Christian apologists – concerned, as they were, to blend into the intellectual landscape, not to stand out – is notable.

In any event, cathartic destruction was not long deferred: the *Pax Britannica*, like the Antonine peace, would soon be shattered. While the King of Italy, speaking at the Capitol on the fiftieth anniversary of national unification (4 March 1911) could refer to Marcus as 'The sacred and propitiary image of that cult of moral and civil law which our Fatherland wishes to follow,' receiving particular applause, such optimism was short-lived.[4] A new generation experienced total war. The breakdown of European norms surely contributed to a loss of reverence for ancient virtue writers, and indeed the first half of the twentieth century saw little interest, in the Anglophone world, in Hellenistic and later pagan thought. In the age of technology and progress, such thought was not *systematic*, and thus hardly seemed worthy of the name philosophy.

To be sure, Marcus' *Meditations* and correspondence with Fronto featured in the Loeb Classical Library, translated by C.R. Haines, in 1916 and 1919 respectively. While sympathetic to Marcus, Haines in his introduction notes the 'hardness and arrogance of Stoicism,' seeing Marcus' own approach as 'softened' by Platonist leanings.[5] But this too is seen as unsatisfactory: Marcus often wavers and is inconsistent.'[6] There is, in fact, no inconsistency: Marcus' clear precursor is Epictetus, with Epictetus' own role-model being Plato's and Xenophon's Socrates, yet this obvious fact seems to have been overlooked on such a reading.

Another factor which began to affect assessments of Marcus in the period was a 'psychological' turn. A very influential work by A.D. Nock (1902–1963) was *Conversion* (1933). Nock was an English classicist who, aged twenty-eight in 1930, became the youngest Harvard professor – Frothingham Professor of the History of Religion – in half a century. *Conversion* highlighted what it saw as the shift from paganism to Christianity, with the 'conversion experience' a key offering of the new system. In Nock's view, Christianity, even more than other 'Oriental cults,' was best placed to 'answer psychological needs,' while Marcus represented some kind of transitional figure (the 'transition,' of course, being a category retrospectively applied):

> The majority, even of philosophers, had chosen to walk by the light of unreason. Marcus Aurelius himself illustrates the transition. His fundamental attitude to the universe is the old heroic Stoic poise, and yet he thanks the gods for dream revelations which relieved him of blood-spitting and giddiness (I.17.20), and in obedience to an oracle from Abonutichus threw two live lions into the Danube. Whether we do or do not believe the story

> that at the outbreak of the war with the Marcomanni he summoned priests from all sides and performed foreign rites at Rome, there is a queer sign of the times in a coin with the legend *Relig(io) Aug(usta)* and a representation of a temple of an Egyptian deity. His successor, Commodus, was devoted to the rites of Isis and Mithras.[7]

Nock is highly selective in his account. Marcus' piety – that is, to the traditional Roman gods – is underlined repeatedly in the ancient sources, as well as in his *Meditations*. There was no conflict in pre-Christian minds between acceptance of foreign gods alongside native Roman ones; productive assimilation was constantly occurring in an empire composed of dozens of interacting cultures and languages. Nor was there ever a clear demarcation between 'magic' and 'religion,' let alone between 'religion' and 'superstition' (Nock's 'unreason'), notwithstanding repeated official attempts throughout Roman history to ban less official forms of divination.[8] It is also worth noting that even in today's Italy, the pursuit of information via 'occult' practices is far from obsolete: a 2024 article reports that 10 to 13 million Italians, mostly baptised Catholics, have turned to 'sorcerers or witches' at least once in their lives, while 30,000 Italians seek counsel from psychics or visionaries daily.[9]

Surprisingly, from the early twentieth-century environment of indifference, where not outright disdain and misrepresentation, there would at length emerge the most significant work of Marcus Aurelius scholarship in English since the seventeenth century. An Oxford classics specialist who bore the rank of Lieutenant Colonel in the Territorial Army during the First World War (apparently using it freely thereafter), A.S.L. Farquharson (1871–1942) spent many years planning and working on a new scholarly text and translation of the *Meditations*. First discussed with the Oxford Clarendon Press in 1936, it would not be published until 1944, after Farquharson's death, while the Second World War was still going on.

Farquharson's eccentricity had been immortalised in a 1930 letter by C.S. Lewis:

> He came gliding towards me in the dusk, about five feet four inches high, his face exactly like an egg in shape, with sandy-hair fringing a bald patch, a little military moustache, and eyebrows so far up his forehead that it gives him a perpetual air of astonishment. [...] It is an old subject of controversy just how mad the Fark is.[10]

Farquharson's labour of love would be introduced by his friend John Sparrow, who had assisted in seeing it through the press. Farquharson had written to

Sparrow each week from the outbreak of war in September 1939, evidently with 'imposter syndrome,' as he feared both that the work would be inadequate and that he would not live to see it finished.[11] The latter event indeed would come to pass; yet the former fear proved groundless. Farquharson, posthumously, joined that band of readers and translators who truly, as Bowra wrote of Pater, understand Marcus with profound sympathy. As Sparrow wrote, Farquharson had that 'admiration and reverence for "the Emperor,"' without which a writer cannot approach an understanding of his great subject.[12]

Farquharson's erudite textual discussions will not be of interest to the general reader, except in underlining the tenuousness of the surviving manuscript transmission (one of the two manuscripts of *Meditations* which survived from antiquity was lost during the Early Modern period). Yet his judgments are of importance. Unusually for his time, Farquharson seems to have valued Stoicism for its own sake. He says of Julian:

> [His] work belongs to an epoch which had absorbed the practical truths of Stoicism and Christianity, but which had submerged the distinctive reflective attitude of the Porch [Stoa] under a flood of orientalism and mystical writing.[13]

Whether or not this was fair to Julian, it was certainly kinder to Stoicism than many current writers. We can see the prevailing mood in the words of a contemporary American, Whitney J. Oates of Princeton, whose 1940 reissue of George Long's translation sold many copies worldwide. Oates seems to have had such a low opinion and scant understanding of Stoicism that the only wonder is that he undertook the work at all:

> In the Stoics we find a lack of systematic completeness, and a kind of rigour which often seems to advise men to curb and outlaw some of their most valued human emotions and relationships. Perhaps this goes back to their inadequate theory of evil ... [14]

For our purposes and for his part, Farquharson's most important insight was to identify what Marcus was doing in writing the *Meditations*. This may sound obvious enough. Yet the work's form – in the views of many scholars, unique and idiosyncratic – had led to a multitude of theories over the centuries. These included that the work had at first been far differently arranged; or had been corrupted and excerpted into the result that we see (there were almost certainly *Florilegia* or collections of sayings extant from later antiquity); or that the work as we know it was only the 'handbook' version of a larger, coherent moral treatise which has been lost, Marcus' *Enchiridion* to a lost *Discourses*, if we were to use the parallel of Epictetus' works.[15] Some interpreters, such as Jean-Pierre de Joly in the eighteenth century, had rearranged the text to their own taste, and published 'a more or less orderly composition.'[16]

Farquharson writes that by his time there was a consensus that the 'disorder and inconsequence' were adequately explained by the work's status as a private journal. He entertains the possibility – but no more – that Marcus at one time may have planned a book which he was never in a position to complete, and that the *Meditations* represents its 'elements.'[17]

More significantly, though, Farquharson concludes that the work includes both hints and reminders to Marcus himself, and more consciously literary images and reflections. It is an original combination:

> Is not much of the *Meditations* an attempt to create a novel form of literature and to find the proper vehicle for its expression? Marcus at times seems to aim at conveying into his Greek sentences something of the lapidary force of the Latin tongue.[18]

Further, Farquharson writes:

> Marcus has hit upon a form of self-expression not previously used in Greek letters, and has written a manual of admonitions useful for the philosophic life, Spiritual Consolations, in fact a *Religio Imperatoris*. He is gradually feeling his way to the right expressional use of his new instrument, and has often failed to reach the final and sufficient shape.[19]

Here, buried within Farquharson's formidable textual scholarship, we find critically important insights about Marcus' literary and philosophical practice. Decades before French scholar Pierre Hadot attracted controversy in calling the writing of notes to oneself, in the ancient pagan tradition, 'spiritual exercises,' Farquharson had explicitly used even more suggestive language.

Farquharson, then, considered that Marcus was experimenting with a 'novel' literary form; Hadot, rather, situated Marcus' practice in longstanding tradition, going back to Socrates, of care for the soul: self-transformation through the habitual reminder of *dogmata*, key principles. In 1972, in his first published article, Hadot put it:

> In order to understand what the *Meditations* are, we must recognize the literary genre to which they belong, situating them in the general perspective of the teaching and philosophical life of the Hellenistic era.

> In this period, philosophy is essentially spiritual direction: it does not aim to give an abstract teaching. Rather, every dogma is intended to transform the soul of the disciple.[20]

In the words of John Sellars, broadly following Hadot, Marcus was 'attending to [him]self.'[21]

We have lost so many ancient works that, in the end, we are poorly placed to assess whether Marcus' text was, in fact, either as strikingly original as Farquharson suggested, or as consonant with tradition as Hadot maintained. To be sure, Epictetus, in claiming that Socrates (contrary to the better-known tradition that he did not write philosophy) wrote notes to himself, may have offered a precedent for Marcus.[22] Further, against Farquharson's position, there is nothing about Marcus' surviving record or personality to suggest that he was likely to have been an innovator simply for its own sake, even if such a thing were familiar from ancient literature in general. Rather, as Hadot insists, each literary genre imposed a structure and a set of features to which a writer was expected to conform, even if he or she varied one or another element of style or emphasis. Nonetheless, it is surely the case that Marcus' luminous intellect and insistence on virtue were of an uncommon degree, if not novel in kind: a view underlined by the ancient judgments which do survive.

It would be with Hadot, whose works received English translation by Michael Chase in the 1990s, and with Martha Nussbaum's ground-breaking 1994 *The Therapy of Desire*, alongside Wolfe's and Lebell's popular books inspired by Epictetus, that Stoicism would once again appear in popular Anglophone culture. The Hellenistic schools – over years, in important works by A.A. Long, David Sedley, Julia Annas, Brad Inwood, and others – had slowly been reinvented, as key subjects not only for academic study, but towards something more practical. In this context, another watershed was Long's comprehensive *Epictetus: A Stoic and Socratic Guide to Life* (2002). All these developments represented some of the background to the revival which we now know as Modern Stoicism.

Chapter Seventeen

Marcus Goes to Hollywood

Fan-fiction as film – The Fall of the Roman Empire (1964) – Alec Guinness' Marcus – Once again, the importance of horses – Gladiator (2000) – Gladiator II – scope for a Young Marcus

It is a fitting outcome that Marcus, whose own prose was able to convey at times almost cinematically visual detail and action, should at last, himself, have been immortalised on screen. In 1964, *The Fall of the Roman Empire* appeared, directed by Anthony Mann and starring Stephen Boyd, Sophia Loren, Christopher Plummer, and, as Marcus Aurelius, Alec Guinness.

The decade of the 1960s was not, as we have seen, an era which was likely to have celebrated Stoicism; there is no mention in the film of the philosophy, nor of the virtue which Marcus pursued. Nonetheless, *FOTRE* represents a key development in Marcus fan-fiction, one which continues to be significant on several cultural fronts.

The budget was huge, and it shows. Filmed on location in Spain, nearly the entire first half is set in the gloomy wastes of the Danube frontier; when the scene shifts to Rome, on Commodus' accession, brilliant sunshine lights the stunning replica of the Forum which was purpose-built. Later, we are taken to the eastern frontier of the empire, Armenia or Cappadocia (the startling giant heads of Mount Nemrut/Commagene are featured), in desert and sierra country. In this way, the immense extent of the Roman empire is effectively conveyed. Where the action occurs in an interior set, these also are both authentic and stunningly beautiful: the black marble of Commodus' palace (filmed at the Cinecittà Studios in Rome), strikes a suitably menacing note, while the grandeur within Rome's Temple of Jupiter is the more effective in its simplicity.

Reportedly, the film director Anthony Mann, who had recently completed filming *El Cid* (1961) also in Spain, happened to see a copy of Gibbon's *Decline and Fall*, and 'read it,' being then inspired to undertake a dramatic version. This is about as unconvincing as any origin story; it is very unlikely that Mann read the whole six volumes of Gibbon's work. Nonetheless, he may have read enough of Volume I to have conceived the idea of developing the death of Marcus and the Commodus disaster into a drama. In the event, the film takes considerable liberties with the known facts.

The screenplay was created by Ben Barzman (1910–1989), a Canadian journalist and unrepentantly blacklisted communist. Barzman and his wife Norma were members of the Communist Party of the USA (CPUSA), and during the 1950s moved to Paris.[1] Philip Yordan, who provided cover for several blacklisted writers, was also listed as a contributor to the screenplay (as Yordan had also been for *El Cid*).[2]

It is the actors who make or break a film, and here *FOTRE* was on the whole poorly served. Sophia Loren does not so much act badly, as not act at all: she conveys not Lucilla (the other daughters are omitted from the film), but remains simply Sophia, beautiful but somehow colourless. Her love-interest, the imaginary officer Gaius Marcellus Livius, played woodenly by Stephen Boyd, is similarly a let-down. James Mason plays Marcus' friend, the (imaginary) Greek philosopher Timonides, moderately well, at least projecting a character of bravery: he undergoes torture by the Germanic barbarians, in a gripping scene.

Among these generally underwhelming performances, Alec Guinness stands out. At the time, he was among Britain's most popular actors, and must have been a drawcard for audiences. He is physically made to resemble Marcus, the curly hair and distinctive beard are featured; he comes across as frail. When he has to stand and greet dozens of leaders and princes from all around the empire, parading before him, we understand how fatiguing Marcus' duties were, and how committed he must have been to perform them with diligence, particularly in the bitter winds of the northern frontier. The film has Marcus, in his final days, appoint Livius, not Commodus, to be his heir.

In dialogue with Timonides, Livius, and Lucilla, Guinness' Marcus speaks calmly, briefly, and often with a wry smile. As noted, it was unlikely that Stoicism would explicitly feature in a 1960s screenplay, but it is as if the *Meditations,* at least, had been wafted over Barzman's script. Stoicism's insistence on the corporeal was something a communist could endorse, and one of Marcus' more striking, and authentic, speeches has him reminding Lucilla that his nerves and other bodily parts would soon be dissipated. In another scene, Marcus moves about his tent, his voice-over musing in a manner very much 'to himself,' interspersed effectively with speaking monologue. We are shown Marcus, by now, dwelling more in his own contemplation than in the world outside, and this is a powerful means of bringing the man and his work to life. Less happily, Barzman's communism is probably responsible for the repetitive and clunky 'peace' rhetoric: before and during the Cold War, the Soviet line was that the US was the global warmonger, Rome evidently standing in for the modern 'imperial' power.

For whatever reason, Mann and Barzman chose to ignore the reported information about Marcus' last moments. Guinness' Marcus lies barely able to speak, finally uttering, indistinctly, 'Livius' to Lucilla. She takes this to mean that

Marcus wanted Livius, not Commodus, to inherit the empire, although when no document is found to support this decision, she has no evidence and no case.

Along with Guinness' Marcus, Christopher Plummer's Commodus perhaps saves the film's acting. Seemingly commonplace to begin with, he transforms, alongside his burgeoning power, into a convincing psychopath. He briskly tells the court and senate that he will overturn all his father's arrangements, and instead of conciliating the provinces, he increases their taxes and tribute, while punishing dissent.

One interesting innovation is the decision – portrayed as one of Marcus' final decrees – that Lucilla should marry Sohaemus, King of Armenia (Omar Sharif, contributing much-needed charisma in a minor role) in order to improve relations with the client nation. While this did not occur in fact, Lucilla and her sisters – like all noblewomen in the Roman world – were indeed subject to marriages organised for political ends. The film shows the entire eastern empire rising in revolt against Commodus' impositions. In effect, this transposes the actual Avidian revolt of 175 into the later reign. Livius defeats the rebels, and on returning to Rome is condemned to death by Commodus.

In reality, as we have seen, Lucilla and her husband were executed by Commodus after the unsuccessful rising of 182, with Commodus himself surviving another near-decade before being assassinated in his turn. In the film, no doubt to foreground the love-interest and a 'happy ending,' Livius defeats Commodus in single gladiatorial combat, then escaping a chaotic Rome alongside Lucilla.

These liberties with the plot, while perhaps hardly justified as art, do not detract from the film's overall impact. At times, *FOTRE* feels like a western, and this is no accident: Anthony Mann had directed classics such as *Winchester '73* (1950), *The Naked Spur* (1953), and *The Man From Laramie* (1955). His insistence on dramatic locations, and particularly the (fictional) sequence in *FOTRE* in which a Roman troop led by Commodus lures the Germans into a tight encounter, followed by Livius' supporting forces, very much recall similar incidents in westerns (the 'barbarians' here assuming the role of the Indians, Mexicans, or outlaws).

This effect is heightened by the score. Dimitri Tiomkin (1894–1979), of Ukrainian heritage and an émigré from Russia following the Revolution, had contributed scores for several westerns, including some of the very greatest, such as *High Noon* (1952) and *Gunfight at the O.K. Corral* (1957). Tiomkin's signature ballad for *High Noon* has been credited with saving the film from critical disaster, as well as becoming a hit song in its own right. Both his classical European background, and the western 'American frontier' feel, can be discerned in the music of *FOTRE*, which attracted the film's only major award, a Golden Globe for Best Original Score (1965).

This western heritage no doubt contributed another spectacular effect which it is hardly within the power of films in the CGI age to achieve: *the horses*. We have seen more than once that horses were key to Marcus' legacy, from the equestrian statues and the Sarmatian steeds, to the cavalry of northern Britain. We have seen young Marcus, who enjoyed hunting, leading his own 'mini squad' through the Roman countryside. In *FOTRE*, cavalry dominates much of the lengthy film: in the first half, we hear the constant crunch on snowy tracks of squadron after squadron, mounted on beautiful, big beasts. Livius and Commodus, along with the other Roman commanders, seemingly spend their lives on horseback. There is a breath-taking chariot race between Livius and Commodus (doubtless in emulation of that in *Ben-Hur*, 1959), along mountain roads, wheels catching the side walls, the amazing horses bounding over obstacles. Sparks are struck from the wheels in contact with each other. At each moment it appears a crash must occur, yet on it whirls. Such scenes are confronting now in part because we know that animal welfare was not a priority in the golden age of Hollywood, and that injuries and deaths were common. Indeed, stunt work remains highly risky even for humans, as some high-profile recent cases have reminded us.[3]

After 1940, film productions had to consult the organisation American Humane about the use of animals on set.[4] But it is not clear how much matters had improved. A writer on the treatment of horses in westerns has claimed:

> The horses were routinely whipped by stage drivers, they were forced up and down steep hills, and they were forcibly driven through raging rivers. Horses were forced to pull heavy loads in the blazing sun. They were spurred, shot at, forced to jump through windows, and ridden through burning buildings. What horses endured in Westerns is similar to that which the heroes themselves endured, with one exception; the horses were not acting voluntarily.[5]

Of course, if we find this confronting, we should find the Rome of Marcus even more disturbing in its routine ill-treatment of animals. The slaughter of men and animals in the arena for entertainment should shock us, but equally, we should never lose sight of the more mundane suffering of cavalry horses throughout history. One of the least dubious benefits of the petrol/diesel age has surely been the long peace granted to the horses.

Supposedly, it was the animals of the arena which provided the 'origin story' for Ridley Scott's 2000 hit film *Gladiator*. We are told that David Franzoni, who with John Logan and William Nicholson wrote the screenplay, was inspired by the 1958 book *Those About to Die*, by Daniel P. Mannix. Mannix (1911–1997) was a journalist, carnival performer, and animal trainer. The book covered all aspects of animals used in the ancient arena, and the gladiators themselves, consulting primary sources. The other element of the 'origin story' is that two DreamWorks producers showed Scott the 1872 painting by Jean-Léon Gérôme, *Pollice Verso* ('Thumbs Down'), showing a triumphant gladiator poised over his defeated rival. This dramatic vision, it appears, was enough to convince Scott to undertake the project.

Such elaborate pretexts do little to obscure the similarities between *FOTRE* and *Gladiator*, although they may have diverted observers from making instant and direct comparisons. The influence of *FOTRE* upon *Gladiator* is obvious. For a start, both cover the same period, from the end of Marcus' reign into the death of Commodus. In *Gladiator*, Russell Crowe plays the imaginary Maximus, very much the same role as Boyd's Livius in the earlier film: both are military leaders, both are former lovers of Lucilla, and both are named by Marcus as his heir. That the later film's creators independently came up with such an imaginary character is highly unlikely. If we are to be generous, both Livius and Maximus owe something to the real Pompeianus, Lucilla's second husband and Marcus' trusted lieutenant.

In the introduction to this book, we noted that Richard Harris' depiction of the emperor is seriously wanting, and – in contrast to *FOTRE* – there is no indication that anyone in the production had any familiarity with the *Meditations*. Nonetheless, Marcus' legacy is repeatedly invoked during the later scenes of the film: it turns out that the gladiator trainer Proximo (a scene-stealing cameo by Oliver Reed) had, himself a successful gladiator, been given his freedom by Marcus. Marcus' supposed dream of restoring the Republic is invoked at times. In these ways, he is shown to have been an influential, indeed unforgettable, figure, which only underlines the disappointment attending Harris' portrayal: there is surely internal inconsistency in the repeated appeals to a figure as ambiguous and lightweight as Harris.

A sequel, *Gladiator II*, is in production at the time of writing. It is to be set in the reign of Septimius Severus, who as we have seen emulated Marcus Aurelius even to the extent of adopting himself into the Antonine family, his son Caracalla accorded the name 'Marcus Aurelius Antoninus.' This, then, will take Marcus fan-fiction to another level and a later generation. It remains to be seen if the sequel will follow historical events more closely than its forebears, although most importantly it will be judged as a success or otherwise on the strength of its entertainment value.

Directors, writers and producers should also be reminded that there must be scope for a 'prequel,' a *Young Marcus* perhaps, covering his youth and adulthood from *gravissimus* and *verissimus* to reconciler of friends, grieving father, leader of men. It is unfortunate that Hollywood's focus on the Commodus story – the 'decline and fall' narrative – has obscured so much of the greatness of the best of emperors, in favour of the decline into insanity of one of the worst.

Walking With Marcus V: Scotland's Antonine Wall

Neither Antoninus Pius, Marcus, nor Commodus ever visited Britain; Hadrian, in 122 CE*, was the last imperial visitor before the chaos which ensued on Commodus' death. Pertinax was governor of Britain during the 180s, before succeeding Commodus in 193, with the support of the army. Septimius Severus would be the next emperor to attempt to restore order in northern Britain, before his sudden death at York, from disease, in 211.*

Half an hour's drive from Edinburgh airport, the visitor can explore remaining stations on the Antonine Wall, the earth rampart constructed on Antoninus' orders. This would remain the northern limit of Roman control in Europe, and it was short-lived. It is estimated that the Antonine fortifications were only effective for about forty years at most, from the 140s until Marcus' death in 180.

Rough Castle, outside Falkirk, lies peacefully within a forest. Defensive ditches, still visible, and turf ramparts surrounded the fort. The garrison consisted of the Cohors VI Nerviorum, from the Belgic tribes of northern Gaul. Traces of the commander's house, a granary, and the obligatory bath-house were excavated early in the twentieth century, before being abandoned or filled in (accounts vary). Dog-walkers with happy pooches frequent the site, where only the odd stone remains to be seen.

This, then, for just a few decades, was the frontier, under constant pressure from the tribes to the north. It was a cold and wild setting. Yet this chain of outposts has yielded some of the most interesting and important artefacts from anywhere in the Roman world, including the 'distance slabs.' These are inscriptions in stone, which proudly record each section's construction. A very long way from the Palatine Hill or the Forum, the troops honoured Antoninus Pius:

IMP C.T.
AEL. HADRIANO
ANTONINO AVG PIO
P.P. VEX. LEG.
XX V.V [Twentieth Legion Valeria Victrix]
P.P. FEC. III

This section had been built by the Twentieth Legion, with its emblem of a wild boar.[6] *Other items found from the vicinity of the Wall, such as altars and tombstones, reveal that however remote, the area shared in the cults and culture of the rest of the Roman world.*[7]

One of the most poignant scenes from Roman Scotland is at Newstead, not far from Sir Walter Scott's remarkable estate of Abbotsford. This was, in the first and second centuries CE, *the fortress of Trimontium, 'of the three hills.' It was built on Dere Street, the Roman road stretching north from Hadrian's Wall. Legio XX Valeria Victrix, once again, had taken part in building one phase of the fort. Finds from Trimontium have included impressive cavalry helmets, including those used for ceremonial displays. It was evidently a key centre for the cavalry which, as we have seen, were key to Roman identity and power in Britain. Several impressive pieces can be seen in the National Museum of Scotland, Edinburgh.*

It was during the reign of Marcus that Trimontium's role changed from rear centre to front line, as the Antonine Wall was gradually less effective. In turn, the civilian population around Trimontium seems to have decreased, and thus the fort was reduced in importance. The latest coin found at Trimontium was from 180, the year of Marcus' death. It has been conjectured that the site was finally abandoned in the reign of Commodus. Following investigations early in the twentieth century, today there is nothing to be seen in the rolling fields outside Newstead, except for a somewhat twee 'waymarker' stele, its inscription in imitation of Roman lettering, erected in the early decades of the twentieth century.

Only in recent years has another Scottish link with Marcus been established. North of the Antonine Wall, the great castle of Stirling, on its mighty rock, was for centuries a royal palace. King James V of Scotland (1512–1542) was a patron of the arts, and it was no doubt as an on-trend Renaissance prince that he commissioned a series of wooden medallions depicting great figures both contemporary and from history, the 'Stirling Heads.'

James, a significant player in the power politics of both Britain and France, employed craftsmen from across Europe in adorning his palaces, and the Stirling Heads included depictions of Roman leaders such as Julius Caesar and Marcus Aurelius, alongside James' own relatives. We saw in an earlier chapter that the Marcus fan-fiction of Antonio de Guevara was hugely popular in the 1530s, and Marcus was coming into fashion as a role-model for princes.

Stirling's surviving heads have been collected and are on display safely behind glass, while reproductions have been created in what is considered to be the original gaudy colours. James' own conspicuous consumption may not, in the end, betray much acquaintance with Marcus' guidance, but at least we can see that Scotland had not forgotten, indeed that it celebrated, its Roman cultural ties.

A tramp in the damp lowlands, then, brings us to the end of our walks with Marcus and his influence. We have traced his impacts through books, and in artefacts; in Rome and at Carnuntum; on the Yorkshire moors and in Scottish fields. Undoubtedly, there is more to be discovered, both in libraries and in excavations, about the legacies of the man whom his successors considered to be the best of the Roman emperors.

Notes

Chapter One: Out of Oblivion

1. Long, *Meditations* (1862 translation), adapted and slightly modernized.
2. MacIntyre (1984), p. 2.
3. Buddensieg (1965), p. 47.
4. Highet (1976), pp. 59–67.
5. Celenza (2021).
6. Aulus Gellius, *Attic Nights* 19.1.4–14.
7. Hard translation, *Handbook* 1.1.
8. Robertson and Codd (2019).
9. Stephens (2000) gives a detailed summary.
10. Farquharson vol. I, p. xxii.
11. Author translation, *Meditations* Book 2.1.

Chapter Two: Succession

1. McLynn (2009), p. 60.
2. '*HA MA*' is the *Historia Augusta* Life of Marcus Aurelius; 'HA Hadrian' that of Hadrian, etc.
3. Author translation.
4. Here, as so often, Marcus was doing something unusual. His French translator André Dacier would write:

   'An extraordinary piece of Gratitude this, which as 'twas an Original in him; for nobody since has had the Ingenuity to Copy after it. When people have any good Qualities, they are apt to thank themselves for the getting them. To impute their Virtue to the Assistance of another, is the way, they fancy to tarnish the Lustre, and lose the Credit on't.' Biographical essay on Marcus, translated by George Stanhope, ?1697; included in Jeremy Collier's 1701 translation of the text of *Meditations*, pp. v-vi.

Walking With Marcus II: Villa Adriana

5. E.g. most recently Robertson (2024), p. 59, pp. 72–3.

Chapter Three: A Knight Called Marcus

1. Nichols (1889), pp. 42–3.
2. Gregorovius (1894), p. 161.
3. Nichols (1889), p. 43.
4. Nichols (1889), pp. 42–5.
5. Higden, *Polychronicon*, I.228–9, translation from Latin by the author. The reading 'under four bronze pillars' (*sub quatuor columnas aereas*) conflicts with accounts which suggest the statue may have originally rested *on top of* four supporting columns: Fehl, pp. 363, 366; and a variant reading of *super* instead of *sub* is cited in textual notes.
6. Higden, *Polychronicon*, I.231–2, translation from Latin by the author.

7. Fehl (1974), p. 366.
8. Birley (1987), pp. 140, 147.
9. Birley (1987), p. 161.
10. Birley (2008), pp. 168–9.
11. Birley (2008), p. 171.
12. Birley (1987), p. 174.
13. Birley (2008), p. 173.
14. Cassius Dio, 72.22.16.
15. Nickel (1989), p. 22.
16. *Historia Augusta* (henceforth *HA*), *Life of Marcus* 24.5.
17. *HA MA* 25.6.
18. *HA MA* 21.3–5.
19. *HA MA* 17.4–5.
20. Cassius Dio, 72.32.
21. Scholars consider that Cassius Dio wrote of events after about 180 from personal knowledge: Barnes (1984), p. 242.
22. Niles (2016), p. 141.
23. Cassius Dio, 72.11.
24. Nickel (1989) p. 20.
25. Beckmann (2012), Figure 15.3, reproducing an engraving by A. Lafreri, c. 1550.
26. Mezzatesta (1984), p. 624.
27. Mezzatesta (1984), p. 625.
28. Carley (2004).
29. In Buddensieg (1965), p. 58.
30. Ibid.
31. Fehl (1974), p. 362.
32. Mezzatesta (1984), pp. 626–7; Woloch (1969) p. 469.
33. Mezzatesta (1984), pp. 628–9.
34. Rees (2000) shows that Bryennius has thus provided important and seemingly independent testimony on textual issues in the *Meditations*.
35. Nickel (1989), p. 17.
36. Dieckmann and Seznec (1952), p. 202.
37. Ala Samartarum: https://www.roman-britain.co.uk/places/bremetenacum/
38. Littleton and Thomas (1978), pp. 514–519.
39. Wadge (1987), p. 208.
40. Nickel (1989), p. 23.
41. Nichols (1889), p. 117.

Chapter Four: In the Hands of the Sophists (Or were They in His?)

1. The term usually refers to the composite of three elements: the surface, the earlier text/s, and the later text/s.
2. http://www.frontoonline.com/history-of-the-collection.html
3. Fleury (2012), p. 64.
4. Haines (1919), Introduction, p. xvii.
5. Haines (1919), p. xxi.
6. The letters are conventionally named as *Ad Marcum Caesarem*, 'To Marcus Caesar.'
7. Intro to LCL 134 (2023, revised), p. 4.
8. Rakovec-Felser Z. Domestic Violence and Abuse in Intimate Relationship from Public Health Perspective. Health Psychol Res. 2014 Oct 22;2(3):1821. doi: 10.4081/hpr.2014.1821. PMID: 26973948; PMCID: PMC4768593.

9. Diogenes Laertius is our major source for the early Stoic writers. LCL 185, vol. II, 1920, adapted.
10. *Boulēsis* can also be rendered as 'wishing' or 'planning' or 'intending.'
11. In stating that 'Antoninus … never had the tolerance for Greek philosophers and (especially) sophists that Marcus had, or, in the latter case, taught himself to have' (p. 67), McLynn, as not infrequently, seems to have the matter 180 degrees wrong. Antoninus – despite having fallen foul personally of Herodes' temper – seems to have had, perhaps in not being an intellectual himself, a reverence for Herodes and Fronto which the better-judging Marcus did not share, notwithstanding his personal attachments to both.
12. Fleury (2012), p. 64.
13. Haines (1919), p. 81; Gellius, *Attic Nights* 19.10.1.
14. Richlin (2008), p. xix; *Phaedrus*: p. xxvi.
15. Fleury (2012), p. 65, notes that Marcus seems to have copied expressions from Roman comedy.
16. Haines (1919), p. 87.
17. Haines (1919), p. 97.
18. Haines (1919), p. 97.
19. Haines (1919), p. 109.
20. Richlin, unfortunately arriving at the obvious: '[Marcus'] use of diminutives verges, I think, on the sarcastic or facetious' (p. xxxviii).
21. *Meditations* 6.30.
22. Haines (1919), p. 113.
23. Haines (1919), p. 125.
24. Haines (1919), p. 129.
25. Haines (1919), p. 143.
26. Haines (1919), p. 151.
27. Fleury (2012): 'What is disconcerting in these letters is the humor,' p. 73.
28. Haines (1919), p. 207.
29. 144–5 CE, *Epist. Graec.* 3, Haines (1919), p. 171.
30. Haines (1919, p. 183.
31. Foucault (1988), p. 29. Fleury (2012) also usefully pushes back on Foucault's stress here on 'care for the self,' p. 69.
32. Haines (1919), p. 185.
33. Haines (1919), p. 185.
34. Haines (1919), p. 193.
35. Haines (1919), p. 197.
36. Haines (1919), p. 207.
37. Haines (1919), p. 221.
38. Haines (1919), p. 217.

Walking With Marcus III: Appian Way and Borghese Gardens

39. Translation by Davies and Pomeroy (2012), p.9.

Chapter Five: A Golden Book

1. Long translation, adapted.
2. Tradition, from Lilius Giraldus (1479–1552): *Demum et M. Antonius* [sic] *Caesar et philosophus de piscibus nonnihil scripsit, cuius etiam quaedam extant adhuc* (1545), noted in Farquharson, vol. I, p. xxii, n. 3.

3. McLynn (2009), pp. 135–6.
4. Suda, omicron, 452.
5. Lennox (2021).
6. Volk (2020), p. 213.
7. Lytle (2022).
8. Translations from Oppian, *Halieutica* are adapted from the Loeb LCL 219, transl. A. Mair, 1928.
9. 'How intelligent are whales and dolphins?' au.whales.org/whales-dolphins/how-intelligent-are-whales-and-dolphins/ accessed 28 May 2024.
10. Long and Sedley, p. 508.
11. Imperadore et al (2017).
12. Notoriously, by the wealthy Crassus: Aelian, *On the Characteristics of Animals* 8.4.1.
13. Zapato (2008).
14. Lytle (2011), p. 350.
15. M. Frontonis Arion (c. 140–143 CE), Haines (1919), pp. 54–59.
16. As *Halieutica* consists of about 3,500 lines, this Suda account would seem to be exaggerated, unless Oppian also performed other of his poems on the same occasion.
17. Author translation. Hays' 'Criminal psychology' – rendering the final sentence here – seems excessively gnomic, even for Marcus.

Chapter Six: Roman Joy: Marcus and Hilaritas

1. Börner (2012), p. 282.
2. Mattingly (1927), p. 4.
3. Börner (2012), p. 279.
4. Mattingly (1927), p. 4.
5. Walton (1957).
6. Mattingly (1927), pp. 5–6.
7. 'Hilaritas,' *Dictionary of Roman Coins,* Numiswiki, The Collaborative Numismatics Project.
8. RIC III Antoninus Pius 425; 428A (date 145–160), 432A; 432B.
9. RIC III Antoninus Pius 1375.
10. RIC III Marcus Aurelius 375, 610, 684, 769.
11. RIC III Commodus 150.

Chapter Seven: Losing a Child

1. Frier (2008), p. 804.
2. McLynn (2009), p. 111.
3. Birley (1987), Appendix F.
4. See, e.g. Shaw and Saller (1984), contesting claims by Goody (1983).
5. Shaw and Saller (1984), p. 432.
6. Frier (2016).
7. Shaw and Saller (1984), p. 435.
8. Birley (1987), Appendix C.
9. Outlined by Frier (2016).
10. Birley (1987), Appendix F.
11. Woods (2007).
12. Woods (2007), p. 375. McLynn (2009), typically, inaccurate: 'The issue of the death rate is reasonably clear-cut' (p. 108).
13. Frier (2008), p. 789.

14. Woods (2007), p. 383.
15. Scheidel (1999), p. 266.
16. Woods (2007), p. 384.
17. Scheidel (1999).
18. Scheidel (1999), p. 269.
19. Scheidel (1999), p. 267–8.
20. Scheidel (1999), p. 269.
21. Scheidel (1999), p. 274.
22. Martial 10.63, in Scheidel (1999), p. 275.
23. Seneca, *Ad Marciam.*
24. Hard translation.
25. McLynn (2009), p. 146, n. 120 referring to *Much Ado About Nothing* V.1.137 as Leonato's speech; the reference given is actually a minor line from Claudio.
26. Lucian, *Demonax* 24.
27. Fronto, *De Nepote Amisso* (Haines, vol. 2, p. 223), quoted in Scheidel (1999), p. 267.
28. Haines (1919), pp. 223–227.
29. Details from Birley (1987) Appendix F.
30. Author translation.
31. Author translation.
32. Author translation. Epictetus: Hard translation.
33. Galen (2016), vol. II, 11.12, pp. 549–553. Discussion at Papavramidou et al (2010), pp. 665–6.
34. HA Comm.11.7.
35. Birley (1987), p. 248.
36. Hekster (2002), p. 34.
37. *Meditations* 1.17.6.
38. Full discussion in Segvic (2000).
39. Frisell et al (2012).
40. Ellis and Walsh, chapter 16, 'Crime, delinquency and intelligence: a review of the worldwide literature,' (2003).
41. London Borough of Redbridge, 'Children's health and parents related by blood,' 2013, p. 4.
42. Hwang et al (2023).
43. Haines (1919), p. 202. There seems to be confusion around this daughter's naming and dates. Birley (1987) gives 'Domitia Faustina, b. 30 November, 147, d. 151' (Appendix F, p. 239). But Haines, as above, notes: 'Annia Galeria Faustina, born probably early in 146. She died in infancy, and Herodes set up an inscription to her at Olympia (Dessau ii.8803).'
44. https://www.mayoclinic.org/diseases-conditions/peripheral-neuropathy/symptoms-causes/syc-20352061
45. McLynn (2009), p. 97.
46. Lead poisoning: Tayeh (2020).

Chapter Eight: Marcus and His Monuments

1. Games: *HA MA* 6.1; tomb: *HA Hadrian* 27.3.
2. *HA MA* 7.10.
3. So Davies (2000), p. 40, citing (n. 98, p. 190), CIL 6.986 = ILS 346. The CIL is the *Corpus Inscriptionum Latinarum*, the standard collection of Latin inscriptions which has been assembled slowly since the nineteenth century. However, some of these,

including 6.986, have disappeared at some stage after being recorded, and a search of the online CIL database (cil.bbaw.de) currently (June 2024) yields no result for that reference number. Fortunately, however, some 'lost' inscriptions have been preserved in other collections, including the *Inscriptiones Latinae Selectae (*ILS), edited by Hermann Dessau (1856–1931), which in their turn have partially been digitised (e.g. in the Internet Archive series). Thus, we can view online several of the burial inscriptions long since vanished from Hadrian's Mausoleum.

4. Davies (2000), p. 40. Ridley (2018), p. 261, explains that the pedestal reliefs underwent restoration in the eighteenth century, fortunately with less catastrophic results than occurred for the column.
5. Torelli (1992), p. 9.
6. Davies (2000), p. 97.
7. Davies (2000), pp. 22–3, fig. 13.
8. Davies (2000), p. 117 reproducing conjectured restorations of the relief.
9. Sellars (2021) discusses Marcus' preoccupation with time, pp. 95–6.
10. Ridley (2018), p. 265. Ridley, depressingly, pieces together, from confused or misleading accounts, several disastrous attempts in the early 1700s to recover the column, which seem to have resulted – rather – in its destruction.
11. Hekster (2002), p. 204, Appendix 1.
12. 176: Beckmann (2012), p. 251. Beckmann's monograph on the column hereafter '2011;' his shorter account hereafter '2012.' After 180: Hekster (2002), p. 204.
13. Beckmann (2012) p. 251, CIL 6.1585=ILS 5920. Texts available at EDSC (Epigraphik-Datenbank Clauss/Slaby, db.edcs.eu.
14. *Mirabilia* 14. Of the twelfth century, this work drew on earlier topographic surveys.
15. Beckmann (2012), p. 253.
16. Ammianus Marcellinus 16.10.14.
17. Beckmann (2012), p. 254.
18. Stevenson (2008), p. 43.
19. Beckmann (2011), p. 59 and p. 65, respectively.
20. Beckmann (2011), p. 4, on which more later.
21. Beckmann (2011), p. 34.
22. Kovács (2012), p. 82.
23. Davies (2000), p. 135.
24. Vitruvius *De Architectura* 9.2.1 (Pythagoras, Democritus, Plato); 9.4.3 (the pre-Socratic philosophers).
25. Dio *Chrysostom Discourses on Kingship* 1.50–84.
26. LCL 276, Emlyn-Jones and Preddy, 2013, pp. 471–3.
27. Pliny, Letters 10.81, 82.
28. Summary in Hays, Index of Persons, p. 188, 'Plato.'
29. McLynn (2009), p. 458.
30. Herodian 1.5.1.
31. Ps.-Aurelius Victor, *Epitome de Caesaribus* 16.12; Tertullian, *Apology* 25.5.
32. Kovács (2012), p. 82.
33. CIL 6.36996.
34. *Schedae scriptor*: Antonella Ferraro (Feraudi), 22-03-2012, EAGLE (Electronic Archive of Greek and Latin Epigraphy), http://www.edr-edr.it/edr_programmi/res_complex_comune.php?do=book&id_nr=EDR092977 accessed 13 June 2024.

35. S. Rowland Pierce (1926), pp. 77–8. ILS 346 (Antoninus), 349 (Faustina I), 350 and 351 (the young sons of Antoninus and Faustina), and 352 (their other daughter): https://archive.org/details/inscriptioneslat01dessuoft/page/86/mode/2up?q=346, pp. 87–8.
36. 'The Arch of Portugal,' http://roma.andreapollett.com/S6/roma2-01e.htm. See earlier in this chapter for a reference to the Sabina relief and one reconstruction, shown in Davies (2000), p. 117.
37. Boschung (2012), pp. 308–313.
38. Boschung (2012), p. 313.

Chapter Nine: Marcus Magus

1. Andrikopolous (2009), p. 94.
2. E.g., influentially, Whiting and Konstantakos (2019), p. 7.
3. Cassius Dio 72.8–10.
4. Israelowich (2008), p. 86.
5. Wallach (1941), p. 280.
6. Wallach (1941), p. 261.
7. Wallach (1941), p. 269.
8. Wallach (1941), p. 270.
9. Thus Wallach (1941), pp. 280–81.
10. Wallach (1941), p. 282.
11. Translations from Hebrew and Aramaic text in Wallach kindly provided by K. Walker, 2024. He adds in a note that the verbal root *paqad* can mean, on the one hand, deposit/give in charge (thus providence), or it can mean for a man to 'visit' his wife maritally, thus also to give in charge.
12. Walker (2024), translation.
13. Formula in McCown (1923), p. 129.
14. Classical Wisdom, 'Do You Believe in Magic? Marcus Aurelius and Ephesia Grammata' (Ed Whalen, 'Ephesia Grammata: Magic Words in the Greek World,' 22 April 2024, https://classicalwisdom.substack.com/p/do-you-believe-in-magic?utm_source=post-email-title&publication_id=335372&post_id=142801569&utm_campaign=email-post-title&isFreemail=true&r=uaf9v&triedRedirect=true&utm_medium=email
15. McCown (1923), p. 135, n. 26.
16. Author translation.
17. Farqhuarson, (1944), p. 418, citing Sen. *Ep.* 11.8.
18. https://finds.org.uk/database/artefacts/record/id/1013510
19. Martin Henig, quoted in database summary in previous note.

Chapter Ten: Julian the Apostate's Marcus Fan-Fiction

1. Traditionally, this strand has been called Neoplatonism, to distinguish it from the classical teachings of Plato; but there is good reason to consider that the ancients observed no such formal distinction.
2. See, e.g., Socrates Scholasticus in Buck (2003), p. 303.
3. Hilton (2017), p. 39.
4. Translation is the LCL 29 of Wright (1913), adapted by the author.
5. Zanker (1996).
6. Cassius Dio 72.6.
7. Ceporina (2012), p. 47.
8. *Eu poiein hōs ho ti malista pleistous.* It is possible that this expression would go on to influence Francis Hutcheson, translator of the *Meditations* and author of the formula most famous as the definition of utilitarianism; see a later chapter.

Chapter Eleven: A Superior Genius: Marcus Among the Anglicans

1. Jeremy Collier, Preface to *The Emperor Marcus Antoninus: His Conversation With Himself* (1701), preface.
2. Justin, *The First Apology* 1, at New Advent, https://www.newadvent.org/fathers/0126.htm
3. 'St. Justin Martyr,' in Cross (1961), pp. 756–7.
4. Birley (1987), pp. 260–1, summarises some of the issues.
5. Waterfield, p. 255, on 11.3.
6. Augustine, *City of God* 18.52. Trajan as restrainer: Pliny *Ep.* 10.96–7.
7. Vitto (1989), p. 11.
8. Durand et al. (2023).
9. Author translation.
10. Kitzler (2015), pp. 46, 49, 54–5.
11. Cross (1961), p. 1274, s.v. 'Soul.'
12. St Athanasius of Alexandria, early-fourth century, Cross (1961), p. 994, s.v. 'Original Sin.'
13. Cross (1961), p. 576, s.v. 'Grace.'
14. Vitto (1989), pp. 43–4.
15. *Discourses* II.1.19 and elsewhere.
16. *City of God* I.20.
17. Papy (2019).
18. Collis (2016), pp. 263–4.
19. Salmon (2004).
20. Collier, Preface.
21. Chignell and Pereboom (2020).
22. Gascoigne (2004).
23. Taylor (2004).
24. Berman (1988), p. 9.
25. Taylor (2004).
26. Gibson (1733), p. 191.
27. *Ib.* p. 183.
28. *Ib.* pp. 184–5.
29. Fulton (2007), pp. 228–30.

Chapter Twelve: Marcus Incognito: The Strange Case of Defoe's *Dumb Philosopher*

1. An earlier version of this chapter appeared in *Stoicism Today*, 10 December 2022.
2. Long translation.
3. Moore (1940), p. 107.
4. Watt (1963) p. 73,
5. Probably a paraphrase of *Meditations* 4.50.
6. Moore (1940), p. 107 (colorless, innocuous), p. 117 (groundwork).
7. Watt (1963), pp. 73–4.
8. Hill and Nidumolu (2021), p. 4.
9. Novak (2013), p. 41.
10. "Tis the Short-hand of the Mind, and crowds a great deal into a little room:' *Miscellanies upon Moral Subjects, the Second Part*. First edition 1695. "shorthand, n. and adj." OED Online, Oxford University Press, September 2022, www.oed.com/view/Entry/178611. Accessed 18 November 2022.
11. Quoted in Watt (1963), p. 241.
12. Watt (1963), p. 242.

Chapter Thirteen: Saint Antoninus: Enlightenment and Revolution

1. Detailed discussion in Dorsey (2021).
2. Ahnert (2010), p. 52.
3. Signatories listed at Miller (1738), p. 20.
4. Moore and Silverthorne (2008), p. 5.
5. Moore and Silverthorne (2008), pp. 6–7.
6. Moore and Silverthorne (2008), p. 21.
7. Moore and Silverthorne (2008), p. 21.
8. Moore and Silverthorne (2008), p. 33.
9. Moore and Silverthorne (2008), p. 34.
10. Moore and Silverthorne (2008), p. 34.
11. Ahnert (2010), p. 52.
12. Often muddled, both about Stoicism and the Christian context; see Clarke (2000), featuring multiple confusions, but at least arriving at the most likely conclusion, that Smith was considerably influenced by Stoicism, probably mediated by Hutcheson.
13. Matson (2020).
14. Smith (1887), p 421.
15. Smith, (1887), p. 422: 'the loss of a child,' which as we have seen is a phrase from Book I, has been inserted here by Smith into 5.8.
16. Smith (1887), p. 423.
17. Stewart, 'A Biographical and Critical Memoir of the Author [of Theory of Moral Sentiments],' pp. xiv-xv.
18. Matson (2020)
19. Sept. 13, 1749. Pennington, vol. I, p. 168.
20. Montesquieu, *The Spirit of Laws* (translated Nugent), fifth edition, 2 vols., London, 1773, vol. II, p. 180.
21. Quoted at Gay (1967), pp. 50–1.
22. Stove (2019), pp. 57–8.
23. La Harpe, quoted in Thomas (1808), p. xi. Some accounts give 1770 as the work's first appearance, others 1775 (the variance perhaps arising from this reported delay between first reading and first printed publication).
24. William Drennan to Samuel McTier, 21 May 1791, https://www.irishphilosophy.com/category/person/long- 18th-century/william-drennan/
25. Biographical information on Warden in Gillmore, Parkhill, Rouston (2018), chapter 5, but this work, and the Dictionary of Irish Biography, strangely omit the 'Republic of Newtownards' information, which is from the Wikipedia article on Newtownards.
26. Thomas (1808), p. 8.
27. Thomas (1808), p. 9.
28. O'Donnell (2004).
29. Thomas (1808), pp. 29–30.
30. Thomas (1808), p. 34.
31. Thomas (1808), p. 37.
32. Thomas (1808), p. 46.
33. Thomas (1808), p. 64.
34. Gillmore et al. (2018), p. 35.
35. Van der Zanden (2020), p. 55.
36. Van der Zanden (2020), p. 42.
37. Ibid., p. 41.

38. Brooke (2006), p. 393.
39. Enfield (1840), vol. 1, pp. 183–4.
40. Brooke (2006), p. 402.

Chapter Fourteen: Decline and Fall: Marcus and His Heirs

1. Nicholls (2011).
2. *Flagitia regis pena urbis insequitur:* John of Salisbury, *Policraticus*, quoted in Buddensieg (1965), p. 46.
3. Gibbon (1838), vol. I, pp. 136–7.
4. Gibbon (1838), vol. I, p. 146.
5. Gibbon (1838), vol. I, p. 147.
6. Gibbon (1838), vol. I, pp. 149–50.
7. Pocock (1976), p. 155.
8. Gibbon (1838), pp. 98–9.
9. *Journal* (1937) p. 147.
10. *Journal* (1937) pp. 156–7.
11. *Salon de 1845 (2de article)*, Press Serial 18 March 1845, https://web.archive.org/web/20100302121432/http://www.theophilegautier.net/salon1845.htm
12. *Journal* (1937) p. 187.
13. Note 17, ibid.
14. Hannoosh (2013), p. 87.
15. Hannoosh (2013), pp. 76–93 p. 89.
16. Quoted in Geer (1936), p. 47.
17. Geer (1936), pp. 50–1.
18. Robertson (2024), p. 166.
19. Birley (1987), p. 131.
20. ILS 388, H. Dessau (ed.), *Inscriptiones Latinae Selectae*, vol. 1, 1892, p. 94.
21. Discussion in Nicols (1989).
22. Hekster (2002), p. 190.
23. Nicols (1989), pp. 119–122, 131.
24. Cicero, On Ends 3.6/22.

Chapter Fifteen: Marcus for the Modern Age

1. Schulman (2005), p. 4 (no page numbers).
2. Schulman (2005), p. 7.
3. Schulman (2005), p. 13.
4. Nelson, 'Joseph Selden, 1787–1824,' *Encyclopedia of Arkansas*, updated June 2023, https://encyclopediaofarkansas.net/entries/joseph-selden-8900/
5. Hedgcock (2020).
6. Wroth and Jones (2004).
7. Hedgcock (2020).
8. Ibid.
9. Wroth and Jones (2004).
10. Long (1880), p. 24.
11. Long (1880), p. 3.
12. Long (1880), pp. 20–2.
13. 'Used for many years': p. 25; language: p. 26.
14. Long (1880), p. 27.

15. National Park Service, 'Captain John Smith – Historic Jamestowne Part of Colonial National Historic Park Virginia,' updated 2 September 2022, https://www.nps.gov/jame/learn/historyculture/life-of-john-smith.htm
16. Long (1880), p. 43.
17. Quoted in Long (1880), p. 49.
18. Both at Long (1880), p. 78.
19. 'Truly modern': Arnold (1940), p. 595; 'us moderns', p. 598.
20. Collini (2008).
21. 'Little of striking incident': p. 598; 'few of much importance': p. 599.
22. Arnold (1940), p. 602.
23. Arnold (1940), p. 610 (note, original has *tendebantque*; Arnold may have adjusted for his singular subject in Marcus); Ebel (1963), p. 566.
24. Long (1880), 'Note.' No date, but evidently likely to date from between the Confederate defeat at Gettysburg (July 1863) and Lincoln's assassination in April 1865.
25. Buckler (1958), pp. 465–7.
26. Arnold (1940), p. 602.
27. Brake (2006).
28. Pater (1990), Postscript to 'Appreciations,' 1876, pp. 63–4.
29. Pater (2021), p. 10, loc. 230 Kindle.
30. Pater (2021), p. 13, loc. 295 Kindle.
31. Pater (2021), p. 81, loc. 1876 Kindle.
32. Pater (2021), p. 127, loc. 2964 Kindle.
33. Pater was owed better from Richlin (2008) than her casual, and inaccurate, characterisation of his 'dainty Victorian pedantry,' p. xxxvi.
34. Bowra (1949), pp. 385–6.
35. Farrar (2020), loc. 3246 Kindle.
36. *The Letters of Franz Liszt to Olga von Meyendorff, 1871–1886* (Harvard UP, 1979), p. 409. Thanks to Dr R.J. Stove for this reference.
37. Author version.
38. Both by the author.
39. Ginzburg (1996) uses Farquharson's translation.
40. Ginzburg (1996), p. 11.
41. Shklovsky, 1919 version, translated A. Berlina (2015), p. 162.
42. Ginzburg (1996), pp. 12–7.
43. Ginzburg (1996), p. 18; p. 26, n. 40, attributes the anecdote to Valentin Bulgakov, *Leone Tolstoj nell'ultimo anno della sua vita* (1930), 431, and the reference to Pier Cesare Bori.

Chapter Sixteen: Nadir and Renewal

1. Chesterton (1959), pp. 75–6. Thanks to Dr R.J. Stove for this reference.
2. Ibid. p. 76.
3. Ibid. p. 77.
4. Haines (1916), 'Introduction,' p.xiv.
5. Haines (1916), *Meditations* p. xiii.
6. Haines (1916), p. xiii.
7. Nock (1972), 'psychological needs' p. 75; Marcus p. 128. Edwards (2012), pp. 200–02, usefully queries Nock's and associated interpretations.
8. Pharr (1932), p. 277 and *passim.*
9. Gomes (2024).

10. C.S. Lewis to A. Greeves, 26 January 1930, Wikipedia (*The Letters of C.S. Lewis to Arthur Greeves 1913–1963*, Collier Books, 1986, pp. 335–6.
11. Sparrow, 'Preface' to Farquharson (1944), p. vi.
12. Sparrow, 'Preface' to Farquharson (1944), p. vii.
13. Farquharson (1944), 'Introduction,' p. xv.
14. Oates (1940), p. xxiv.
15. Sellars (2021), p. 20; Farquharson (1944) p. lx.
16. Farquharson (1944), p. lxii.
17. Farquharson (1944), p. lxiv.
18. Farquharson (1944), p. lxvii, a thought which the author is gratified to have found expressed by such an authority, having had it occur to herself.
19. Farquharson (1944), p. lxxvi.
20. Hadot (2020, first published 1972), p. 211. Controversy around 'spiritual exercises': briefly in Sharpe and Testa (2020), p. 7. While Farquharson is not referenced in 'Physics as Spiritual Exercise,' his edition of *Meditations* receives a paragraph on page 27 of Hadot (1998), a work which develops and expands much of the 1972 article's scope. As in the later work Hadot refers explicitly to Farquharson's placement of *Meditations* among religious texts, it appears that he may indeed have owed something to Farquharson's insights.
21. Sellars (2021), pp. 20–22.
22. Epictetus *Disc.* 2.1.32, with W. Oldfather suggestion (LCL 131, p. 217 *ad loc.*) that Socrates may in fact have 'written copiously.' Thanks to John Sellars for this reference.

Chapter Seventeen: Marcus Goes to Hollywood

1. Proyect (1997).
2. Rode (2009), p. 15.
3. E.g. stunt performer David Holmes, paralysed from the chest down during stunts in place of Daniel Radcliffe, https://www.theguardian.com/film/2023/nov/11/harry-potter-stunt-double-david-holmes-interview, S. Hattenstone, 11 November 2023.
4. https://humanehollywood.org/about-us/our-history/.
5. Jane Tompkins, *West of Everything: the Inner Life of Westerns* (1992), quoted at Kelly Chase, 'Horses abused for entertainment?' https://www.racc.edu/sites/default/files/imported/StudentLife/Clubs/Legacy/vol_1/Horses_in_Film.html#:~:text=So%2C%20in%201980%2C%20the%20entertainment,be%20used%20in%20their%20productions.

Walking With Marcus V: Scotland's Antonine Wall

6. Distance slab, Hutcheson Hill, 'Key Artefacts,' https://www.antoninewall.org/about-the-wall/key-artefacts, inscription in Hunterian Museum, Glasgow.
7. Ibid.

Bibliography

Primary Sources

Epictetus, *Discourses, Fragments, Handbook* (translated by Robin Hard, Oxford World's Classics, 2014)

Marcus Aurelius, *Meditations*. Editions used in this book include:

Collier, Jeremy, *The Emperor Marcus Antoninus: His Conversation With Himself* (London, 1701)

Farquharson, A.S.L., *ΜΑΡΚΟΥ ΑΝΤΩΝΙΟΥ ΑΥΤΟΚΡΑΤΟΡΟΣ ΤΑ ΕΙΣ ΕΑΥΤΟΝ: The Meditations of the Emperor Marcus Antoninus,* 2 vols. (Oxford University Press, 1944)

Haines, C.R. *Marcus Aurelius* (Loeb Classical Library 58, Cambridge, MA: Harvard University Press, 1916)

Haines, C.R. *The Correspondence of Marcus Cornelius Fronto with Marcus Aurelius Antoninus, Lucius Verus, Antoninus Pius, and Various Friends*, 2 vols. (LCL 112, Cambridge, MA: Harvard University Press, 1919)

Hays, Gregory, *Marcus Aurelius Meditations* (New York: The Modern Library, 2002; 2012 e-Book edition)

Long, George, *The Thoughts of the Emperor M. Aurelius Antoninus,* second edition (London: George Bell & Sons, 1880)

Moore, James, and Michael Silverthorne (eds.), *The Meditations of the Emperor Marcus Aurelius Antoninus, Translated by Francis Hutcheson and James Moor* (Indianapolis, Liberty Fund, 2008)

Oates, Whitney J. Oates (ed.), *The Stoic and Epicurean Philosophers: The Complete Extant Writings of Epicurus, Epictetus, Lucretius, Marcus Aurelius* (New York: Random House, 1940)

Waterfield, Robin, *Marcus Aurelius Meditations: The Annotated Edition* (New York, Basic Books, 2021)

Principal Loeb Classical Library texts

LCL 195 [Aulus] Gellius, *Attic Nights, Volume I: Books 1–5* (transl. J.C. Rolfe, Cambridge, MA: Harvard University Press, 1927)

LCL 32 Dio Cassius [=Cassius Dio], *Roman History, Volume I: Books 1–11* (transl. Earnest Cary, Herbert B. Foster, Cambridge, MA: Harvard University Press, 1914)

LCL 257 Dio Chrysostom, *Discourses I-II* (transl. J.W. Cohoon, Cambridge, MA: Harvard University Press, 1932)

LCL 185 Diogenes Laertius, *Lives of Eminent Philosophers, Volume II* (transl. R.D. Hicks, Cambridge, MA: Harvard University Press, 1970)

LCL 523 Galen, *On the Constitution of the Art of Medicine, The Art of Medicine, A Method of Medicine to Glaucon* (ed. and transl. Ian Johnston, Cambridge, MA: Harvard University Press, 2016)

LCL 454 Herodian, *History of the Empire, Volume 1: Books 1–4* (transl. C.R. Whittaker, Cambridge, MA, Harvard University Press, 1969)

LCL 139 *Historia Augusta, Volume 1* (transl. David Magie, revised by David Rohrbacher, Cambridge, MA: Harvard University Press, 2022)

LCL 29 Julian, *Orations 6–8, Letters to Themistius, To the Senate and People of Athens, To a Priest, The Caesars, Misopogon* (transl. Wilmer C. Wright, Cambridge, MA: Harvard University Press, 1913)

LCL 14 Lucian, *Volume 1* (transl. A.M. Harmon, Cambridge, MA: Harvard University Press, 1979)

LCL 219 Oppian, Colluthus, Tryphiodorus, *Oppian, Colluthus, and Tryphiodorus* (transl. A.W. Mair, Cambridge, MA: Harvard University Press, 1928)

LCL 134 Philostratus, Eunapius, *Lives of the Sophists, Lives of the Philosophers and Sophists* (ed. and transl. Graeme Miles, Han Baltussen, Cambridge, MA: Harvard University Press, 2023)

LCL 176, Plato, *Republic*, Volume II: Books 6–10 (ed. and transl. Christopher Emlyn-Jones and William Preddy (Cambridge, MA: Harvard University Press, 2013)

Other Primary Sources

De Guevara, Antonio, *The Golden Boke of Marcus Aurelius, Emperour, and Eloquent Oratour* (transl. John Bourchier, London: Thomas East, 1586)

Higden, Ranulf, *Polychronicon Ranulphi Higden, Monachi Cestrensis, together with the English translations of John Trevisa and of an unknown author of the fifteenth century* (London: Longman & Co., 1865) https://archive.org/details/polychroniconra00lumbgoog/page/n6/mode/2up

Nichols, Francis Morgan, *Mirabilia Urbis Romae: The Marvels of Rome, or a Picture of the Golden City (*London: Ellis and Elvey, Rome: Spithoever, 1889)

Standard Modern Reference Works

Ackeren, M. van, (ed.), *A Companion to Marcus Aurelius* (Chichester: Wiley-Blackwell, 2012)

Birley, Anthony, *Marcus Aurelius: A Biography* (revised edition, New Haven and London: Yale University Press, 1987)

Birley, Anthony, 'Hadrian to the Antonines,' in A. Bowman, P. Garnsey, & D. Rathbone (eds.), *The Cambridge Ancient History* (Cambridge: Cambridge University Press, 2008), 132–194, doi:10.1017/CHOL9780521263351.004

Hadot, Pierre (transl. Michael Chase), *The Inner Citadel: The Meditations of Marcus Aurelius* (Cambridge, Massachusetts and London: Harvard University Press, 1998)

Long, A.A. and David Sedley, *The Hellenistic Philosophers, Volume 1* (18th printing, Cambridge University Press, 2012)

McLynn, Frank, *Marcus Aurelius: Warrior, Philosopher, Emperor* (London: Vintage Books, 2009)

Robertson, Donald J. *Marcus Aurelius: The Stoic Emperor* (New Haven and London: Yale University Press, 2024)

Sellars, John, *Marcus Aurelius* (London and New York: Routledge, Taylor and Francis Group, 2021)

Selected Secondary Works

Ahnert, Thomas, 'Hutcheson and the Heathen Moralists,' *Journal of Scottish Philosophy* vol. 8 (2010), 51–62

Andrikopoulos, Georgios, *Magic and the Roman Emperors* (University of Exeter, 2009)

Arnold, Matthew, 'An Essay on Marcus Aurelius,' reproduced in Oates (ed., 1940), 593–610

Barnes, T.D. 'The Composition of Cassius Dio's "Roman History,"' *Phoenix*, vol. 38, no. 3 (Autumn 1984), 240–255

Beckmann, Martin, 'The "Columnae Coc(h)lides" of Trajan and Marcus Aurelius,' *Phoenix*, vol. 56, no. 3/4 (Autumn-Winter 2002), 348–357

Beckmann, Martin, *The Column of Marcus Aurelius: The Genesis and Meaning of a Roman Imperial Monument* (Chapel Hill: University of North Carolina, 2011)

Beckmann, Martin, 'The Column of Marcus Aurelius,' in Ackeren, M. van (2012), 251–263

Berman, David, *A History of Atheism in Britain: from Hobbes to Russell* (London/New York/Sydney: Croom Helm,1988)

Börner, Susanne, 'Coins,' in Ackeren, M. van (2012), 278–293

Boschung, Dietrich, 'The Reliefs: Representations of Marcus Aurelius' Deeds,' in Ackeren, M. van (2012), 305–314

Bowra, C.M. 'Walter Pater,' *The Sewanee Review,* vol. 57, no. 3 (Summer 1949), 378–400.

Brake, Laurel, 'Pater, Walter Horatio (1839–1894), author and aesthete.' *Oxford Dictionary of National Biography* 23 Sep. 2004; accessed 25 Jun. 2024

Brooke, Christopher, 'How the Stoics Became Atheists,' *The Historical Journal* 49, 2 (2006), 387–402

Buck, David F. 'Socrates Scholasticus on Julian the Apostate,' *Byzantion* vol. 73, no. 2 (2003), 301–318

Buckler, William E. 'Matthew Arnold in America: The "Reason,"' *American Literature* vol. 29, no. 4 (January 1958), 464–470

Buddensieg, Tilmann, 'Gregory the Great, the Destroyer of Pagan Idols: The History of a Medieval Legend Concerning the Decline of Ancient Art and Literature,' *Journal of the Warburg and Courtauld Institutes,* vol. 28 (1965), 44–65

Carley, James P. 'Bourchier, John, second Baron Berners (c. 1467–1533), soldier, diplomat, and translator,' *Oxford Dictionary of National Biography* 23 Sep. 2004; accessed 25 Jun. 2024

Celenza, Christopher S. 'Marsilio Ficino,' *The Stanford Encyclopedia of Philosophy* (Winter 2021 edition). Edward N. Zalta (ed.), https://plato.stanford.edu/archives/win2021/entries/ficino

Ceporina, Matteo, '*The Meditations*,' in Ackeren, M. van (2012), 45–61

Chesterton, Gilbert. K. *Orthodoxy,* (New York: Image Books, 1959)

Chignell, Andrew and Derk Pereboom, "Natural Theology and Natural Religion", *The Stanford Encyclopedia of Philosophy* (Fall 2020 Edition), Edward N. Zalta (ed.), URL = <https://plato.stanford.edu/archives/fall2020/entries/natural-theology/>.

Clarke, P. H. 'Adam Smith, Stoicism and Religion in the 18th Century,' *History of the Human Sciences* vol. 13, no. 4 (2000), 49–72

Collini, Stefan, 'Matthew Arnold (1822–1888),' *Oxford Dictionary of National Biography,* 23 September 2004

Collis, Karen, 'How Shaftesbury read Marcus Aurelius: Two "Curious and Interesting" Volumes with his Manuscript Annotations,' *Journal of the Warburg and Courtauld Institutes,* vol. 79 (2016), 263–293

Cross, F.L. (ed.) *The Oxford Dictionary of the Christian Church* (Oxford: Oxford University Press, 1961)

Davies, M. and S. B. Pomeroy, 'Marcellus of Side's Epitaph on Regilla (IG XIV 1389): An Historical and Literary Commentary,' *Prometheus* vol.38, no. 1 (2012), 3–34

Davies, Penelope, *Death and the Emperor: Roman Imperial Funerary Monuments from Augustus to Marcus Aurelius* (Cambridge: Cambridge University Press, 2000)

Defoe, Daniel, *Serious Reflections During the Life and Surprising Adventures of Robinson Crusoe: with his Vision of the Angelick World* (London: W. Taylor, 1720).

Defoe, Daniel. *Dickory Cronke: the Dumb Philosopher, or, Great Britain's Wonder.* [1719]. Project Gutenberg EBook #2051 (2000), transcribed from the 1889 George Bell & Sons edition

Delacroix, Eugène, *The Journal of Eugène Delacroix,* translated from the French by Walter Pach (New York: Covici-Friede Publishers, 1937)

Dieckmann, H., and Seznec, J. 'The Horse of Marcus Aurelius: A Controversy between Diderot and Falconet,' *Journal of the Warburg and Courtauld Institutes*, vol. 15, no. 3 / 4 (1952), 198–228.

Dorsey, Dale, 'Francis Hutcheson,' *The Stanford Encyclopedia of Philosophy* (Summer 2021 edition), Edward N. Zalta (ed.), https://plato.stanford.edu//archives/sum2021/entries/hutcheson/

Durand, Marion, Simon Shogry, and Dirk Baltzly, "Stoicism", *The Stanford Encyclopedia of Philosophy* (Spring 2023 Edition), Edward N. Zalta & Uri Nodelman (eds.), URL = https://plato.stanford.edu/archives/spr2023/entries/stoicism/

Ebel, Henry, 'Matthew Arnold and Marcus Aurelius,' *Studies in English Literature, 1500–1900,* vol. 3, no. 4, Nineteenth Century (Autumn 1963), 555–566

Edwards, Mark J. 'Religion in the Age of Marcus Aurelius,' in Ackeren, M. van (2012), 200–216

Ellis L. and A. Walsh, chapter 16, 'Crime, delinquency and intelligence: a review of the worldwide literature,' in H. Nyborg (ed.), *The Scientific Study of General Intelligence: Tribute to Arthur R. Jensen* (New York: Pergamon Press, 2003), 343–366

Enfield, William, *The History of Philosophy, from the Earliest Periods, Drawn Up from Brucker's* Historia Critica Philosophiae (London: Thomas Tegg and Son, 1840)

Farrar, F.W. *Seekers After God.* Project Gutenberg Kindle edition (2020)

Fehl, Philipp, 'The Placement of the Equestrian Statue of Marcus Aurelius in the Middle Ages,' *Journal of the Warburg and Courtauld Institutes*, vol. 37 (1974), 362–367

Fleury, Pascal, 'Marcus Aurelius' Letters,' in Ackeren, M. van (2012), 62–76

Foucault, Michel, 'Technologies of the Self,' in L.M. Martin, H. Gutman, P. Hutton (eds.), *Technologies of the Self: A Seminar with Michel Foucault* (London: Tavistock Publications, 1988), 16–49

Frier, Bruce W., 'Demography,' Chapter 27, *The Cambridge Ancient History*, Cambridge Histories Online, Cambridge University Press, 2008, doi: 10.1017/CHOL9780521263351.028

Frier, Bruce W., 'Regulating Incestuous Marriage in the Roman Republic,' in A. de Robillant, J. Witte Jr., S. MacDougall (eds.), *Texts and Contexts in Legal History: Essays in Honor of Charles Donohue* (Boston University: The Robbins Collection, 2016), 23–35

Frisell T, Pawitan Y, Långström N. 'Is the association between general cognitive ability and violent crime caused by family-level confounders?' *PLoS One* (2012);7(7):e41783. doi: 10.1371/journal.pone.0041783

Fulton, Gordon D. '*Evidences of the Christian Religion*: Using Pascal to Revise Addison in Eighteenth-Century Scotland,' *Lumen* 26 (2007), 227–241

Gascoigne, John, 'Clarke, Samuel (1675–1729), theologian and philosopher,' *Oxford Dictionary of National Biography* 23 Sep. 2004; accessed 27 Jul. 2023

Gay, Peter, *The Enlightenment: An Interpretation: The Rise of Modern Paganism* (London: Weidenfeld and Nicolson, 1967)

Geer, Russell Mortimer, 'Second Thoughts on the Imperial Succession from Nerva to Commodus,' *Transactions and Proceedings of the American Philological Association*, vol. 67 (1936), 47–54.

Gibbon, Edward, *The History of the Decline and Fall of the Roman Empire* (ed. Rev. H.H. Milman), 12 vols (London: John Murray, 1838)

Gibson, Edmund (ed.) *The Evidences of the Christian Religion, by the Right Honorable Joseph Addison, Esq.* Second edition (London, 1733)

Gillmore, Peter, Trevor Parkhill, William Roulston, *Exiles of '98: Ulster Presbyterians and the United States* (Belfast: Ulster Historical Foundation, 2018)

Ginzburg, Carlo, 'Making Things Strange: The Prehistory of a Literary Device,' *Representations*, special issue, The New Erudition, no. 56 (Autumn 1996), 8–28

Gomes, Jules, 'Italian Catholics reverting to ancient Roman gods, seers, and sorcerers,' *Catholic Herald*, 5 March 2024, https://catholicherald.co.uk/italian-catholics-reverting-to-ancient-roman-gods-seers-and-sorcerers/?fbclid=IwAR2ppRy4MZyWVr-fc6Wg4SeVlEEOuLZPi8QVb8XPIyee9R_zDItwSmAUTEI

Gregorovius, Ferdinand, *The History of the City of Rome in the Middle Ages (*transl. by Annie Hamilton), vol II (London: George Bell and Sons, 1894)

Hadot, Pierre, 'Physics as Spiritual Exercise, or Pessimism and Optimism in Marcus Aurelius,' 1972, in Sharpe and Testa (2020), 207–226

Hannoosh, Michèle, 'Delacroix and the Ends of Civilisation,' in *Delacroix and the Question of Finish*, exhibition catalogue, ed. Eik Kahng, Santa Barbara Museum of Art (New Haven: Yale University Press, 2013)

Hedgcock, Deborah, 'Special Reflective Post: Remembering Jacob Walker, from Virginia, in Hornsey, 2020, https://groups.io/g/TottenhamCivicSociety/topic/fw_special_reflective_post/76382508?p=

Hekster, Olivier, *Commodus: An Emperor at the Crossroads* (Leiden, 2002)

Highet, Gilbert, *The Classical Tradition: Greek and Roman Influences on Western Literature* (Oxford: Oxford University Press, 1976)

Hill, Lisa and Prasanna Nidumolu, 'The Influence of Classical Stoicism on John Locke's Theory of Self-Ownership.' *History of the Human Sciences*, vol. 34 (3–4) (2021), 3–24

Hilton, John, 'Myth and Narrative Fiction in the Work of the Roman Emperor Julian,' *Listy filologické/Folia philologica* vol. 140, no. 1/2 (2017), 39–70

Hwang, Sam and Jakob, Deaglan and Squires, Munir, 'Health Effects of Cousin Marriage: Evidence From U.S. Genealogical Records' (18 October 2023) https://ssrn.com/abstract=4632501 or http://dx.doi.org/10.2139/ssrn.4632501

Imperadore, Pamela, Sameer B. Shah, Helen B. Makarenkova, Graziano Fiorito, 'Nerve degeneration and regeneration in the Cephalopod mollusc *Octopus vulgaris*: the case of the pallial nerve,' *Nature Scientific Reports* (20 April 2017), 7:46564, doi: 10.1038/srep46564

Israelowich, Ido, 'The Rain Miracle of Marcus Aurelius: (Re-)Construction of Consensus,' *Greece & Rome*, second series, vol. 55, no. 1 (April 2008), 83–102

Kitzler, Petr. 'Tertullian's Concept of the Soul and His Corporealistic Ontology,' in J. Lagouanere – S. Fialon (eds.), *Tertullian Afer: Tertullien et la literature chrétienne d'Afrique.* Turnhout: Brepols, Instrumenta Patristica et Mediaevalia 70 (2015), 43–62

Kovács, Péter, 'Epigraphic Records,' in Ackeren, M. van (2012), 77–91

Lennox, James, 'Aristotle's Biology,' *The Stanford Encyclopedia of Philosophy* (Fall 2021 edition), Edward N. Zalta (ed.) url= https://plato/stanford.edu/archives/fall2021/entries/aristotle-biology/

Littleton, C. Scott, and Thomas, Ann C., 'The Sarmatian Connection: New Light on the Origin of the Arthurian and Holy Grail Legends.' *The Journal of American Folklore*, vol. 91, no. 359 (Jan-Mar 1978), 513–527

London Borough of Redbridge, 'Children's Health and Parents Related by Blood,' Redbridge LSCB (2013)

Lytle, Ephraim, 'The Red Sea Aristotle,' *The Journal of Hellenic Studies* 142 (2022), 100–143, doi 10.1017/S0075426922000106

Lytle, Ephraim, 'The Strange Love of the Fish and the Goat: Regional Contexts and Rough Cilician Religion in Oppian's *Halieutica* 4.308–73,' *Transactions of the American Philological Association (1974–2014)* , vol. 141, no. 2 (Autumn 2011), 333–386

MacIntyre, Alasdair, *After Virtue: A Study in Moral Theory (*second edition, Notre Dame: University of Notre Dame Press, 1984)

Matson, Erik W. 'A Brief History of the Editions of *TMS*: Part 2,' (4 December 2020), https://www.adamsmithworks.org/documents/erik-matson-brief-history-of-the-editions-of-tms-part-2

Mattingly, H., *'Hilaritas,' Proceedings of the Cambridge Philological Society*, Second Meeting, no. 136–138 (Lent, Easter and Michaelmas Terms, 1927), 3–9

McCown, Chester C., 'The Ephesia Grammata in Popular Belief,' *Transactions and Proceedings of the American Philological Association*, vol. 54 (1923), 128–140

Mezzatesta, Michael P. 'Marcus Aurelius, Fray Antonio de Guevara, and the Ideal of the Perfect Prince in the Sixteenth Century,' *The Art Bulletin,* vol. 66, no. 4 (Dec. 1984), 620–633

Miller, the Rev. Henry, et al, *A Vindication of Mr Hutcheson from the Calumnious Aspersions of a Late Pamphlet* (1738)

Moore, John Robert, 'Defoe's Political Propaganda in 'The Dumb Philosopher,''' *Huntingdon Library Quarterly*, vol. 4, no. 1 (October, 1940), 107–117

Nicholls, Matthew C. 'Galen and Libraries in the Peri Alupias,' *The Journal of Roman Studies* vol. 101 (2011), 123–142

Nickel, Helmut, 'The Emperor's New Saddle Cloth: The Ephippium of the Equestrian Statue of Marcus Aurelius,' *Metropolitan Museum Journal*, vol. 24 (1989), 17–24

Nicols, John, '*Patrona civitatis:* Gender and Civic Patronage,' *Studies in Latin Literature and Roman History* V, Collection Latomus, vol. 206 (1989), 117–142

Niles, John D. 'Hawks, Horses, and Huns: The Impact of Peoples of the Steppe on the Folk Cultures of Northern Europe,' *Western Folklore,* vol. 75, no. 2 (Spring 2016), 133–164

Nock, A.D. *Conversion* (Oxford: Oxford University Press, 1972)

Novak, Maximillian, 'Imaginary Voyages in *Serious Reflections* and *A Vision of the Angelick World,*' *Digital Defoe: Studies in Defoe & His Contemporaries 5*, no. 1 (Fall, 2013), 34–44

O'Donnell, Ruan, 'Castle Hill and Vinegar Hill: The Australian Rising of 1804,' *18th-19th-Century History* (Summer 2004), News, The United Irishmen, vol. 12, https://www.historyireland.com/castle-hill-and-vinegar-hill-the-australian-rising-of-1804/#:~:text=Counter%2Dinsurgency%20measures%20in%20Ireland,at%20least%20600%20republican%20prisoners

Papavramidou, Niki, Theodossis Papavramidis, and Thespis Demetriou, 'Ancient Greek and Greco-Roman Methods in Modern Surgical Treatment of Cancer,' *Annals of Surgical Oncology*, 17:665–667 (2010), doi:10.1245/s10434-009-0886-6

Papy, Jan, 'Justus Lipsius,' *The Stanford Encyclopedia of Philosophy* (Spring 2019 Edition), Edward N. Zalta (ed.), URL = <https://plato.stanford.edu/archives/spr2019/entries/justus-lipsius/>

Pater, Walter, *Essays on Literature and Art* (ed. and with an introduction by Jenny Uglow), Everyman's Library (London: J.M. Dent & Co., 1990)

Pater, Walter, *Marius the Epicurean: His Sensations and Ideas* Project Gutenberg Kindle (2021)

Pennington, Rev. Montagu, *Memoirs of the Life of Mrs. Elizabeth Carter, with a New Edition of her Poems, &c*, 4th edition, 2 vols. (London: James Cawthorn, 1825)

Pharr, Clyde, 'The Interdiction of Magic in Roman Law,' *Transactions and Proceedings of the American Philological Association*, vol. 63, (1932), 269–295

Pierce, S. Rowland, 'The Mausoleum of Hadrian and the Pons Aelius,' *The Journal of Roman Studies,* vol. 15 (1925), 75–103

Pocock, J.G.A. 'Between Machiavelli and Hume: Gibbon as Civic Humanist and Philosophical Historian,' *Daedalus* vol. 105, no. 3 (Summer, 1976), 153–169

Proyect, Louis, review of *Tender Comrades: Interviews with Blacklisted Hollywood Reds* (eds. P. Buhle and P. McGilligan, St. Martins, 1997), https://www.columbia.edu/~lnp3/mydocs/culture/tender_comrades.htm

Rees, D.A. 'Joseph Bryennius and the Text of Marcus Aurelius' "Meditations,"' *The Classical Quarterly* vol. 50, no. 2 (2000), 584–596

Richlin, Amy, *Marcus Aurelius in Love: Marcus Aurelius and Marcus Cornelius Fronto* (University of Chicago Press, 2006, e-book 2008)

Ridley, Ronald T. 'The Fate of the Column of Antoninus Pius,' *Papers of the British School at Rome* vol. 86 (2018), 235–269

Robertson, Donald, and T. Codd, 'Stoic Philosophy as a Cognitive-Behavioral Therapy,' *The Behavior Therapist*, vol. 42, no. 2 (February 2019), https://medium.com/stoicism-philosophy-as-a-way-of-life/stoic-philosophy-as-a-cognitive-behavioral-therapy-597fbeba786a

Rode, Alan K. 'The Philip Yordan Story,' *Noir City Sentinel* (November-December 2009), 12–15

Salmon, Eric, 'Collier, Jeremy (1650–1726), anti-theatrical polemicist and bishop of the nonjuring Church of England,' *Oxford Dictionary of National Biography* 23 Sep. 2004; accessed 27 Jul. 2023

Scheidel, Walter, 'Emperors, Aristocrats, and the Grim Reaper: Towards a Demographic Profile of the Roman Elite,' *The Classical Quarterly*, vol. 49, no. 1 (1999), 254–281

Schils, Griet, 'Plato's Myth of Er: The Light and the Spindle,' *L'Antiquité Classique*, t. 62 (1993), 101–114

Schulman, Gayle M. 'Slaves at the University of Virginia,' *Latin American Studies* (2005)

Schwarz, Daniel R. 'The Importance of Ian Watt's *The Rise of the Novel*,' *The Journal of Narrative Technique*, vol. 13, no. 2 (Spring, 1983), 59, 61–73

Segvic, Heda, 'No One Errs Willingly: The Meaning of Socratic Intellectualism,' *Oxford Studies in Ancient Philosophy* vol. xix (Winter 2000), 1–46

Sharpe, Matthew, and Federico Testa (transl.), *The Selected Writings of Pierre Hadot: Philosophy as Practice* (London, New York: Bloomsbury Academic, 2020)

Shaw, Brent D. and Richard P. Saller, 'Close-Kin Marriage in Roman Society?' *Man*, new series, vol. 19, no. 3 (September 1984), 432–444

Shklovsky, Viktor, 'Art as Device,' [1917], translated and introduced by A. Berlina, *Poetics Today*, 36:3 (September 2015), doi:10.1215/03335372-3160709

Smith, Adam, *The Theory of Moral Sentiments; To Which is Added a Dissertation on the Origin of Languages,* new edition (ed. with introduction by Dugald Stewart) (London: George Bell and Sons, 1887)

Stephens, William O. 'Real Men are Stoics: An Interpretation of Tom Wolfe's *A Man in Full*,' *Stoic Voice Journal*, vol. 1, no. 3, April 2000. https://web.archive.org/web/20091231170452/http://puffin.creighton.edu/phil/Stephens/Stoicism/Real_Men_Are_Stoics.htm

Stevenson, Tom, 'On Dating the Frieze of Trajan's Column,' *Mediterranean Archaeology* vol. 21 (2008), 43–58

Stove, Judith, *Jane Austen's Inspiration: Beloved Friend Anne Lefroy* (Barnsley: Pen & Sword, 2019)

Tayeh, Jordan Reece, 'Blood, Lead and Tears: The Cult of Cybele as a Means of Addressing Ancient Roman Issues of Fertility,' *Discentes* (August 28, 2020) https://web.sas.upenn.edu/discentes/2020/08/28/blood-lead-and-tears-the-cult-of-cybele-as-a-means-of-addressing-ancient-roman-issues-of-fertility/

Taylor, Stephen, 'Gibson, Edmund (bap. 1669, d. 1748), bishop of London,' *Oxford Dictionary of National Biography* 23 Sep. 2004; accessed 27 Jul. 2023

Thomas [Antoine-Léonard], *Eulogium on Marcus Aurelius* (transl. David Bailie Warden) (New York: Bernard Dornin, 1808)

Torelli, Mario, *Typology and Structure of Roman Historical Reliefs* (Ann Arbor: University of Michigan Press, 1992)

Van der Zanden, Jos, *Beethoven's Interest in Greco-Roman Antiquity and Its Impact on His Life and Music* (University of Manchester, 2020)

Vitto, Cindy L. 'The Virtuous Pagan: In Middle English Literature,' *Transactions of the American Philosophical Society*, vol. 79, no. 5, (1989), 1–100

Volk, Katharina, 'Plumbing the Ovidian *Halieutica*,' in T.E. Franklinos and L. Fulkerson, *Constructing Authors and Readers in the* Appendices Virgiliana, Tibulliana, and Ovidiana, (Oxford University Press, 2020), 212–222

Wadge, Richard, 'King Arthur! A British or Sarmatian Tradition?' *Folklore*, vol. 98, no. 2 (1987), 204–215

Walker, Khyel, 'The Antoninus Questions,' translations from Hebrew and Aramaic in Wallach (1941) (2024)

Wallach, Luitpold, 'The Colloquy of Marcus Aurelius with the Patriarch Judah I,' *The Jewish Quarterly Review*, new series, vol. 31, no. 3 (January 1941), 259–286

Walton, F. R. 'Cybele,' in M. Cary et al (eds.), *The Oxford Classical Dictionary* (Oxford at the Clarendon Press, 1957), 246–7

Watt, Ian, *The Rise of the Novel: Studies in Defoe, Richardson and Fielding* (fourth impression, London: Chatto and Windus, 1963)

Whale and Dolphin Conservation, 'How Intelligent Are Whales and Dolphins?' au.whales.org/whales-dophins/how-intelligent-are-whales-and-dolphins/ accessed 28 May 2024.

Whiting, Kai, and Leonidas Konstantakos, 'Stoic Theology: Revealing or Redundant?' *Religions* (2019), 10,93; doi:10.3390/rel10030193

Woloch, Michael, 'A Note on the Equestrian Statue of Marcus Aurelius,' *American Journal of Archaeology*, vol. 73, no. 4 (Oct 1969), 469

Woods, Robert, 'Ancient and Early Modern Mortality: Experience and Understanding,' *The Economic History Review*, new series, vol. 60, no. 2 (May 2007), 373–399

Wroth, W. W., and Martin D. W. Jones, 'Long, George (1800–1879), classical scholar,' *Oxford Dictionary of National Biography* 23 Sep. 2004; accessed 25 Jun. 2024

Zapato, Lyle, 'Olive Loving Tree Octopuses of Antiquity,' *ZPI/Blog* (26 September 2008), https://zapatopi.net/blog/?post=200809266800.olive_loving_tree_octopuses_of_antiquity

Zanker, Paul, *The Mask of Socrates: The Image of the Intellectual in Antiquity* (Berkeley, Calif: University of California Press, 1996)

Index